D1379344

BRONX ACCENT

BRONX ACCENT

A

LITERARY AND PICTORIAL
HISTORY OF THE BOROUGH

LLOYD ULTAN AND BARBARA UNGER

RUTGERS UNIVERSITY PRESS
New Brunswick, New Jersey

Publication of this book was supported, in part, by a grant from Furthermore, the publication program of the J. M. Kaplan Fund.

LIBRARY OF CONGRESS CATALOGING-IN-PUBLICATION DATA

Bronx accent : a literary and pictorial history of the borough / [compiled by] Lloyd Ultan and Barbara Unger.

p.   cm.

Includes bibliographical references and index.

ISBN 0–8135–2863–1 (cloth : acid-free paper)

1. Bronx (New York, N.Y.)—Literary collections. 2. American literature—New York (State)—New York. 3. Bronx (New York, N.Y.)—Pictorial works. 4. Bronx (New York, N.Y.)—History. I. Ultan, Lloyd. II. Unger, Barbara, 1932–

PS549.N5 B86 2000

810.8'032747275—dc21

00–028081

British Cataloging-in-Publication data for this book is available from the British Library

Text design and composition by Jenny Dossin.

Manufactured in the United States of America

CONTENTS

PREFACE

IN THE PAST FEW DECADES, PERHAPS NO PLACE ON EARTH HAS BEEN AS CON-
demned and vilified by public pundits as The Bronx. The image burned into the
minds of people is that of a devastated region of torched and abandoned buildings
reduced to rubble in which a feral population preys upon each other and the unwary
visitor. This stereotype has never borne a resemblance to reality, even during the
period of the arson fires. Indeed, recently The Bronx has experienced a powerful
renaissance.

The current resurgence of this northernmost borough of New York City has
created an advantageous moment for a new book about The Bronx based on one of
its treasured assets—its rich literary heritage. In works touching upon the borough,
over one hundred authors reveal the development of The Bronx over a period of
some three hundred years, from the days of landed gentry, gaslight, sweatshops, and
horse-drawn carriages, through its internationally known urban crisis, to its hard-
won contemporary rebirth.

This book captures the *Zeitgeist* of The Bronx through the words of its celebrated writers and, because of its historical foundation, it also provides the reader
with an insight into the kaleidoscopic shifts in Bronx life over the centuries. Filtered
through the imaginations of authors of different times, social classes, and literary
styles, the borough of The Bronx emerges not only as a shaper of destinies and lives,
but as an important center of urban literature.

The result of a collaboration between a historian and a literary scholar, this
book groups the works of authors by the era explored in their content, rather than
by publication date. In order for a work to be included in this book, it must be set in
The Bronx or in the area that eventually became The Bronx. Most, but not all,
authors in this book lived in the borough during some period in their lives. Some
still do.

For years, New York literature was defined primarily as the literature of Manhattan. To compensate for this oversight, recent anthologies that celebrate the literary life in Brooklyn and Queens have appeared. Although not an anthology, this book is the first to explore in depth the rich literary heritage of the northernmost borough.

Among the illustrious authors who wrote about The Bronx are giants of American literature. Some are winners of Nobel and Pulitzer Prizes and of other major literary awards. Such talents and their connections to the borough deserve a permanent place in any book about New York in literature. We have also included many promising and emerging literary talents.

In order to maintain a historical perspective, we have drawn from many sources—fiction, nonfiction, drama, memoir, poetry, letters, journals, magazines, and newspapers. Despite great efforts, we were unable to discover literary works dealing with some Bronx neighborhoods, while other areas of the borough were blessed with an abundance of literature.

Whenever possible, the original spelling, punctuation, and grammar in the source material have been retained even if they do not conform to today's standard English. In addition, foreign words and names originally written in languages that do not use the Latin alphabet are sometimes given variant renderings in English by different translators. Thus, alternate or different spellings from these translated sources remain unchanged within their context.

We were also forced to be selective in choosing literature for this book. If every work by every published author who ever wrote about The Bronx were included in this book, it would extend over several volumes. Space also dictates that, except for short poems, only excerpts of entire selections appear. What is found here is only a sampling, therefore, although a rich one, of the vast range of literature about New York City's northernmost borough.

This book strives for a realistic balance without bathing the borough in a rosy glow of nostalgia or stressing years of neglect or decay. This exploration of literature about The Bronx reveals changing literary perspectives of the borough, the interaction of diverse cultures, and human efforts against the odds to achieve the American Dream.

ACKNOWLEDGMENTS

NO WORK OF THIS INTRICACY AND MAGNITUDE CAN REACH FRUITION WITHOUT behind-the-scenes help. For aiding us to uncover the many literary works that focus on The Bronx and for their professional expertise, we would like to thank the reference librarians at The Bronx County Historical Society Research Library, the Fairleigh Dickinson University Library, the New York Public Library, the Rockland Community College Library, the Suffern Free Library, and the YIVO Institute for Jewish History and Research. For their help in providing photographs, great thanks go to Deborah Bershad of the Art Commission of the City of New York, Janet Butler of the Lehman College Archives, William R. Rodriguez, Laura Tosi of The Bronx County Historical Society Research Library, and Rose Young, assistant director of Highbridge Voices. For their photographic services, we thank Layle Silbert and Suffern Camera. A grant-in-aid from Fairleigh Dickinson University provided some very necessary financial support. We would also like to thank Barnes and Noble–Union Square in New York City, Fairleigh Dickinson University, the New York Public Library, and the Rockland Community College Library for providing places where we could meet to confer on our developing and ever-changing manuscript. For proofreading that manuscript, our gratitude and thanks go to Ted Sakano.

For their personal assistance, great and small, we have many to thank. They include Dina Abramowicz, Michael Bergman, David Bodansky, Renée Breitbarth, Joseph Camaratta, Janice Eidus, Frederick Feirstein, Gella Fishman, Estelle Gilson, Bella Gottesman, Arlene Gross, Jerry Gross, Gary D. Hermalyn, the late Irving Howe, Mr. and Mrs. Joseph Mlotek, Marcus Olitski, Norma Fain Pratt, the late Gabriel Preil, Poets and Writers, Inc., Al Ramrus, Naomi Replansky, Marcia Rock, William Robert Rodriguez, Msgr. Donald Sakano, Frank Sauer, Mordechai Schaechter, the family of the late Ruth Lisa Schecter, Virginia Scott, Myra Shapiro,

Grace Walsh, Deborah Williams, Writers' Community, Hinde Zaretsky, and others too numerous to mention.

We would especially like to thank our agent, Bob Silverstein of Quicksilver Books Literary Agents, and our editor at Rutgers University Press, Leslie Mitchner, for their many suggestions and active support that made this book possible.

We also wish to thank the authors and publishers who gave us permission to quote from their works. Every effort has been made to trace holders of publishing rights and acknowledge them properly. Of these, some demand special recognition.

Sholem Aleichem, "On America," trans. Curt Leviant, in *Stories and Satires by Sholem Aleichem*. Reprinted with permission of Curt Leviant.

Cathy Asato, "Old Furniture Is Big News on Port Morris Antique Row," *Bronx Beat* (March 13, 1995). Copyright © 1999 Graduate School of Journalism, Columbia University. *Bronx Beat* is a publication of the Graduate School of Journalism, and this excerpt is used with permission.

Melissa August et al., "Hip-Hop Nation," *Time* (February 8, 1999).Copyright © 1999 Time Inc. Reprinted by permission.

Cindy Beer-Fouhy, "Bronx Childhood," by permission of the author.

Ed Bullins, "Whiteness in the '80s (Short Ode to a Lost Generation)," by permission of the author.

N. R. Charvat-Nagle, "The Fig Trees of Arnow Avenue," by permission of the author.

Avery Corman, "Grand Concourse: A Writer's Return," *New York Times Magazine* (November 20, 1988). Reprinted by permission of the author.

George Diamond, "I Remember Tremont: 1911–1918," *The Bronx County Historical Society Journal* (Fall 1974). Reprinted by permission of The Bronx County Historical Society.

Cleveland E. Dodge, "Recollections of Riverdale," in *The Bronx in the Innocent Years: 1895–1925*, ed. Lloyd Ultan and Gary Hermalyn. Reprinted by permission of The Bronx County Historical Society.

Joan Renzetti Durant, "Old World, New World," by permission of the author.

Janice Eidus, "Vito Loves Geraldine," from *Vito Loves Geraldine: A Collection of Stories*. Copyright © 1989 Janice Eidus. Reprinted by permission of City Lights Books.

Sandra María Esteves, "Father's Day on Longwood Avenue," from *Bluestown Mockingbird Mambo*. Reprinted by permission of Arte Público Press.

Gil Fagiani, "The Battle of Bean Hill," reprinted by permission of the author; "East Harlem and Vito Marcantonio: My Search for a Progressive Italian-American Identity," reprinted by permission of the author and *Voices in Italian America* (1994); and "Stirrings in the Bronx," *Forward Motion* (October–November 1985), by permission of *Forward Motion*.

Frederick Feirstein, "The Boarder," from *New and Selected Poems* (Brownsville, Ore.: Story Line Press, 1998). Story Line Press is currently located in Ashland, Oregon.

Alan Finder, "Nonprofit Community Groups Rebuild Housing in the Bronx," *New York Times* (March 11, 1990). Copyright © 1990 by the New York Times Co. Reprinted by permission.

Richard Foerster, "The Superintendents of 3152 Hull Avenue" first appeared in *Poets On:* and is reprinted from *Sudden Harbor* by Richard Foerster, published by Orchises Press. Copyright © 1992 by Richard Foerster. Reprinted by permission.

Bill Fullham, "Friday Night Dances," *Back in The Bronx* 7 (25). Reprinted by permission of *Back in The Bronx*.

Michael Gilmartin, "Summer Nights Italian Bronx, 1959," reprinted by permission of the author. Michael Gilmartin, a Bronx native, has been Professor of English at Corning (N.Y.) Community College since 1969.

Allen Ginsberg, excerpt from "Kaddish," from *Collected Poems 1947–1980* by Allen Ginsberg. Copyright © 1959 by Allen Ginsberg. Copyright renewed. Reprinted by permission of HarperCollins Publishers, Inc.; and excerpt from "White Shroud," from *White Shroud: Poems 1980–1985.* Copyright © 1986 by Allen Ginsberg. Reprinted by permission of HarperCollins Publishers, Inc.

Aaron Glanz-Leyeles, "November," from *Rondeaux and Other Poems* by A. Leyeles (1929), in *American Yiddish Poetry: A Bilingual Anthology*, ed. Benjamin and Barbara Harshav (Berkeley and Los Angeles: University of California Press, 1986). Copyright © 1986 The Regents of the University of California.

David Gonzalez, "An Immigrant's Field of Dreams Transforms a Dingy Patch of the Bronx," *New York Times* (November 12, 1991). Copyright © 1991 by the New York Times Co. Reprinted by permission.

Arlene C. Gross, "What Does Holloween Have to Do with It: A Story about People in the 1940s Who Call Halloween 'Holloween.'" Copyright © 1999 Arlene C. Gross.

Trish Hall, "A South Bronx Very Different from the Cliché," *New York Times* (February 14, 1999). Copyright © 1999 by the New York Times Co. Reprinted by permission.

Florence Holzman, "The Death of the Bronx," *Impulse* (May 1995). Reprinted by permission of the author.

Irving Howe, excerpts from "A Memoir of the Thirties," in *Steady Work: Essays in Politics and Democratic Radicalism 1953–1966*, copyright © 1966 by Irving Howe and renewed 1994 by Nicholas Howe and Nina Howe, reprinted by permission of Harcourt, Inc.

Marc Kaminsky, "All That Our Eyes Have Witnessed: Memories of a Living History Workshop in the South Bronx," in *Twenty-five Years of the Life Review: Theoretical and Practical Considerations*, ed. Robert Disch. Reprinted by permission of The Haworth Press, Inc.

Milton Kessler, "Mover," first appeared in *The Grand Concourse* (1990, 1993). Reprinted by permission of the author.

Irena Klepfisz, excerpt from "*Der mames shabosim*/My Mother's Sabbath Days" in *A Few Words in the Mother Tongue: Poems Selected and New (1971–1990)* (Portland, Ore.: The Eighth Mountain Press, 1990). Copyright © 1990 by Irena Klepfisz. Reprinted by permission of the author and publisher.

Jack M. Kugelmass, "The Miracle of Intervale Avenue," *Natural History* (December 1980). Reprinted by permission of the author.

Zische Landau, "A Little Park, with Few Trees," in *A Century of Yiddish Poetry*, ed. and trans. Aaron Kramer. Reprinted by permission of Cornwall Books.

Daniel S. Levy, "Surviving Urban Blight," *Metropolis* (July 8, 1989). Copyright © 1989 Bellerophon Publications, Inc. Permission granted by *Metropolis*.

Anna Margolin, "Girls in Crotona Park," trans. Norma Fain Pratt, by permission of the translator.

Vito A. Merola, "Memories of a One-Way Passage," *The Bronx County Historical Society Journal* (Spring 1990). Reprinted by permission of The Bronx County Historical Society.

Marianne Moore, "Baseball and Writing." Copyright © 1961 Marianne Moore, © renewed 1989 by Lawrence E. Brinn and Louise Crane, Executors of the Estate of Marianne Moore. Used by permission of Viking Penguin, a division of Penguin Putnam Inc.

Joan Murray, "Building Inspector," in *Egg Tooth* (Sunbury Press, 1975). Reprinted by permission of the author. "Coming of Age on the Harlem," and "The Unmolested Child," in *The Same Water* (Wesleyan University Press, 1990). Reprinted by permission of the author and publisher.

Ogden Nash, excerpt from "Random Reflections: Geographical," *The New Yorker* (July 12, 1930), reprinted by permission; and untitled poem, *The Bronx County Historical Society Journal* (July 1964), reprinted by permission of The Bronx County Historical Society.

Maria Newman, "Émigrés Who Want to Assimilate Pick Co-op City," *New York Times* (February 9, 1992). Copyright © 1992 by the New York Times Co. Reprinted by permission.

Joseph Opatashu, "Yiddish Literature in the United States," trans. Shlomo Noble, in *Voices from the Yiddish: Essays, Memoirs, Diaries*, ed. Irving Howe and Eliezer Greenberg. Reprinted by permission of the YIVO Institute for Jewish Research.

Cynthia Ozick, "A Drugstore Eden," *The New Yorker* (September 16, 1996). Copyright © 1996 by Cynthia Ozick. Reprinted by permission of the author and her agents, Raines & Raines.

Grace Paley, excerpt from *Just as I Thought*. Copyright © 1998 by Grace Paley. Reprinted by permission of Farrar, Straus and Giroux, LLC. Distribution in the

United Kingdom and the Commonwealth by permission of Grace Paley. "The Loudest Voice," in *The Little Disturbances of Man* (New York: Doubleday & Company, Inc., 1959). Copyright © 1959 by Grace Paley. Reprinted by permission. "Tough Times for a City of Tenants," *New York Times* (January 25, 1998). Copyright © 1998 by Grace Paley. Reprinted by permission of the author.

Sophie Paul, excerpt from "I Remember the Bronx," by permission of the author.

Shirley Pollan-Cohen, "Turns," by permission of the author.

Chaim Potok, "Cultural Confrontation in Urban America: A Writer's Beginnings," in *Literature and the Urban Experience*, ed. Michael C. Jaye and Ann Chalmera Watts. Reprinted by permission of the author.

Gabriel Preil, "Grand Concourse," trans. Estelle Gilson, by permission of the translator.

Naomi Replansky, "An Inheritance" from *The Dangerous World: New and Selected Poems 1934–1994* (Another Chicago Press). Copyright © 1994 by Naomi Replansky. Reprinted by permission of the author.

Abraham Rodriguez, Jr., "Elba," in *The Boy without a Flag: Tales of the South Bronx* (Milkweed, 1992, 1999). Copyright © 1992, 1999 by Abraham Rodriguez, Jr. Excerpts reprinted with permission from Milkweed Editions.

w r rodriguez, "blinky" and "grandfather," from *the shoe shine parlor et al.* (Ghost Pony Press, 1984), reprinted by permission of the author; "logic," originally appeared in *Dusty Dog*, copyright © 1991 by w r rodriguez, reprinted by permission of the author; "roosevelt's bust," copyright © 1994 by w r rodriguez, reprinted by permission of the author; "saint mary's park," copyright © w r rodriguez, reprinted by permission of the author.

Joseph Rolnick, "Neighbors," trans. Irving Feldman, from *The Penguin Book of Modern Yiddish Verse*, ed. Irving Howe, Ruth R. Wisse, and Khone Shmeruk. Copyright © 1987 by Irving Howe, Ruth R. Wisse, and Khone Shmeruk. Used by permission of Viking Penguin, a division of Penguin Putnam Inc.

Max Rosenfeld, "Goat in the Backyard" and "A Temporary Job," by permission of the author.

Ruth Lisa Schechter, "Bronx," *The Bronx County Historical Society Journal* (July 1971). Reprinted by permission of The Bronx County Historical Society.

I. J. Schwartz, "The Light of Summer's End," trans. Etta Blum, from *A Treasury of Yiddish Poetry*, ed. Irving Howe and Eliezer Greenberg. Copyright © 1969 by Irving Howe and Eliezer Greenberg. Reprinted by permission of Henry Holt and Company, LLC.

Virginia Scott, "Limoges," in *The Witness Box* (Motheroot Publications, 1984). Reprinted by permission of the author.

Myra Shapiro, "Across from Bronx Park," copyright © Myra Shapiro. Reprinted by permission of the author.

Katherine Soniat, "Skirting It: The Bronx," from *Cracking Eggs* (University Presses of Florida, 1990). Reprinted by permission of the author.

Jonathan Stempel, "From Gaseteria to Gastronome," *Bronx Beat* (April 12, 1999). Copyright © 1999 Graduate School of Journalism, Columbia University. *Bronx Beat* is a publication of the Graduate School of Journalism, and this excerpt is used with permission.

Marie Syrkin, "Morris High School, Class of '16," *The New Republic* (November 7, 1983). Reprinted by permission of *The New Republic*.

Gayl Teller, "Nets," in *Shorehaven* (The Edwin Mellen Press, 1996). Reprinted by permission of the author and publisher.

Calvin Trillin, "U.S. Journal: The Bronx: The Coops," *The New Yorker* (August 1, 1977). Copyright © 1977 by Calvin Trillin. This usage is granted by permission of Lescher & Lescher, Ltd.

Terence Winch, "Six Families of Puerto Ricans," in *Irish Musicians/American Friends* (Coffee House Press, 1985). Reprinted by permission of the author and publisher.

Vic Ziegel, "Promises Keep Him in Bronx," *Daily News* (March 20, 1999). Copyright © 1999 by the New York Daily News, L.P. Reprinted with permission.

BRONX ACCENT

GENESIS

THE COLONIAL AND REVOLUTIONARY BRONX

1639–1800

THE FIRST INHABITANTS OF THE BRONX WERE AMERICAN Indians. They had no written language and left no written record. Information about American Indian life is sketchy at best. However, remnants of the original forested landscape traversed by local tribes were later preserved in large parklands in a highly urbanized Bronx. Modern writers have tried to imagine areas like Van Cortlandt Park as pristine wilderness. Amid this park setting, which included the colonial-era Van Cortlandt House and a recently built golf course, J. J. Meehan set his 1923 poem "The Song of Mosholu," a romanticized view of local American Indian life. Mosholu is the Algonquin name for a brook running through the park.

> A little brook that tinkles low,
>   Beyond the Harlem's tide,
> O'er many a rocky, shingled slope
>   Adown the green hillside.
>
> Oft have I trod its mossy ways
>   In wood of pine and leaf,
> Where wound his spear or trimmed his bow
>   Some brave Mohican chief.
>
> Here burned his camp-fires long ago
>   And rose his bright tepee,
> Where now the golfer swings his club,
>   Or builds his sanded tee.

Gone are the war dance and the cry
That echoed hill and glade;
Long hushed the voice of swarthy sire,
And lithesome, dusky maid.

But still Van Cortlandt's storied wall
Looks out on skies of blue;
Still comes the twilight's mystic hour
The song of Mosholu.

—J. J. Meehan, "The Song of Mosholu," in *Valentine's Manual of Old New York: 1924*, ed. Henry Collins Brown (New York: Museum of the City of New York, 1923).

In 1639, Swedish-born Jonas Bronck, who had lived in the port of Amsterdam, sailed to the New World with his wife and a few indentured farmhands. He became the first European settler to live on the mainland across the Harlem River north and east of the island of Manhattan. Bronck settled south of today's 150th Street. The Bronx River received its name from him. In 1898, the river's name was given to the borough.

The area that was to become today's Bronx was used as a locale by writers on the colonial period, both great and obscure. Some, such as diarists and men of letters, lived during the era about which they wrote. Others, such as literary titans Washington Irving and James Fenimore Cooper, lived and wrote centuries after the period in which their works were set. All were suffused by a deep love of their unique American heritage and a desire to preserve it for coming generations.

Conditions faced by the early settlers were primitive and dangerous. Few had time for literary production. Thus, it took authors who lived in later centuries to write of the era when The Bronx was a frontier, although their efforts reflect the time in which their work was written as much as the conditions of the period. Poet and humorist Arthur Guiterman evoked the frontier nature of Jonas Bronck's original settlement in his 1920 poem "The Legend of The Bronx," and provided an amusing tale purporting to explain why Bronck chose that location. In Guiterman's

Mosholu, the brook in Van Cortlandt Park, in 1918. "Oft have I trod its mossy ways / In wood of pine and leaf."—J. J. Meehan. The Bronx County Historical Society Research Library.

time, it was believed that Jonas Bronck came from Denmark, rather than from Sweden, but the poet used the correct Indian name for the Bronx River, Ah-qua-hung.

> With sword and Bible, brood and dame,
> Across the seas from Denmark came
> Stout Jonas Bronck. He roved among
> The wooded vales of Ah-qua-hung.
> "Good sooth! on every hand," quoth he,
> "Are pleasant lands and fair to see;
> But which were the best to plow and till
> and meetest both for manse and mill?"

"Bronck! Bronck! Bronck!"
> Called the frogs from the reeds of the river;
"Bronck! Bronck! Bronck!"
> From the marshes and pools of the stream.
"Here let your journeyings cease;
> Blest of the Bounteous Giver,
Yours is the Valley of Peace,
> Here is the home of your dream."

> "Oho!" laughed Jonas Bronck; "I ween
> These pop-eyed elves in bottle green
> Do call my name to show the spot
> Predestined!—Here I cast my lot!"
> So he reared his dwelling-place
> And built a mill, with wheel and race.

> —Arthur Guiterman, "The Legend of The Bronx,"
> *Ballads of Old New York* (New York: Harper &
> Brothers, 1920).

Based upon the initial discovery of the area in 1609 by Henry Hudson, the Netherlands claimed the area and placed it under the control of the Dutch West India Company. Because of clashing cultural attitudes toward land ownership, conflict with local American Indians arose. In addition, some New England religious dissidents moved into the region from the north and east.

In 1642, John Throckmorton, a follower of Rhode Island's founder, Roger Williams, led a group of English settlers to today's Throggs Neck, which was named after Throckmorton. At the same time, Anne Hutchinson, exiled from Massachusetts for dissenting from Puritan orthodoxy, established herself and her family north of today's Co-op City on the banks of a river that empties into Eastchester Bay. The site was across from modern Pelham Bay Park, which the American Indians called Lapechwahacking. The European settlers in both these areas angered the tribes because they never bothered to ask their permission to reside there. In addition, the Dutch governor, William Kieft, adopted high-handed policies that antagonized almost all the colony's tribes, including the local Siwanoy, which attacked these new settlements in the area that would become The Bronx.

Novelist Jesse Browner drew upon these historical events in his imaginative 1997 novel, *Turnaway*. In his fantasy tale, a modern canoeist, caught in a storm on Long Island Sound, wrecks his craft and saves himself by crawling upon a hitherto uncharted island called Turnaway, supposedly located among the many islets off the coast of Pelham Bay Park. Here he meets the fictional Elias, a contemporary American Indian who claims to be a descendant of both Anne Hutchinson and Wampage, the American Indian leader who killed her. Elias recounts these historical events to the canoeist.

> "Wampage approached the house alone, and the man named Collins met him. Wampage asked Collins to tie up the mastiffs, who were none too friendly to Indians and had been known to bite, and Collins was happy to comply. But the moment the dogs were immobilized the war party came whooping down out of the woods and began the slaughter. None who were found were spared. The cows and pigs were burned in the barns, Collins and Anne's children, Francis, William, Mary, and little Anne, were all hacked to death. Young Katherine tried to flee but was caught at the fence, dragged back into the barnyard by her hair, and had her head chopped off in one blow by Cokoe's temahikan.
>
> "In the meantime, Wampage had entered the house and found Anne cowering in the larder with her youngest daughter Susannah."

Wampage sends Susannah to the kitchen, and then turns to Anne.

> "Wampage hesitated only a moment before burying his hatchet deep in her forehead and then, in one swift arc, removing her scalp with his blade and tucking it neatly into the belt of his sakutakan. When he stepped into the kitchen he found Pemgaton holding young Susannah by the arm and about to plunge an iron dagger into her chest. Wampage called to him to stop and he obeyed immediately.
>
> "'This girl is reparation for my dead wife. I will take her.'
>
> "Wampage did take her. When the last traces of Anne's settlement had

burned to the ground, Wampage and his warriors vanished with their families deep into the hills of Cantito, beyond the frontier, where they remained for some years before returning to Lapechwahacking to sell their lands once and for all to Thomas Pell. But from the moment he killed Anne, Wampage renamed himself Annhook, in honor of his slain enemy, and that was how he was known until his death."

On hearing the story, the narrator is puzzled.

"There's something I don't understand," I eventually said; in that silence my voice sounded loud and stupid, but I pressed on. "If Wampage killed Anne, how is it you're related to her?"

"Wampage took Susannah with him into the wilderness, and there, when she was old enough, she bore him a child. When she was ransomed by the Dutch, at the age of fifteen, she was already a mother, a secret that was kept from her so-called benefactors. Actually, she was very reluctant to leave the Siwanoy, whom she had grown to love, and Wampage the father of her son. But it was part of a peace treaty—she had to go. She took her son with her and renamed him William."

Later, the skeptical canoeist researches the matter.

What is known: Wampage did live in Lapechwahacking, he did murder Anne Hutchinson and take her name in 1643, he did kidnap Susannah into the wilderness of Westchester then return her to her uncle several years later, and he and Maminepoe did sign away their lands under the Pelham Oak in 1654. . . . But there is no way of knowing if William was his son or not, none at all.

—Jesse Browner, *Turnaway* (New York: Villard, 1997).

Although no evidence exists that Susannah bore a child in captivity, Anne Hutchinson and Wampage were historical persons. Both a river and a parkway in The Bronx bear Anne Hutchinson's name to honor her advocacy of religious freedom.

The land where Bronck, Throckmorton, and Hutchinson settled was, at the time, located in the Dutch colony of New Netherland. Englishmen from Connecticut migrated to The Bronx in increasing numbers and, in 1664, an English fleet anchored off the southern Manhattan shoreline to wrest the colony from the Dutch. The Dutch governor, Peter Stuyvesant, tried to rally the indifferent population of New Amsterdam at the tip of Manhattan to oppose the invasion. In 1809, almost 150 years later, Washington Irving, America's first great literary figure, writing as Diedrich Knickerbocker, provided an amusing burlesque of the incident in a book now considered the first important work of comic literature written by an American. In the process, Irving, who later created Ichabod Crane and Rip Van Winkle, also created a legend to explain the odd name given to Spuyten Duyvil Creek, the northernmost section of the Harlem River, and to the abutting area in today's northwestern Bronx. Stuyvesant was irate at the refusal of his fellow Dutchmen to arm themselves to resist the invasion.

Resolutely bent, however, upon defending his beloved city, in despite even of itself, he called unto him his trusty Van Corlear, who was his right-hand man in all times of emergency. Him did he adjure to take his war denouncing trumpet, and mounting his horse, to beat up the country, night and day—Sounding the alarm along the pastoral borders of the Bronx—startling the wild solitudes of Croton, arousing the rugged yeomanry of Weehawk and Hoboken—the mighty men of battle of Tappan Bay—and the brave boys of Tarry Town and Sleepy hollow,—together with all the other warriers of the country round about; charging them one and all, to sling their powder horns, shoulder their fowling pieces, and march merrily down to the Manhattoes.

Now there was nothing in all the world, the divine sex excepted, that Antony Van Corlear loved better than errands of this kind. So just stopping to take a lusty dinner, and bracing to his side his junk bottle, well charged with heart inspiring Hollands, he issued jollily from the city gate, that looked out upon what is at present called Broadway; sounding as usual a farewell strain, that rung in sprightly echoes through the winding streets of New Amsterdam—Alas! never more were they gladdened by the melody of their favourite trumpeter!

It was a dark and stormy night when the good Antony arrived at the creek (sagely denominated Haerlem river) which separates the island of Manna-hata from the mainland. The wind was high, the elements were in an uproar, and no Charon could be found to ferry the adventurous sounder of brass across the water. For a short time he vapored like an impatient ghost upon the brink, and then bethinking himself of the urgency of his errand, took a hearty embrace of his stone bottle, swore most valourously that he would swim across, en spijt den Duyvil (in spite of the devil!) and daringly plunged into the stream.—Luckless Antony! Scarce had he buffetted half way over, when he was observed to struggle violently as if battling with the spirit of the waters—instinctively he put his trumpet to his mouth and giving a vehement blast—sank forever to the bottom!

The potent clangour of his trumpet, like the ivory horn of the renowned Paladin Orlando, when expiring in the glorious field of Roncesvalles, rung far and wide through the country, alarming the neighbours round, who hurried in amazement to the spot—Here an old Dutch burgher, famed for his veracity, and who had been a witness of the fact, related to them the melancholy affair; with the fearful addition (to which I am slow of giving belief) that he saw the duyvel, in the shape of a huge Moss-bonker with an invisible fiery tale, and vomiting boiling water, seize the sturdy Antony by the leg, and drag him beneath the waves. Certain it is, the place, with the adjoining promontory, which projects into the Hudson, has been called Spijt den Duyvel or Spiking devil, ever since—the restless ghost of the unfortunate Antony still haunts the surrounding solitudes, and his trumpet has often been heard by the neighbours, of a stormy night, mingling with the howling of the blast. No body ever attempts to swim across the creek after dark; on the contrary, a bridge has been built to guard against such melancholy accidents in the future—and as to Moss-bonkers, they are held in such abhorrence, that no true Dutchman will admit them to his table, who loves good fish and hates the devil.

> —Diedrich Knickerbocker [Washington Irving], *A History of New York, from the Beginning of the World to the End of the Dutch Dynasty* (New York: Inskeep & Bradford, 1809).

Spuyten Duyvil Creek in 1865. "He . . . swore most valourously that he would swim across, en spijt den Duyvil (in spite of the devil!) and daringly plunged into the stream."—Diedrich Knickerbocker [Washington Irving]. The Bronx County Historical Society Research Library.

Largely because of the indifference of the Dutch inhabitants Irving so irreverently spoofed, the English easily conquered the colony and renamed it New York. Under English rule, beginning in 1664, the remaining Dutch continued their way of life but gradually acquired English ways. The area to become The Bronx shed some of its frontier roughness. By the end of the seventeenth century, the area became the southern part of New York's Westchester County, a status it was to retain until the last quarter of the nineteenth century. By the first decade of the eighteenth century, towns were organized and a settled Anglican clergy established. No longer menaced by American Indian attacks, the population slowly grew.

The county took its name from the town of Westchester, now part of The Bronx, which served as the first county seat. Part of the town of Eastchester also extended into today's northeastern Bronx. Characteristic of the area and of the time were the manors, huge land grants owned by wealthy families, worked either by slave labor or by tenants as family farms. In the southwestern portion of the modern Bronx was the manor of Morrisania, owned by the Morris family. To its north lay the manor of Fordham, owned by the New York City Dutch Reformed Church. North of Fordham was the manor of Philipsburgh, owned by the Philipse family, which extended along the Hudson River shoreline well into modern Westchester County. Jacobus Van Cortlandt married into the Philipse family and received much of the land that now constitutes the northwestern corner of the modern Bronx. In the northeast area of The Bronx, and also extending into modern Westchester, was the manor of Pelham, held by the Pell family. This handful of large landowners constituted the region's aristocracy in the eighteenth century, and they attempted to reconstruct English society in what was to become The Bronx.

Colonial life and the stratification of its society were depicted in *Satanstoe*, a novel of manners written by another early American literary giant, James Fenimore Cooper. The novel was set in the Westchester County countryside he knew so well. Young Cooper and his bride, a daughter of John Peter Delancy, a Revolutionary War Tory leader, inherited land at Mamaroneck, where he explored the region, absorbing its local legends. Long after he became famous for *The Leatherstocking Tales* and retired to Cooperstown in upstate New York, Cooper drew upon those scenes to write the Littlepage trilogy, of which *Satanstoe* is a part. The novel reflects the author's admiration for the manners of the colonial gentry and support of traditional property rights. It is considered the finest portrait of colonial life in American literature. Cooper's story is told by his main character, Cornelius Littlepage, who grew up on his father's fictional farm called Satanstoe, located where Mamaroneck is today in Westchester County. Littlepage recounts an old legend to explain the strange name of his family's farm and the area of rocks and eddies off the shoreline of today's southeastern Bronx.

The neck lies in the vicinity of a well-known pass that is to be found in the narrow arm of the sea that separates the island of Manhattan from its neighbour, Long Island, and which is called Hell Gate. Now, there is a tradition, that I confess is somewhat confined to the blacks in the neighborhood, but which says that the Father of Lies, on a particular occasion, when he was violently expelled from certain roystering taverns in the New Netherlands, made his exit by drawing his foot somewhat hastily from among the lobster-pots that abound in those waters, leaving behind him as a print of his passage by that route, the Hog's Back, the Pot, and all the whirlpools and rocks that render navigation so difficult in that celebrated strait, he placed it hurriedly upon the spot where there now spreads a large bay to the southward and east-ward of the neck, just touching the latter with the ball of his great toe, as he passed Down East; from which part of the country some of our people used to maintain he originally came.

Littlepage also ranked his family's status in the local hierarchy in the years before the American Revolution. All of the families mentioned owned property in today's Bronx.

We happened to be in a part of Westchester in which were none of the very large estates, and Satanstoe passed for property of a certain degree of importance. It is true, the Morrises were at Morrisania, and the Felipses, or Philipses, as these Bohemian counts were then called, had a manor on the Hudson, that extended within a dozen miles of us, and a younger branch of the de Lanceys had established itself even much nearer, while the Van Cort-landts, or a branch of them, too dwelt near Kingsbridge; but these were all the people who were at the head of the colony, and with whom none of the minor gentry attempted to vie. As it was, therefore, the Littlepages held a very respectable position between the higher class of the yeomanry and those who, by their estates, education, connections, official rank, and hereditary consideration, formed what might be justly called the aristocracy of the Colony.

In Cooper's novel, Littlepage and his best friend, Dirck, ride from Satanstoe to New York City. They stop at a tavern in Kingsbridge, named after a small span cross-ing Spuyten Duyvil Creek.

We dined and baited at Kingsbridge, intending to sup in town. While the dinner was cooking, Dirck and I walked out on the heights that overlook the

The Van Cortlandt House in Van Cortlandt Park in the 1890s. A postcard photograph. "The Van Cortlandts, or a branch of them, too dwelt near Kingsbridge."—James Fenimore Cooper. Barbara Unger Collection.

Hudson; for I knew less of this noble river than I wished to know of it. We conversed as we walked; and my companion, who knew the river much better than myself, having many occasions to pass up and down it, between the village of Haverstraw and town, in his frequent visits to his relatives below, gave me some useful information.

They spot a wooded cove on the river in which the country house of fictional merchant Herman Mordaunt is located. Dirck tells Littlepage of his love for Mordaunt's daughter, Anneke. Littlepage attempts to solicit information from the innkeeper about the status of the Mordaunt family.

"Pray, Mrs. Light," I asked when there was an opening, which was not until the good woman had exhausted her breath in honour of the Littlepages, "do you know anything of a family, hereabouts, of the name of Mordaunt?"

"Do I happen to know, sir!—Why, Mr. Littlepage, you might almost as well have asked me, if I had ever heard of a Van Cortlandt, or a Philipse, or a Morris, or any other of the gentry hereabouts. Mr. Mordaunt has a country-place, and a very pretty one it is, within two miles and a half of us; and he and Madam Mordaunt never passed our door, when they went into the country to see Madam Van Cortlandt, without stopping to say a word and leave a shilling.

> —James Fenimore Cooper, *Satanstoe, or the Little-page Manuscripts: A Tale of the Colony* (New York: Burgess, Stringer & Company, 1845).

While the established landed gentry, like those portrayed by Cooper, presided over the colonial government, economy, and society, most residents of the area to become The Bronx were hard-working farmers who barely eked out a living raising flax for the linen market, sheep for the woolens trade, wheat to be made into flour, and apples to be pressed into cider. Discontent with British rule was growing. The First Continental Congress imposed an embargo on the exporting and importing of specific items to and from Britain in reaction to the British Parliament's passage of the Intolerable Acts following the Boston Tea Party. The town of Westchester had been granted privileges in a royal charter and its residents were reluctant to sacrifice them. They also thought that the American retaliatory measures went too far and were highly destructive to the local farmers. For these reasons, many Westchester residents tended to support the British. Samuel Seabury, the Anglican rector in the town of Westchester, wrote a pamphlet, effectively using biting ridicule to make points in support of the farmers against the actions of the Congress. He disguised his identity, posing as a simple farmer residing in the town. Considering the embargo on the sale of flaxseed, Seabury suggested that paying the nominal tea tax to Great Britain was preferable to following the congressional will.

> You know, my Friends, that the sale of your seed not only pays your taxes, but furnishes you with many of the little conveniences, and comforts of life; the loss of it for one year would be of more damage to you, than paying the three-penny duty on tea for twenty. . . . I use in my family about six pounds of tea: few farmers in my neighbourhood use so much; but I hate to stint my wife and daughters, or my friendly neighbours when they come to see me. Besides, I like a dish of tea too, especially after a little more than ordinary fatigue in hot weather. Now 200 pounds of tea, at six pounds a year, will last just 33 years, and eight months. So that in order to pay this monstrous duty upon tea, which has raised all this confounded combustion in the country, I have only to sell the produce of a bushel of flax-seed once in THIRTY-THREE years. Ridiculous! . . .
>
> Look well to yourselves, I beseech you. From the day that exports from this province are stopped, the farmers may date the commencement of their ruin. . . . And unless you can sell your produce, how are you to get money?

Nor will the case be better, if you are obliged to sell your produce at an under-rate; for then it will not pay you for the labour and expence of raising it. But this is the least part of the distress that will come upon you.

Unhappily, many of you are in debt, and obliged to pay the enormous interest of seven pounds on the hundred, for considerable sums. It matters not whether your debts have been contracted through necessity or carelessness: You must pay them, at least the interest, punctually; the usurer will not wait long; indeed you cannot expect he should: You have had his money, and are obliged, in justice, to pay him the principal and interest, according to agreement. But without selling your produce, you can neither pay the one, nor the other; the consequence will be that after a while, a process of law will be commenced against you, and your farms must be sold by execution; and then you will have to pay not only principal and interest, but Sheriffs fees, Lawyers fees, and a long list of *et cæteras*.

> —a W. Farmer [Samuel Seabury], *Free Thoughts, on The Proceedings of the Continental Congress, Held at Philadelphia Sept. 3, 1774 . . .* (N.p., 1774).

Seabury's pamphlet provided a rallying cry for those opposed to the actions of the Congress. By August 1776, the British army and navy massed in upper New York Bay, menacing the American-held city on Manhattan Island. Since the King's Bridge crossing Spuyten Duyvil Creek constituted the back door to the city, and the heights overlooking the upper portion of the Harlem River commanded the approaches to the bridge, fortifications had to be built on the mainland. Thus, the area became a battlefield in the war of independence.

American Maj. Gen. William Heath recorded in his memoirs the incidents as the conflict came ever closer. There, he referred to himself as "our general," Throggs Neck as "Frog's Point," City Island as "New City Island," Randall's Island as "Montresor's Island," and today's Pelham Bay Park as "Pell's Neck." His "Williams's Bridge" spanned the Bronx River at today's Gun Hill Road, and Morrisania was the home of Lewis Morris, a signer of the Declaration of Independence.

[August] 27th. [1776] —Early in the morning, two ships and a brig came to anchor a little above Frog Point. Our general immediately detached Col. Graham with his regiment, to prevent their landing to plunder or harm. Before he arrived, several barges full of men landed on New City Island, and killed a number of cattle. Two companies of the regiment, immediately on their arrival, ferried over to the island. The enemy carried off one man and 14 cattle—the remainder of the cattle were secured. . . .

[September] 5th. [1776] —Our general ordered a chain of videttes and centinels to be formed at Morrisania, Hunt's and Frog's Point &c....

10th. —The British landed a number of troops on Montresor's Island....

18th. — ...A picket from our General's division, of 450 men, constantly mounted, by relief, at Morrisania; from which a chain of centinels, within a half gunshot of each other, were planted, from the one side of the shore to the other, and near the water passage, between Morrisania and Montresor's Island, which in some places is very narrow. The centinels on the American side were ordered not to presume to fire at those of the British, unless the latter began; but the British were so fond of beginning, that there was frequent fire between them.

A British officer was wounded by an American picket in an exchange of fire. Another British officer, in retaliation, threatened to cannonade the house of Lewis Morris, where the American officers commanding the soldiers at Morrisania were quartered. An agreement was made that the pickets would not fire on one another.

[October] 3rd. [1776] —The Brigadier-Generals of our General's division were in council, and several new works were laid out; among others, a redoubt on the hill above Williams's Bridge. Our General, in reconnoitring his position, accompanied by Col. Hand, below the camp of the rifle corps, being appreciative that the British might land on Frog's Neck, took a view of the causeway between West Chester and the point. Upon the creek, which runs between these two, is a tide-mill and a plank bridge: at the mill, at the west end of the causeway, (the side of the American army) was at this time a range of cord-wood, as advantageously situated to cover a party to defend the pass, as if constructed for the very purpose.

Heath told Colonel Hand to select his best men to guard the pass and, if necessary, to take up the planks of the bridge and set fire to the mill. He also ordered Hand to dispatch more soldiers to the headwaters of the creek to hold off a possible British attack at that position.

12th. —Early in the morning, 80 or 90 British boats, full of men, stood up the sound, from Montresor's Island, Long Island, &c. The troops landed at Frog's Neck, and their advance pushed towards the causeway and the bridge, at West Chester mill. Col. Hand's riflemen took up the planks of the bridge, as had been directed, and commenced a firing with their rifles. The British moved towards the head of the creek, but found there also the

Americans in possession of the pass. Our General immediately (as he assured Col. Hand he would do) ordered Col. Prescott, the hero of Bunker Hill, with his regiment, and Capt. Lieut. Bryant of the artillery, with a 3 pounder, to reinforce the riflemen at West Chester causeway; and Col. Graham of the New York line, with his regiment, and Lieut. Jackson of the artillery, with a 6 pounder, to reinforce the head of the creek; all of which was promptly done, to the check and disappointment of the enemy. The British encamped on the Neck....

16th. — ... The General Officers of the army rode to reconnoitre the ground at Pell's Neck, &c. and it was determined that the position of the American army should be immediately changed; the left flank to be extended more northerly, to prevent its being turned by the British....

18th. — ... The wind was now fresh at south-west. The British crossed to the other side of Frog's Neck, embarked on board their boats, crossed over the cove, landed on Pell's Neck, and moved briskly upwards. Three or four of the American regiments advanced towards them, and took a good position behind a stone fence. When the British had advanced sufficiently near, they gave them a pretty close fire, which checked them, and even obliged them to fall back; but being immediately supported, they returned vigorously to the charge. The action was sharp, for a short time; but the Americans were soon obliged to give way to superior force.

—William Heath, *Memoirs of Major-General Heath*
(Boston: J. Thomas and E. T. Andrews, 1798).

The Battle of Pell's Point, or as Heath called it, Pell's Neck, in today's Pelham Bay Park, was also described in a letter written on October 22, 1776, by the American commander on the spot, Col. John Glover, whose nominal superior, Maj. Gen. Charles Lee, had not yet taken up his post when the battle began to develop. Since Glover, like many American officers, was untrained in the military arts, he experienced great anxiety at the British approach.

I arose early in the morning and went on the hill with my glass, and discovered a number of ships in the Sound under way; in a very short time saw boats, upwards of two hundred sail, all manned and formed in four grand divisions. I immediately sent off Major Lee express to General Lee, who was about three miles distant, and without waiting his orders, turned out the brigade I have the honour to command, and very luckily for us I did, as it turned out afterwards, the enemy having stole a march of one and a half miles on us. I marched down to oppose their landing with about seven hundred and fifty men and three field-pieces, but had not gone more than half the distance before I met their advanced guard, about thirty men; upon which I detached a captain's guard of fifty men to meet them, while I could dispose of the main body to advantage.

Glover posted Colonel Reed's men behind a wall to the left of the road. Colonel Shepard's unit was placed diagonally across the road, and Colonel Baldwin's still farther back, but on the same side of the road as Reed's troops.

The enemy gave a shout and advanced, Colonel Reed's laying under cover of a stone wall undiscovered until they came within thirty yards, then rose up and gave them the whole charge; the enemy broke and retreated for the main body to come up. In this situation we remained about an hour and a half, when they appeared about four thousand, with seven pieces of artillery; we kept our post under the cover of the stone wall before mentioned, till they came within fifty yards of us; rose up and gave the whole charge of the battalion, they halted, and returned the fire with showers of musketry and cannon balls. We exchanged seven rounds at this post, retreated and formed in the rear of Colonel Shepard and on his left; they then shouted and pushed on till they came on Shepard, posted behind a fine double stone wall; he rose up and fired by grand divisions, by which he kept up a constant fire, and maintained his post till he exchanged seventeen

The Battle of Pell's Point, October 18, 1776, mural by James Monroe Hewlitt in the Mario Merola Bronx County Building. "The enemy gave a shout and advanced, Colonel Reed's laying under cover of a stone wall undiscovered until they came within thirty yards, then rose up and gave them a whole charge." —John Glover. Municipal Art Commission of the City of New York.

rounds with them, and caused them to retreat several times, once in particular so far that a soldier of Colonel Shepard's leaped over the wall and took a
hat and canteen off a captain that lay dead on the ground they retreated from.
However, their body being so much larger than ours, we were for the preservation of the men forced to retreat, and formed in the rear of Baldwin's Regiment.

> —John Glover, "A Letter to a Friend," *Freeman Jour-*
> *nal and the New Hampshire Gazette* (November 26,
> 1776).

Glover continued to retreat while holding the far larger British forces to a virtual standoff. His quick thinking and the bravery of his men at Pell's Point delayed
the British advance long enough to enable George Washington to escape encir-
clement and safely evacuate his forces from northern Manhattan and The Bronx.
That action left most of the area, already a hotbed of Tory sentiment, under the control of the British military and their Hessian mercenaries for the remainder of the
conflict. The British were also aided by the Tories who fled from behind American
lines to live in refugee settlements in what is today's Bronx. A great many resided in
huts erected for them in Morrisania. Some local Tories organized into militia units,
such as DeLancey's Loyal Refugees, to raid farms situated between the armies, the
so-called Neutral Ground, and to steal cattle to feed the British soldiers. Angry
Patriots called them Cowboys, the first use of the term. American militiamen retal-
iated by raiding suspected Tory farmers. Irate Tories called them Skinners. Private
Joseph Plumb Martin described a Skinner raid on a gang of Cowboys who had
stolen provisions from a Patriot colonel.

> [The Colonel] solicited some men from the Light Infantry, to endeavour
> to capture some of the gang whom he was personally acquainted with, who
> belonged to, or were often at, Westchester, a village near King's Bridge.
> Accordingly, a captain and two subaltern officers and about eighty men, of
> which I was one, was sent from our regiment, then lying at a village called
> Bedford, to his assistance....
> ... We staid here through the day, drew some pork and biscuit, and pre-
> pared for our expedition against the Cow Boys. At dark we set off, accompa-
> nied by the Militia Colonel and three or four subaltern Militia officers;—this
> was the third night I had been on my feet, the whole time without any sleep,
> but go we must. We marched but a short way in the road, and then turned
> into the fields and pastures, over brooks and fences, through swamps, mire
> and woods, endeavouring to keep clear of the inhabitants as possible. About
> midnight we crossed a road near a house, the inmates of which, I suppose,

were friendly to our cause, as the officers ordered us to stand still and not to speak nor leave our places on any account whatever, while they all entered the house for a few minutes, upon what errand I know not. As soon as the officers joined us again we marched off. . . .

. . . About two o'clock we took to the high road when we were between the village of Westchester and King's Bridge, we then came back to the village, where we were separated into small divisions, each led by an officer, either of our own or of the Militia, and immediately entered all the suspected houses at once; what we had to do must be done quickly, as the enemy were so near that they might have been informed of us in less than half an hour; there were several men in the house to which I was led, but one only appeared to be obnoxious to the officer who led us; this man was a Tory Refugee, in green uniform; we immediately secured him. An old man blind as a bat, came out of the bedroom, who appeared to be in great distress, for fear that there would be a murder committed, as he termed it. I told him it was impossible to commit murder with Refugees. We directly left the house with our prisoner, and joined the other parties and hurried off with all possible speed.

When we got away and day light appeared, we found that we had twelve or fourteen prisoners, the most or all of whom had been concerned with the destruction of the Colonel's stores.

> —Joseph Plumb Martin, *A Narrative of Some of the Adventures, Dangers and Sufferings of a Revolutionary Soldier . . .* (Hallowell, Me.: Glazie, Masters & Co., 1830).

The heated emotions of the era were captured in another poem by Arthur Guiterman writing in 1920. He described a victorious Patriot raid made by people from the Hudson Highlands in modern Putnam County and upper Westchester County. Starting at the Nepperhan Valley in today's Yonkers and going down the Tibbett's Brook valley, these Skinners (Patriots) aimed to engage a Cowboy (Tory) troop led by James DeLancey of West Farms outside Fort Number Eight, a fortification overlooking the Harlem River where Bronx Community College stands today. They also encountered some German mercenaries hired by the British, the Hessian riflemen, or Yägers, at the King's Bridge and at the parallel Dyckman's Bridge, both of which spanned the northern part of the Harlem River called Spuyten Duyvil Creek.

> "Up! bully boys of the Nepperhan!
> Gather! ye troopers, grim and rough;
> Ye of the hardy homespun clan,
> Ye who have trained in the Blue and Buff.

Come from the Highlands, grandly free,
      Barring the stream to the baffled foe;
Come from your farms by the Tappan Zee,
      Come from the Vale of Pocantico!"
Dark of the moon; and shadows deep
      Curtain the road on field and ridge;
Laggardly watch the redcoats keep,
      Calling the word at Dyckman's Bridge.

Down in the dell by the Sawmill ford
      Fourscore men to the muster throng;
Scarred are some by the British sword,
      Scarred are some by the deeper wrong:
Murdoch—he of the Monmouth fray:
      Dirksen, wreck of a massive bulk,
One of the hundreds racked away,
      Starved in the Jersey's prison hulk;
Dyckman breathing his dead boy's name;
      Young, God knoweth, a vengeful man,
Brooding and dark since the Tory flame
      Blackened his home by the Nepperhan.
Oh, give and take is the way of war,
      And of cloven helmets our own swords tell;
But the turncoat curs of the Tory corps
      We hate as we hate the gates of hell.

Only the beaver, sunk from view,
      Watched us pass with a furtive eye;
Only the owl of Mosholu
      Challenged us as we skirted by;
Only the stars, through a drift of gray
      Silently beckoning, led us straight
There where De Lancey's Tories lay
      Under the guns of Number Eight.

"Brands!" And the bridge upon Haarlem's breast
      Melts in a broken chain of fire;
Every hut has a flaming crest,
      Every shack is a blazing pyre.

Blundering out to the lurid night
  Rally the shreds of the hated corps;
Speak to them! gun of the Trenton fight,
  Bell-muzzled piece of the Indian War!
Reavers and harriers, each and all,
  Traitors with blood of their country wet—
Ply them with rifle and musket-ball!
  At them with saber and bayonet!

Loosen your horses! Burn the hay!
  Kill whom ye must and take whom ye can,
For the Yägers are up on the King's Bridge Way.
  So it's back! through the Valley of Nepperhan!
Three miles up through the well-known glade,
  Helmeted Yägers hard on our track,
Laughing, we turned at our ambuscade,
  Hurling the Hessians staggering back.

Dark were our deeds of the steel and brand?
  Aye. But they wearied a stubborn foe,
Held him at bay, while our leader planned,
  Cautious and wise, for the final blow.

King's Bridge in 1865. "Kill whom ye must and take whom ye can, / For the Yägers are up on the King's Bridge way." —Arthur Guiterman. The Bronx County Historical Society Research Library.

> Judge us fairly, if judge ye may;
>   Freed is our country of hostile ban;
> Redcoat and Hessian have had their day;
>   Peace rules the Vale of the Nepperhan.
>
>> —Arthur Guiterman, "A Raid of the Neutral
>> Ground," *Ballads of Old New York* (New York:
>> Harper & Brothers, 1920).

Even before the 1783 peace treaty confirming the final American victory, the new government of New York State acted to strip the Tories of their property. Many were exiled, their lands divided into family farms and sold. The members of the old ruling gentry who supported the American cause and owned such manors as Morrisania and Pelham were also affected by the war's outcome. Even though these Patriots retained ownership of their estates, their manors were declared towns in 1788, making it easier for small farmers to purchase land from them. The colonial stratified society was gone. Independence was established in the new United States. A decade was needed to repair the extensive damage caused by the war but, by the end of the century, the politically independent people of the area to become The Bronx once more settled back into an agricultural life. Primarily, Bronx farmers served the market of a growing New York City, already one of the country's largest municipalities. That growth was to have a profound effect on the area's future.

2

OUT OF TOWN

THE SUBURBAN BRONX

1800–1898

AT THE ONSET OF THE NINETEENTH CENTURY, THE STILL SPARSELY populated Bronx was seen as a rural Arcadia. With time, the construction of new roads and, in 1841, of the first railroad, transformed it into a pleasant suburb of New York City. Some writers celebrated the lush countryside. Others observing the scene lamented the incursions of industry and increased population. Thus, all writers of this era stressed the unspoiled natural beauty of the landscape. Small villages and hamlets such as Mott Haven, Fordham, and Kingsbridge formed tightly knit communities surrounded by open farmland and forests.

At first, the changes wrought by both the American Revolution and the continued growth of New York City slowly caused statesman Gouverneur Morris, the half brother of Lewis Morris, a signer of the Declaration of Independence, to become concerned. As a member of the Constitutional Convention, Gouverneur Morris had contributed many important ideas enshrined in the Constitution of the United States. Because he put the literary polish on the document, he was called the "Penman of the Constitution." Just before the century began, he returned to Morrisania after spending more than a decade in Europe both as American minister to France and as a private citizen. Morris vainly opposed continual efforts to build roads through his large sylvan farm to New York City. In 1800, a thoroughfare, roughly today's Boston Road, had to be created to connect the town of Westchester to New York over the newly built Harlem Bridge, on the site of today's Third Avenue Bridge. Later, the Westchester Turnpike Company sought to take part of Morris's land to build a toll road, roughly modern Westchester Avenue. In his diary, Morris jotted down notes about his struggle to hold off development.

Monday 17 March 1800
This Morning I am occupied in drawing a Map of the Road in West Chester to shew the Commissioners who have been called to run a Road thro my farm. Two of them[,] Mr Delancey and Mr Williams[,] dine with me and

so does Captain Kelly. They are to meet again on Monday for the Purpose of hearing the Determination of the Applicants on the ground that they are to pay for the Road.

Tuesday 11 Aug. [1801]

    I attend at Hunt's Tavern on the Bronx a Jury of View on the petition of Ludlow and others to get a Road thro my Land. Kept till late and obtain a Verdict. Very warm weather. . . .

Friday 21 Aug.

    At ten oClock I leave this and go on about thirteen miles to Mr. Wilkins's. . . . The new Turnpike lies over a hilly Country and has occasioned much Heartburning in the Country—I breakfast here and get home at Noon. . . .

Morris was also preoccupied over a dispute with the Leggett family, who claimed that the western boundary of their lands extended to the Mill Brook, today's Brook Avenue, which would give them the ownership of his property.

The Hunt Inn in 1900. This site today is where Southern Boulevard, Westchester Avenue, and 167th Street converge and a short distance from the Bronx River. "I attend at Hunt's Tavern on the Bronx." —Gouverneur Morris. The Bronx County Historical Society Research Library, Randall Comfort Collection.

Saturday 14 Augt. 1802

Go to Squire Leggets at the West Farms to see the map of that grant which he says he has not but he shews me the grant and says the true Western Boundary is the Mill Brook. There is a meeting here about a Road thro' my Land which they wish to try for again. fine Day. . . .

Saturday 9 Octr.

. . . Go to the West Farms to attend a jury summoned about a Road thro' Morrisania. . . .

By 1811, the Turnpike Company was in negotiations with Morris.

Monday 19 [August 1811]

Ludlow Ogden comes to treat on the part of the Turnpike Company— He declares that he is tied up by verbal instructions not to exceed a certain Sum—I tell him in that Case there can be little ground for treaty. He says he supposes I shall not ask any Thing for the Soil—I assure him that this is a Mistake. That as to the fencing I had rather the Company make it Part of their Contract to put up a good Stone Wall on each Side of the Road—and state my Demand for the Land at £100 per Acre for my Orchard and Meadow and £50 per Acre for the Rest. He is not authorized to accede to these Terms but is to make Report to the Comm[issione]rs. . . .

Morris also recorded the beginnings of manufacturing in West Farms, just north of Morrisania, and his continuing feud with the turnpike company.

Monday 9 [September 1811]

Ride to the factories at the West Farms—The various Compositions of Lead are I think going well under the Direction of Mr[.] Vosburgh—The Pottery might do well but there is a Want of Order and Management. Am shewn some Kaolin which is as it seems abundant in this Neighborhood— At least the Substance shewn to me but whether it be Kaolin remains to be Determined. . . .

Tuesday 21 [April 1812]

. . . In the Evening Thomas Leggett and another Person come down to tender me the Sum awarded by the Comm[issio]n for Damages by a Turnpike Road passing thro my farm Which is less than the Company had offered and I had rejected with Contempt. God grant me Patience.

Wednesday 22d [April]

    fine but cool weather—Walk a little and direct fences to cover myself as well as I can against the Depredations by the new Road—The Commodore comes in the Afternoon and[,] full of Indignation himself[,] is not surprised at mine but rather at my Composure[.] he is paid 17 to 10 in Proportion to our respective Land and mine is much more valuable—

By July 1812, Morris, having been forced to sell some of his land to the company, boasted of being the first to take a carriage ride on the turnpike he had once so bitterly opposed.

Tuesday 21 [July]

    Ride before Breakfast and pass (I believe the first Carriage) over the new Turnpike so as to come round by the West farms—Then up to my Harvest field and get Home a little after eight. . . .

        —Gouverneur Morris, Diary, manuscript in the Library of Congress.

Despite the waning authority of the old gentry and the inevitable development of new roads and early manufacturing, much of what would become The Bronx still remained pastoral and bucolic. This Arcadian setting was immortalized by poet Joseph Rodman Drake, one of the nation's earliest recognized poets. In the poem "Bronx," especially in the final stanza, Drake longingly remembers the Bronx River of his youth from a faraway place.

    Yet I will look upon thy face again,
      My own romantic Bronx, and it will be
    A face more pleasant than the face of men.
      Thy waves are old companions, I shall see
    A well-remembered form in each old tree,
      And hear a voice long loved in thy wild minstrelsy.

        —Joseph Rodman Drake, "Bronx," *The Culprit Fay and Other Poems* (New York: George Dearborn, 1835).

Decades later, Drake's Arcadia began to change when, in 1841, the New York and Harlem River Railroad was built through the farmlands along today's Park Avenue and Bronx River valley. Stations erected in the middle of nowhere attracted businesses and people, and new villages, such as Mott Haven, Tremont, and Williamsbridge, sprouted up around them seemingly overnight. These transformed The Bronx over time to a suburb, with residents commuting by railroad to their jobs in New York City. One of these new settlements was the village of Fordham.

In 1846, Edgar Allan Poe, accompanied by his mother-in-law, who was also his aunt, Maria Clemm, came to Fordham from Manhattan hoping that the clean country air could cure his young wife, Virginia, of tuberculosis. Poe was already known for his literary criticism and as the author of such poems as "The Raven" and many short stories, such as "The Gold Bug," "The Masque of the Red Death," and "The Purloined Letter." He rented a small cottage from John Valentine, now standing in Poe Park at the Grand Concourse and Kingsbridge Road, but he could not escape the irate carping of those literary men whose works he had savaged in his reviews, nor his poverty. He wrote to his friend, Dr. Thomas H. Chivers:

> I am living out of town about 13 miles, at a village called Fordham, on the rail-road leading north. We are in a snug little cottage, keeping house,

The Bronx River in Bronx Park in 1909. A postcard photograph. "Yet I will look upon thy face again, / My own romantic Bronx." —Joseph Rodman Drake. Barbara Unger Collection.

The Fordham Railroad Station in 1865. "I am living out of town about 13 miles, at a village called Fordham, on the railroad leading north." —Edgar Allan Poe. The Bronx County Historical Society Research Library.

and would be very comfortable, but that I have been for a long time dreadfully ill. I am getting better, however, although slowly, and shall get *well*. In the meantime the flocks of little birds of prey that always take the opportunity of illness to peck at a sick fowl of larger dimensions, have been endeavoring with all their power to effect my ruin. My dreadful poverty, also, has given them every advantage. . . .

. . . I have not been able to write *one line* for the Magazines for more than 5 months—you can then form some idea of the dreadful extremity to which I have been reduced. . . .

There is one thing you will be glad to learn:—It has been a long time while since any artificial stimulus has passed my lips. When I see you—should that day ever come—this is a topic on which I desire to have a long talk with you. I am done forever with drink—depend upon that—but there is much more in this matter than meets the eye.

Do not let anything in this letter impress you with the belief that I *despair* even of worldly prosperity. On the contrary although I feel ill, and am ground into the very dust with poverty, there is a sweet *hope* in the bottom of my soul. . . .

When you write, address simply "New-York-City." There is no Post Office at Fordham.

Despite Poe's admonition, letters were still addressed to him at Fordham. Three years after his arrival, he informed a correspondent, Edward H. N. Patterson, of the difficulties this had caused him.

I live at the village of Fordham; about 14 miles from New-York on the Harlam Rail-Road—but as there is no Post-Office at the place, I date always from New-York and get all my letters at the city Post-Office. When, by accident or misapprehension, letters are especially directed to me at Fordham, the clerks—some of them who do not know my arrangements—forward them to West-Farms, the nearest Post-Office town, and one which I rarely visit.

> —*The Letters of Edgar Allan Poe*, vol. 2, ed. John Ward Ostrom (New York: Gordian Press, Inc., 1966).

While Poe resided at Fordham, he regularly ambled around the changing rural landscape. He strolled across the new High Bridge, which carried the Croton Aqueduct water across the Harlem River to New York. A regular visitor to the new St. John's College, later Fordham University, nearby, Poe became friendly with the Jesuit instructors and was permitted to use the library. He enjoyed seeing the wild gorge of the Bronx River in today's Botanical Garden in Bronx Park and the flat meadows below it in what would become the Bronx Zoo. Poe used his surroundings at Fordham as the inspiration for a scene in "Landor's Cottage." He described the interior of his own dwelling, but as a mirror image of its real floor plan, and added a fictional north wing. Most of the furnishings were far more expensive than Poe could afford, but a few of those he did detail, such as the rocking chair and the books, were actually in his possession.

> I entered—passing first into a tolerably wide vestibule. Having come mainly to *observe*, I took notice that to my right as I stepped in, was a window, such as those in front of the house; to the left, a door leading into the principal room; while, opposite me, an open door enabled me to see a small apartment, just the size of the vestibule, arranged as a study, and having a large bow window looking out to the north. . . .
>
> The north wing, I now saw, was a bedchamber; its door opened into the parlor. West of this door was a single window, looking toward the brook. At the west end of the parlor, were a fire-place, and a door leading to the west wing—probably a kitchen.
>
> Nothing could be more simple than the furniture of the parlor. On the floor was an ingrain carpet, of excellent texture—a white ground, spotted with small circular green figures. At the windows were curtains of snowy white jaconet muslin: they were tolerably full, and hung *decisively*, perhaps rather formally in sharp parallel plaits to the floor—*just* to the floor. The walls were prepared with a French paper of great delicacy, a silver ground, with a faint green cord running zig-zag throughout. Its expanse was relieved merely by three of Julien's exquisite lithographs *à trois crayons*, fastened to the wall without frames. One of these drawings was a scene of Oriental luxury, or rather voluptuousness; another was a "carnival piece," spirited

beyond compare; the third was a Greek female head—a face so divinely beautiful, and yet of an expression so provokingly indeterminate, never before arrested my attention.

The more substantial furniture consisted of a round table, a few chairs (including a large rocking chair)....

On the table were a few books....

—Edgar Allan Poe, "Landor's Cottage: A Pendant to the Domain of Arnheim," [Boston] *Flag of Our Union* (June 9, 1849).

One of Poe's visitors at Fordham was Mary Gove Nichols, who arrived by railroad at Fordham station in the company of two book reviewers. She later wrote a memoir of her experience. Poe's new poem that she discussed with Mrs. Clemm was "Ulalume."

We made one excursion to Fordham to see Poe. We found him, and his wife, and his wife's mother—who was his aunt—living in a little cottage at the top of a hill. There was an acre or two of greensward, fenced in about the house, as smooth as velvet and as clean as the best kept carpet. There were some grand old cherry-trees in the yard, that threw a massive shade around them. The house had three rooms—a kitchen, a sitting-room, and a bed-chamber over the sitting-room. There was a piazza in front of the house that was a lovely place to sit in the summer, with the shade of cherry-trees before it. There was no cultivation, no flowers—nothing but smooth greens-ward and the majestic trees. . . . So handsome, so impressive in his wonderful intellectual beauty, so proud and reserved, and yet so confidently communicative, so entirely a gentleman on all occasions that I ever saw him—so tasteful, so good a talker was Poe, that he impressed

The Edgar Allan Poe Cottage in 1884. "We made one excursion to Fordham to see Poe. We found him and his wife, and his wife's mother—who was his aunt—living in a little cottage at the top of a hill. . . . There was no cultivation, no flowers—nothing but smooth greensward and the majestic trees." —Mary Gove Nichols. The Bronx County Historical Society Research Library.

himself and his wishes, even without words, upon those with whom he spoke. . . .

Poe's voice was melody itself. He always spoke low, even in a violent discussion, compelling his hearers to listen if they would know his opinion, his facts, his fancies, or philosophy, or his weird imaginings. These last usually flowed from his pen, seldom from his tongue.

On this occasion I was introduced to the young wife of the poet, and to the mother, then more than sixty years of age. She was a tall, dignified old lady, with a most ladylike manner, and her black dress, though old and much worn, looked really elegant on her. She wore a widow's cap of the genuine pattern, and it suited exquisitely with her snow-white hair. Her features were large, and corresponded with her stature, and it seemed strange how such a stalwart and queenly woman could be the mother of her almost petit daughter. Mrs. Poe looked very young; she had large black eyes, and a pearly whiteness of complexion, which was a perfect pallor. Her pale face, her brilliant eyes, and her raven hair gave her an unearthly look. One felt that she was almost a disrobed spirit, and when she coughed it was made certain that she was rapidly passing away.

The mother seemed hale and strong, and appeared to be a sort of universal Providence for her strange children.

The cottage had an air of taste and gentility that must have been lent to it by the presence of its inmates. So neat, so poor, so unfurnished, and yet so charming a dwelling I never saw. The floor of the kitchen was white as wheaten flour. A table, a chair, and a little stove that it contained seemed to furnish it perfectly. The sitting-room floor was laid with check matting; four chairs, a light stand, and a hanging bookshelf completed its furniture. There were pretty presentation copies of books on the little shelves, and the Brownings had posts of honour on the stand. With quiet exultation Poe drew from his side pocket a letter he had received from Elizabeth Barrett Browning. He read it to us. It was very flattering. She told Poe that his "poem of the Raven had awakened a fit of horror in England." This is what he loved to do. To make the flesh creep, to make one shudder and freeze with horror, was more to his relish (I cannot say more to his mind or heart) than to touch the tenderest chords of sympathy or sadness.

On the book-shelf there lay a volume of Poe's poems. He took it down, wrote my name on it, and gave it to me. I think he did this from a feeling of sympathy, for I could not be of advantage to him, as my two companions could. I had sent him an article when he edited the Broadway Journal, which had pleased him. It was a sort of wonder article, and he published it without knowing the authorship, and he was pleased to find the anonymous contributor in me. He was at this time greatly depressed. Their extreme poverty, the sickness of his wife, and his own inability to write, sufficiently accounted for this. We spent half an hour in the house, when some more company came, which included ladies, and then we all went to walk.

Poe and his friends then walked into the nearby woods and played an active game of leaping. Although Poe won, the impoverished poet burst his well-worn gaiters.

> When we reached the cottage, I think all felt that we must not go in, to see the shoeless unfortunate standing in our midst. I had an errand, however—I had left the volume of Poe's poems—and I entered the house to get it. The poor old mother looked at his feet, with a dismay that I shall never forget.
>
> "Oh, Eddie!" said she, "how did you burst your gaiters?"
>
> Poe seemed to have come to a semitorpid state as soon as he saw his mother.
>
> "Do answer Muddie, now," said she, coaxingly.
>
> "Muddie" was her pet name with her children.
>
> I related the cause of the mishap, and she drew me into the kitchen.
>
> "Will you speak to Mr. ———," said she, "about Eddie's last poem?"
>
> Mr. ——— was the reviewer.
>
> "If he will only take the poem, Eddie can have a pair of shoes. He has it— I carried it last week, and Eddie says it is his best. You will speak to him about it, won't you?"...
>
> "Of course they will publish the poem," said I, "and I will ask C to be quick about it."
>
> The poem was paid for at once, and published soon after. I presume it is regarded as genuine poetry in the collected poems of its author, but then it bought the poet a pair of gaiters, and twelve shilling over.
>
> —Mary Gove Nichols, "Reminiscences of Edgar Allan Poe," *Sixpenny Magazine* (February 1863).

The wasting illness and death of Poe's wife, Virginia, in January 1847, strongly influenced his state of mind and, thus, his work. Poe's years at Fordham were productive. He wrote some of his best-loved poems, such as "The Bells" and "Annabel Lee," while living in The Bronx. Poe traveled while maintaining his Fordham cottage as his residence until he died. Years after Poe's death in 1849, his growing fame and association with Fordham attracted other literary figures to live there. Irish poet John Savage resided in the village in a similar cottage during the Civil War, and he recruited his friend, Robert Barry Coffin, to live there, too. Coffin, writing as Barry Gray and referring to his colleague as "my savage literary friend," wrote an amusing account of his move from the high rents and congestion of New York City and of the simple pleasures and economies of Fordham life.

> I resolved to save money by purchasing a place in the country. Other reasons, quite as important—the health of my estimable spouse and also of my little ones, and still others which I will not particularize—had weight in leading me to change my base....
>
> ... So, when a savage literary friend of mine commended the village of Fordham, where he resided, as a desirable location in which to place my household gods, I at once decided to become a Fordhamerer, and the owner of the little woodbine-clad cottage he had selected for me.
>
> The house is small, but, as the maid-of-all-work remarked, "mighty convenient." She declared to my wife that she could stand at the bottom of the stairs, in the hall, and sweep every room in the house without moving more than a foot either way....
>
> Everybody in the country ought to keep a cow,—at least, every one who has a family of young children who like milk. As yet, I have only inquired for a cow. And though several respectable-looking cows did, in an independent manner, make me an early-morning call, and, opening the gate with their horns, walk into the enclosure where my youthful beets, and cabbages, and peas, and beans are growing, and eliminated their tender shoots from the parent roots, I failed to appreciate their visit, or to do them the honor of becoming their owner. On the contrary, I drove them forth with opprobrious epithets, accompanied with sticks and stones; and afterward put up a shingle sign on the fence to the effect that cows could not be pastured in my garden, and that hereafter all such trespassers would be taken to the pound, and there pounded. Since then I am happy to state that my garden-gate has remained unlifted....

Part of the rural village of Fordham in 1890. The site today is Valentine Avenue north of 194th Street. "I at once decided to become a Fordhamerer, and the owner of the little woodbine-clad cottage." —Barry Gray [Robert Barry Coffin]. The Bronx County Historical Society Research Library.

The High Bridge in 1865. "My wife ... had a lingering regard for the High Bridge ... which structure she more than once visited, not only with me, but with other gentlemen friends, before she was married." —Barry Gray [Robert Barry Coffin]. The Bronx County Historical Society Research Library.

... Several days elapsed before we discovered that we were in the receipt, daily, of a hundred pounds of ice. When, however, our large refrigerator began to groan under its burden, and we found that we had a larger quantity of ice on hand than was necessary, mutual explanations revealed the fact that we were obtaining more than our fair share of the product from the polar regions. Of course, we resolved to dispense with one of the Arctic explorers; but which of the two, became the question to be solved. My wife, for her part, advocated the retention of the Harlem River man, because she had engaged him, and, besides, she had a lingering regard for the High Bridge, which spanned it, and which structure she had more than once visited, not only with me, but with other gentlemen friends, before she was married. This, however, had no weight with me, and I strongly advocated the retention of the Bronx River man....

And, as Mrs. Gray vouchsafed no reply, it was duly carried and recorded.

—Barry Gray [Robert Barry Coffin], *Out of Town: A Rural Episode* (New York: Hurd and Houghton, 1867).

Like the cottage dwellers in Fordham, wealthy New York industrialists and commercial leaders came to The Bronx by railroad. They built mansions, villas, and estates along the ridges overlooking the Hudson and Harlem Rivers or along the shores of Long Island Sound and dabbled in raising prize cattle or horses. One newcomer to Morrisania, journalist and historian Henry B. Dawson, described the landscape in Hunts Point, which was dotted with the homes of the wealthy, many of whom are now commemorated in the area's street names. He walked with his son on a sweltering day to seek the grave of poet Joseph Rodman Drake.

The mansion of Edward G. Faile around 1900. "We passed . . . the residence . . . of Edward G. Faile." —Henry B. Dawson. The Bronx County Historical Society Research Library, Randall Comfort Collection.

We passed, successively, the residence of the late Thomas Richardson, concealed from the passer-by, by its dense screen of magnificent evergreens, and that of the late William W. Fox, solid and substantial, yet everywhere exhibiting the cheering comforts of a plentifully supplied country home. The elegant mansions of William and John B. Simpson, in the midst of a carefully ornamented lawn which seemed to be held in common by the two well-known brothers; and the grounds of Richard M. Hoe and J. B. Herrick—the residence of the latter approached through a long vista of willows, were next admired, as we passed along the road; while that of Edward G. Faile—with its appropriate appendages of carefully arranged and scrupulously neat farm buildings—and the elegant but narrowly-confined residence of stone, in the style of the Tudors, lately owned by Peter S. Hoe; the densely wooded entrance to the ample grounds of Mr. Dickey; the large, square, old-fashioned frame house of Paul Spofford and the elegant modern villa, surrounded by elaborately ornamented grounds, of Robert L. Kitching, successively arrested our attention and commanded our admiration. The distant chateau of our

The mansion of Benjamin M. Whitlock around 1900. "The distant chateau of our lamented friend, Benjamin M. Whitlock . . . was occasionally seen in the distance." —Henry B. Dawson. The Bronx County Historical Society Research Library, Walter Jackson, photographer.

lamented friend, Benjamin M. Whitlock, whose memory is cherished by all who knew him in the broad and manly benevolence of his nature, was occasionally seen in the distance, through the trees on our right; and still further, in the same direction, the business-like structures at Port Morris, flanked by the deep waters of the Sound, added to the varied beauties of the scene: on our left, the heavy foliage which gave an air of coolness and comfort to the carefully kept grounds and the cosy gate-house of Mr. Dickey and to the old fashioned farm-buildings of Mr. Spofford, concealed from our curious enquiries, the wide marshes through which the distant Bronx steals its way into the Sound, and from the more distant high lands of the borough of Westchester.

A turn in the road, near Mr. Kitching's and the termination of the screen of woods on our left, to which we have alluded, suddenly opened from that point, an extended view of the marshy meadows and the sluggish Bronx, with the unappropriated, if not unappreciated beauties of Hunt's Point, bounded, in the distance, by the Sound and by the receding shores of Long Island; and thence, leaving the estate of Francis Barretto, on our right, we descended from the highly cultivated ridge along which we had been passing, into the dreary waste below.

Dawson noted a grassy knoll with a roadway through it rising from the meadows. A cottage was on its northeast side. An old oak tree there covered an old burial ground surrounded by a picket fence with an unlatched gate. The graveyard was filled with masses of bushes, briars, and weeds. There, among the graves of the former landowning families of the area, they found the object of their search.

We wandered over the greater part of the ground, picking our way among the bushes and briars, and stopping to read the inscriptions which perpetuate the memory of the Leggetts, the Wards, and the Hunts who, for more than a hundred years, have garnered their dead in this forbidding place; but we failed to see the stone which, more than all others had attracted us to that spot. . . .

At length, as a last resort, in our anxious search, we pushed through the obstructions, and we were rewarded for our labor by finding the particular object of our visit—a neat marble monument, about eight feet in height, enclosed with an iron, picket fence, overhung by a weeping willow. . . .

. . . The monument begins to need repair. The iron pickets, for instance, for the want of paint, are rapidly rusting away, the white marble base being sadly disfigured with the stains; and the whole structure, slightly leaning toward the North, needs a little friendly care from some of the Poet's many admirers. A few hours labor, bestowed occasionally by any of the wealthy and large-hearted citizens who live in the immediate vicinity, would keep it in good order and render it more worthy of the neighborhood and of the youthful bard who rests within its borders—such an evidence of respect for the memory of one of Westchester's sweetest songsters, should at least be shown, by some one, as would ensure the removal of the rubbish from his grave and secure his monument from premature destruction.

—Henry B. Dawson, "The Poet's Grave," *Rambles in Westchester County, New York: A Fragment* (Yonkers, N.Y.: N.p., 1866).

Drake's grave and the small cemetery are preserved and cared for today as part of Joseph Rodman Drake Park at the corner of Hunts Point and Oak Point Avenues.

In the nineteenth century, the railroad was not only used by the wealthy, but also facilitated the movement of Irish and German immigrants from crowded New York City to the suburban Bronx. Many Irish, who actually started to move northward in the first decades of the nineteenth century, became hired farmhands, gardeners, and servants in the homes of the wealthy. Later, they worked on the railroads and in construction and entered politics and the Catholic Church hierarchy. They settled in Highbridge, Mott Haven, Kingsbridge, and elsewhere. German immigrants, who came in large numbers beginning in the 1850s, often became shopkeepers, factory owners, and brewers, and resided primarily in Morrisania. A few German immigrants attained considerable wealth. Gustav Schwab, the North American representative of the North German Lloyd steamship line, resided in a villa commanding a magnificent view. He called it Fort Number Eight, after the Revolutionary fort that once stood on the site overlooking the Harlem River valley in today's University Heights. The building survives today as South Hall on the Bronx Community College campus. One of Schwab's daughters, Lucy Schwab White, recalled growing up in a cultured, tight-knit, and affectionate home, where household employees helped with the

The grave and monument of Joseph Rodman Drake, June 1898. "We were rewarded for our labor by finding the particular object of our visit—a neat marble monument, about eight feet in height, enclosed with an iron, picket fence." — Henry B. Dawson. The Bronx County Historical Society Research Library.

cooking, gardening, and cleaning. The children were tutored at home. Supplies and provisions were purchased in Manhattan and later from horse-drawn wagons, as stores had not yet come to their area. This prosperous German-American family was fond of song and dance and would gather around a table groaning with the weight of huge portions of food at mealtimes.

Then when the meal was over, all would join in singing around the table, the male voices predominating. German songs they were chiefly, which our elder brother Gustav had brought over from Bremen, where he had lived in a highly musical atmosphere.

Music was so much a part of our daily lives that I never knew a house could be without it. Our governess was a trained musician, and she and our sister Henrietta, with Gustav and his friends, sang German part songs, which I thought enchanting.

Sunday evening was given to hymns, English and German, and this practice was continued as long as the home lasted, in spite of occasional disaffection on the part of the younger brothers. Gustav had a good baritone voice, Henrietta and Emily played the piano, Hermann the cello, Henry, in his boyhood, played the violin, but gave it up later, though he was always fond of music in the home. The younger members of the family were chiefly useful as chorus. . . .

We were fortunate in having among our near neighbors two mothers who played exceptionally well for dancing, Mrs. Edson and Mrs. Camp; and at many parties in our house and others, they were untiring in furnishing the young people the waltz, polka, gallop, lancers, and the inevitable Virginia Reel which wound up the evening. . . .

Our Sunday afternoons were altogether given up to visitors, guests staying in the house, neighbors dropping in, and old friends coming up from town. Frequently, we had young Germans who had brought letters to my father, and whom he was always ready to befriend and advise. After the Franco-Prussian War in 1870 there were many young men, just released from the army, who made use of their freedom to travel across the water, some of them making quite a stay in this country.

A wealthy businessman, Schwab also had a public role to play.

Busy man that he was, my father was always ready to do his part in public welfare work as well as in the ordinary duties of citizenship. It was quite a sight to see him on the morning of election day, get into the carriage with his grown sons, the gardener and second man squeezed in somehow, beside the coachman, and all bound for the polls, the employés it must be confessed, under some duress with regard to the disposal of their votes.

Although Schwab had several alternatives to get to his Manhattan office, he often took advantage of the sidewheeler steamships that regularly picked up passengers at docks along the Harlem and East Rivers. One such stop was at Morris Dock. Today, the site is Roberto Clemente State Park.

> My father's working day was long. He left the house before eight, taking the boat in summer, the *Tiger Lily* or *Water Lily* from Morris Dock to Harlem, and the *Sylvan Dell* or others of that line to Peck Slip; at other seasons he used the trains of the Hudson River Railroad. In the early days of Fort Number Eight he was obliged to go back and forth by the Harlem Railroad, driving a mile to the station, whereas the Hudson River station was only a few minutes' drive. It sometimes happened that the boat left before the carriage reached the dock, and by fast driving to High Bridge, the coachman was able to overtake her there.
>
> —Lucy Schwab White, *Fort Number Eight: The Home of Gustav and Eliza Schwab* (Privately printed, 1925).

The sidewheeler steamship Morrisania *at Mott Haven in the 1890s. "[My father] left the house before eight, taking the boat in summer, . . . from Morris Dock to Harlem, and . . . others of that line to Peck Slip." —Lucy Schwab White. The Bronx County Historical Society Research Library.*

As immigration from Europe increased, the population of New York City began to outgrow the confines of Manhattan Island. Civic-minded business leaders and politicians then looked toward the mainland for further expansion. In 1874, the city acquired all of today's Bronx west of the Bronx River, calling it the Annexed District. Journalist John Mullaly viewed the inexpensive land and the sparse population of the Annexed District as an opportunity for the city to purchase parkland at low cost for the crowded city he foresaw developing. In 1888, he was instrumental in getting an appointed committee to buy extensive tracts of land for parks and parkways in The Bronx, both in the lands already annexed and in the area east of the Bronx River that was then still part of Westchester County. Mullaly lauded Pelham Bay Park's proximity to Long Island Sound, calling it the "Newport of the toilers," and praised the variety of shade trees in Crotona Park, the charm of St. Mary's Park, and the rustic beauty of Claremont Park. He went on to describe the blessings of Van Cortlandt and Bronx Parks in similar terms.

Of the area embraced in the new parks and parkways beyond the Harlem, the tract of 1,669 acres included in the Van Cortlandt Park possesses

The view to the northwest toward the Palisades from Vault Hill in Van Cortlandt Park, 1887. "From the commanding eminence known as Vault Hill . . . an extended view of the park is presented on every side." —John Mullaly. The Bronx County Historical Society Research Library.

The Van Cortlandt Mills in the 1890s. The mills were destroyed when they burned down after being struck by lightning in 1911. "Then there is also the ancient mill—over a century old—which stands at the southern extremity of the lake, nestling in the deep shadow of towering elms, and which will long be a favorite resort of the lovers of the picturesque, for the retired nook in which it stands is one of the most beautiful in the whole range of the park." —John Mullaly. The Bronx County Historical Society Research Library, Randall Comfort Collection.

in the picturesque beauty of the surrounding country, as well as in its diversified surface, a rare combination of all that is essential to a great suburban pleasure ground....

From the commanding eminence known as Vault Hill, and which has an elevation of over a hundred feet above the parade ground, an extended view of the park is presented on every side....

Then there is also the ancient mill—over a century old—which stands at the southern extremity of the lake, nestling in the deep shadow of towering elms, and which will long be a favorite resort of the lovers of the picturesque, for the retired nook in which it stands is one of the most beautiful in the whole range of the park....

At this point the overflow of the lake forms a miniature cascade and rapids, which flow between banks bordered with great trees, as the stream courses on its way to join the waters of the Spuyten Duyvil, a mile off in the valley below. The Van Cortlandt Station of the New York & Northern Railroad, which passes through the park, is within a few hundred feet of the old mill and cascade, and as he leaves the station the visitor finds himself in one of the most exquisite rural scenes. . . .

. . . Through the foliage of great ancestral trees the lake is visible, and the sound of falling water mingled with the melody of birds greets the ear as you cross the rustic bridge that spans the brook. This is literally the home of the birds and "the trees are full of song" the whole summer through. . . . Robins, blackbirds, thrushes, orioles, catbirds, bobolinks, all build their nests. . . . The thick, tangled sedge and dense shrubbery that hide the Mosholu as it flows into the lake are still the resort of wood duck, woodcock and quail, for here the park is a wilderness, and in both brook and lake the "lusty trout" is still to be found by the skillful angler, a testimony more truthful than iron-clad affidavit of the purity of the water. The writer has in his possession a well-preserved speckled two-pounder, caught near the mill and at which point an occasional capture is still made. . . .

The Bronx Park has an area of six hundred and fifty-three acres lying on both sides of the "romantic Bronx" and extending from West Farms to Williamsbridge. . . .

It would be difficult to do justice to the exquisite loveliness of this tract without seeming to exaggerate, for the character of the scenery is so varied that every step is a surprise and the artist and "the wayfaring man might love to linger there.". . . The Bronx runs through it from north to south, not confined between parallel banks, but bordering curves, forming at intervals wide lake-like reaches, then closing in until they are scarcely fifty feet apart, where its waters are interrupted by the Lydig Dam, over which they are precipitated in one broad foaming cascade that adds a new charm to the landscape. The banks rise to the height of fifty, eighty and even ninety feet; in some places abrupt and precipitous, in others easily surmounted. Gigantic trees, centuries old, crown these summits, while great moss and ivy-covered rocks project here and there at different heights above the surface of the river, increasing the wildness of the scene. . . .

The Bronx Park has a great attraction for artists, for it affords such opportunities for studying effects; it presents such varieties of color, such mingling of light and shade, such blending of hues, such manifold forms of growth and such opposite types of beauty . . . that it is in fact a scenic reservoir to which they love to resort for inspiration and artistic "points.". . .

No better place could be selected for a model botanical garden than Bronx Park, and no better use could be made of any of the parks than to make them subserve educational purposes, practical schools of horticulture, zoology, arboriculture, etc. where children could learn without studying, acquire

The Lydig Dam or Lower Falls of the Bronx River near the southern end of Bronx Park around 1907. A postcard photograph. "The Bronx runs through [the park] . . . its waters . . . interrupted by the Lydig Dam, over which they are precipitated in one broad foaming cascade." —John Mullaly. The Bronx County Historical Society Research Library.

knowledge without opening a book, and where there could be levied "a tax of profit from their very play."

> —John Mullaly, *The New Parks beyond the Harlem*
> (New York: The Record and Guide, 1887).

Mullaly was right. The New York Botanical Garden was eventually established in the northern part of Bronx Park, and that park and the Bronx River valley did, indeed, become the haunt of artists. One of them, painter and author Francis Hopkinson Smith, wrote a thinly disguised, fictionalized account of a journey he made in the 1890s to the area, where quite a few French immigrants had established inns and restaurants along the stream.

It is the most delightful of French inns, in the quaintest of French settlements. As you rush by in one of the innumerable trains that pass it daily, you may catch glimpses of tall trees trailing their branches in the still stream,—hardly a dozen yards wide,—of flocks of white ducks paddling together, and of queer punts drawn up on the shelving shore or tied to soggy, patched-up landing-stairs.

If the sun shines, you can see, now and then, between the trees, a figure kneeling at the water's edge, bending over a pile of clothes, washing,—her head bound with a red handkerchief.

If you are quick, the miniature river will open just before you round the curve, disclosing in the distance groups of willows, and a rickety foot-bridge perched on poles to keep it dry. All this you see in a flash.

But you must stop at the old-fashioned station, within ten minutes of the Harlem River, cross the road, skirt an old garden bound with a fence and bursting with flowers, and so pass on through a bare field to the water's edge, before you catch sight of the cosy little houses lining the banks, with garden fences cutting into the water, the arbors covered with tangled vines, and the boats crossing back and forth. . . .

So, this being an old tramping-ground of mine, I have left the station with its noise and dust behind me this lovely morning in June, have stopped long enough to twist a bunch of sweet peas through the garden fence, and am standing on the bank waiting for some sign of life at Madame Laguerre's. I discover that there is no boat on my side of the stream. But that is of no moment. On the other side, within a biscuit's toss, so narrow is it, there are two boats; and on the landing-wharf, which is only a few planks wide, supporting a tumbledown flight of steps leading to a vine-covered terrace above, rest the oars.

After the artist calls for Madame Laguerre, Lucette, the woman's eighteen-year-old daughter, rows him across the Bronx River to the charming inn.

As we walk under the arbor and by the great trees, towards the cottage, Lucette following with the oars, I inquire after monsieur, and find that he is in the city, and very well and very busy, and will return at sundown. He has a shop of his own in the upper part where he makes *passe-partouts*. Here, at his home, madame maintains a simple restaurant for tramps like me.

These delightful people are old friends of mine, François Laguerre and their only child Lucette. They have lived here for nearly a quarter of a century. He is a straight, silver-haired old Frenchman of sixty, who left Paris, between two suns, with a gendarme close at his heels, a red cockade under his coat, and an intense Hatred in his heart for that "little nobody," Napoleon III. . . .

His wife is a few years his junior, short and stout, and thoroughly French down to the very toes of her slippers. She is devoted to François and Lucette, the best of cooks, and, in spite of her scoldings, good-nature itself. As soon as she hears me calling there arise before her the visions of many delightful dinners prepared for me by her own hand and ready to the minute—all spoiled by my belated sketches. So she begins to scold before I am out of the boat, or in it, for that matter.

The Bronx River at Williamsbridge, 1892. "As there is no path or road,— all the houses fronting the water,—the Bronx here is really the only highway, and so everybody must needs keep a boat." —Francis Hopkinson Smith. The Bronx County Historical Society Research Library.

Across the fence next to Laguerre's lives a *confrère*, a brother exile, Monsieur Marmosette, who also has a shop in the city, where he carves fine ivories. Monsieur Marmosette has only one son. He too is named François, after his father's old friend. Farther down on both sides of the narrow stream front the cottages of other friends, all Frenchmen; and near the propped-up bridge an Italian who knew Garibaldi burrows in a low, slanting cabin, which is covered with vines. I remember a dish of *spaghetti* under those vines, and a flask of Chianti from its cellar, all cobwebs and plaited straw, that left a taste of Venice in my mouth for days.

As there is only the great bridge above, which helps the country road across the little stream, and the little foot-bridge below, and as there is no path or road,—all the houses fronting the water,—the Bronx here is really the only highway, and so everybody must needs keep a boat. This is why the stream is crowded in the warm afternoons with all sorts of water crafts loaded with whole families, even to the babies, taking the air, or crossing from bank to bank in their daily pursuits.

The artist uses one of the boats to find a spot to sketch.

For half a mile down-stream there is barely a current. Then comes a break of a dozen yards just below the perched-up bridge, and the stream divides, one part rushing like a mill-race, and the other spreading itself softly around the roots of leaning willows, oozing through beds of water-plants, and creeping under masses of wild grapes and underbrush. Below this is a broad pasture fringed with another and larger growth of willows. Here the weeds are breast high, and in early autumn they burst into purple asters, and white immortelles, and goldenrod, and flaming sumac.

If a painter had a lifetime to spare, and loved this sort of materials,—the willows, hillsides, and winding stream,—he would grow old and weary before he could paint it all; and yet no two of his compositions need be alike. I have tied my boat under these same willows for ten years back, and I have not yet exhausted one corner of this neglected pasture. . . .

Now you are ready. You loosen your cravat, hand your coat to some rustic peg in the creviced bark of the tree behind you, seize a bit of charcoal from your bag, sweep your eye around, and dash in a few guiding strokes. Above is a turquoise sky filled with soft white clouds; behind you the great trunks of the many-branched willows; and away off, under the hot sun, the yellow-green of the wasted pasture, dotted with patches of rock and weeds, and hemmed in by the low hills that slope to the curving stream.

Lucette arrives in another boat to call the artist back to the inn for his dinner.

There may be ways of dining more delicious than out in the open air under the vines in the cool of the afternoon, with Lucette, in her whitest of aprons, flitting about, and madame garnishing the dishes each in turn, and there may be better bottles of honest red wine to be found up and down this world of care than "Château Lamonte, '62," but I have not yet discovered them.

Lucette serves the coffee in a little cup, and leaves the Roquefort and the cigarettes on the table just as the sun is sinking behind the hill skirting the railroad.

> —Francis Hopkinson Smith, "A Day at Laguerre's,"
> *A Day at Laguerre's and Other Days: Being Nine
> Sketches* (Boston: Houghton Mifflin and Company,
> 1892).

These picturesque scenes indicate how the area that was to become The Bronx changed in the course of the nineteenth century. It progressed from a rural area devoted to raising the products needed by New York City to a suburb of that metropolis, serviced by railroads and providing homes in the countryside to wealthy businessmen and enterprising immigrant families. When the city absorbed the western half of The Bronx in 1874 and the eastern half in 1895, the newly annexed mainland area, furnished with huge parks, was looked upon as a picturesque retreat from the hustle and crowding of usual urban life. When the city annexed Brooklyn, Queens, and Staten Island in 1898, the previously annexed Bronx became a borough of New York City, equal in political status to the newly acquired territories and to Manhattan. For the first time, the name, The Bronx, was used to describe the area.

Other ethnic groups followed the Irish and Germans into The Bronx. They needed schools, increased municipal services, shops, and houses of worship. Plans were made for the creation of a high school, today's Morris High, the establishment of the Bronx Zoo and the Botanical Garden in Bronx Park, the founding of the Hall of Fame for Great Americans, and the opening of the New York Public Library's Bronx branches. These plans presaged the great upheaval that was about to occur in The Bronx in the course of the following two decades.

3

"LIKE COUNTRY"

THE URBANIZATION OF THE BRONX

1898–1919

FROM THE OPENING OF THE TWENTIETH CENTURY UNTIL THE end of World War I, The Bronx underwent enormous change. Its quiet suburban villages and farms were rapidly transformed into an urban landscape dominated by apartment houses, paved streets, and densely populated neighborhoods. The chief agent of this transformation was the new subway system, which first entered The Bronx in 1904. Many New Yorkers in cramped and crowded tenements quickly realized that for only a nickel, they could commute to Manhattan to work and live in semi-rural Bronx neighborhoods. Landowners sold their farms and estates as the rapid transit lines were being constructed and their land was subdivided into building lots, mostly for apartment houses. Urbanization began in the southwestern part of the borough and fanned out to other areas as the decade advanced. Hundreds of thousands began life anew north and east of the Harlem River. The British novelist Arnold Bennett, on tour in the United States, marveled at this promise of a new beginning.

I was urgently invited to go and see how the folk lived in the Bronx; and, feeling convinced that a place with a name so remarkable must itself be remarkable, I went. The center of the Bronx is a racket of Elevated, bordered by banks, theaters, and other places of amusement. As a spectacle, it is decent, inspiring confidence but not awe, and being rather repellent to the sense of beauty. Nobody could call it impressive. Yet I departed from the Bronx very considerably impressed. It is the interiors of Bronx homes that are impressive. I was led to a part of the Bronx where five years previously there had been six families and where there are now over two thousand families. This was newest New York.

No obstacle impeded my invasion of the domestic privacies of the Bronx. The mistresses of flats showed me round everything with politeness and with obvious satisfaction. A stout lady, whose husband was either an artisan or clerk, I forget which, inducted me into a flat of four rooms, of which the rent was $20 a month. She enjoyed the advantages of central heating, gas, and electricity; and among the landlord's fixtures were a refrigerator, a kitchen range, a bookcase, and a sideboard. Such amenities for the people . . . simply do not exist in Europe; they do not even exist for the wealthy in Europe. But there was also the telephone, the house exchange being in charge of the janitor's daughter—a pleasing occupant of the entrance-hall. I was told that the telephone, with a "nickel" call, increased the occupancy of the Bronx flats by ten per cent. . . .

I visited another house and saw similar interiors. And now I began to be struck by the splendor and the cleanliness of the halls, landings, and staircases; marble halls, tessellated landings, and stairs out of Holland; the whole producing a gorgeous effect—to match the glory of the embroidered pillow-

Rogers Place at 163rd Street, March 16, 1909. "The center of the Bronx is a racket of Elevated. . . . I was led to a part of the Bronx where five years previously there had been six families and where there are now over two thousand families." —Arnold Bennett. The Bronx County Historical Society Research Library.

162nd Street and Washington Avenue about 1914. Washington Avenue, the most elegant street in The Bronx at the time, is decked out for a patriotic celebration. Note the new apartment house to the right. "Then I was lifted a little higher in the social-financial scale to a building of which the entrance-hall reminded me of the foyers of grand hotels." —Arnold Bennett. The Bronx County Historical Society Research Library.

cases in the bedrooms. On the roofs were drying-grounds, upon which each tenant had a rightful "day," so that altercations might not arise. The professional vermin exterminator had just gone—for the landlord-company took no chances in this detail of management.

Then I was lifted a little higher in the social-financial scale to a building of which the entrance-hall reminded me of the foyers of grand hotels.... In this house the corridors were broader, and to the conveniences was added a mail-shoot, a device which is still regarded in Europe as the final word of plutocratic luxury rampant. The rents ran to $18 a month for six rooms....

That the landlord-company was not a band of philanthropists, but a capitalistic group in search of dividends, I would readily admit. But that it should find its profit in the business of improving the standard of existence and appealing to the pride of the folk was to me a wondrous sign of the essential vigor of American civilization and a proof that public spirit . . . must after all have long been at work somewhere....

Nothing, I should imagine, could be more interesting to the sociological observer than that actual creation of a city of homes as I saw it in the Bronx.... Why, I even saw farther out, the ground being leveled and the solid rock drilled where now, most probably, actual homes are inhabited and babies have been born! And I saw farther than that. Nailed against a fine and ancient tree, in the midst of a desolate waste, I saw a board with these words: "A new subway station will be erected on this corner." There are legendary people who have eyes to see the grass growing. I have seen New York growing. It was a hopeful sight, too.

—Arnold Bennett, "Your United States," *Harper's Monthly Magazine* (June 1912).

The noted Russian revolutionary and author Leon Trotsky also came to The Bronx with his wife and two sons and settled in an area where the new apartment houses attracted large numbers of working-class Jewish immigrants. After being expelled from various European countries as a Marxist propagandist, Trotsky arrived in New York on January 13, 1917, and left two months later to help lead the

Trinity Avenue near Pontiac Place, June 26, 1917. "I even saw farther out, the ground being leveled and the solid rock drilled where now, most probably, actual homes are inhabited and babies have been born!" —Arnold Bennett. The Bronx County Historical Society Research Library.

Bolshevik Revolution. His observations of economic progress in the southern part of The Bronx were similar to Bennett's, but more personal.

> We rented an apartment in a worker's district and furnished it on the installment plan. That apartment, at eighteen dollars a month, was equipped with all sorts of conveniences that we Europeans were quite unused to: electric lights, gas, cooking-range, bath, telephone, automatic-service elevator, and even a chute for the garbage.
>
> —Leon Trotsky, *My Life* (Gloucester, Mass.: Peter Smith, 1970).

In this era, a few of the early motion picture companies erected their studios in The Bronx. The Edison Studio was established in 1909 at Decatur Avenue and Oliver Place. D. W. Griffith began his career there when he was hired as an actor in his first film, *Rescued from an Eagle's Nest.* He later became a famous director at Biograph Studios, which built a facility for him on 175th Street near Marmion Avenue. Neighborhood children often gathered near the studios to see the stars, hoping to be plucked from the crowd to work as extras. George Diamond recalled the activity at one such studio in his memoir, "I Remember Tremont: 1911–1918." Wendover Avenue is now Claremont Parkway.

> There was a motion picture studio on Wendover Avenue near Park Avenue. If you were willing to stand in line for a few hours, you might get a job in the moving pictures. You would get two dollars to be in a mob scene. Sometimes they would rent pets from my father's store to put in a picture. Once, I went to the studio with a parrot. It was a picture with Theda Bara. The actors and actresses had a lot of makeup on their faces so that they could photograph better. I had to wait for the parrot and take it home when they got through with it.
>
> —George Diamond, "I Remember Tremont: 1911–1918," *The Bronx County Historical Society Journal* (Fall 1974).

At about the same time, twenty-one-year-old John Kieran, later to become famous as a naturalist and radio show celebrity, resided in the still-countrified area overlooking the northern Bronx village of Kingsbridge. Although the rapid urbanization noted by both Bennett and Trotsky had not yet reached his neighborhood, he was beginning to see its impact and, even at his young age, understood the importance of saving the natural habitat of local wildlife.

> As part of the city water supply-system, there are reservoirs in every borough. These reservoirs serve as feeding areas and refuges for ducks, gulls, and other water fowl, and more than a few rareties have been sighted on such waters.
>
> This matter is close to my heart because it was through the fact that the rear attic window of our house overlooked the waters of the Jerome Reservoir in the Bronx that I became acquainted with two noted ornithologists. . . . It was during the winter of 1913–1914, at which time I had developed a lively interest in birds that I began to take notice of ducks congregating on the reservoir. I saw them first from the rear window of the attic room in which I slept. I immediately armed myself with field glasses and went out to inspect the ducks at closer range by peering at them through the iron picket fence surrounding the reservoir. I remember that the first bird I brought in focus turned out to be a White-winged Scoter and, looking back, I recall seeing Canvasback, Redheads, Goldeneyes, Common Mergansers, and, in all, fourteen different species of water fowl on the reservoir that winter.

The Flying Cage at the Bronx Zoo, May 1907. "Standing in front of a cageful of North American warblers in the Bird House at the Bronx Zoo one cold day, I met three elderly men who, from their talk, evidently were much interested in birds. I told them about the ducks on the reservoir and they were so much stirred by the news that we left the zoo together and plodded westward through the snow to the reservoir, where the ducks were duly seen as advertised." —John Kieran. The Bronx County Historical Society Research Library, New York Zoological Society photograph.

Standing in front of a cageful of North American warblers in the Bird House at the Bronx Zoo one cold day, I met three elderly men who, from their talk, evidently were much interested in birds. I told them about the ducks on the reservoir and they were so much stirred by the news that we left the zoo together and plodded westward through the snow to the reservoir, where the ducks were duly seen as advertised.

—John Kieran, *A Natural History of New York City*
(New York: Fordham University Press, 1982).

One of the men wrote a nature column for a New York newspaper and included Kieran's findings in it. This article brought the young man to the attention of two prominent ornithologists at the American Museum of Natural History and led as well to Kieran's lifelong interest in urban ecology.

Shortly before Kieran's explorations, then-aspiring novelist Theodore Dreiser came to the northern Bronx. He was seeking manual labor as a restorative after a nervous breakdown suffered because of the scandalous reception of his novel *Sister Carrie*, a blow that nearly ended his writing career. Dreiser found work in the New York Central Railroad's Spuyten Duyvil facility and lodging at a boarding house in the village of Kingsbridge, down the hill from where Kieran lived.

> This village, set down among green hills, and partially encircled, as the island portion was by green hills, was one of the fairest and most pleasing pictures of earth that I have ever witnessed. It was a quiet old place, bereft by the flight of time and the near approach of New York of all that had once

*Kingsbridge, 1899. "This village, set down among green hills, and partially encircled, as the island portion was by green hills, was one of the fairest and most pleasing pictures of earth that I have ever witnessed. . . . From the depot, as you dismounted from the train a winding, tree-shaded road led up across Broadway and by the banks of the river (the Harlem) to a little clump of antiquated wooden houses and stores, which served at once as the remnant of the old life and the nucleus of the new."
—Theodore Dreiser. The Bronx County Historical Society Research Library.*

made it interesting and busy as a village and yet superficially endued with a kind of buoyancy and enthusiasm which came from the fact that although New York had killed the old life, it had all but created a new one. From the depot, as you dismounted from the train a winding, tree-shaded road led up across Broadway and by the banks of the river (the Harlem) to a little clump of antiquated wooden houses and stores, which served at once as the remnant of the old life and the nucleus of the new. It was surrounded on every hand by long tree shaded lanes of houses which clustered together in curious isolated groups and then left the roads bare again. Houses covered the green side of a nearby hill to the eastward which when the sun shone on them, stood out from their green setting like little white structures of card board, and houses decorated the tops of a hill or two to the westward, which were always visible by daylight by their white colors and at night by their lamps. Immediately about this tumble down center of old life were a few churches and schools, some half awake business enterprises such as a coal yard, a launch building establishment, and a small hotel, set close down to the waters edge and in the distance, over the waters of the river to the south and on the distant top of a hill stood a notable nunnery its pinnacled roof surmounted by a handsome gold cross and its imposing array of windows gleaming in the evening sun like burnished gold. When night fell and the lamps shown forth, the hills and valleys, rising and falling in darksome rythm [sic] revealed a world of seeming peace and prosperity gathered in little gleaming groups which made it all the more appealing for that was under the extended vault of heaven, and looked down upon by billions of scintillating stars. . . .

I knocked at the door of a pretty house, overlooking the Harlem, and was greeted by a tall woman, gray-haired and handsome who wished to know, in a very direct manner what I wanted. I explained to her, as politely as I could, just what I wished, and why I wished it. She looked at me critically, and I fancied approvingly, out of the most experienced of eyes and finally declared that although she was ordinarily opposed to taking in strangers she might make an exception in my case. . . . On the morrow I returned for I was anxious to get settled and go to work. My money was not too plentiful and I had several things to do before entering the shop. One was to get my working clothes ready and the other to confer with the foreman and find out what, if anything, I would need. The lady was decidedly affable and told me at once that I might come. I immediately went to the local depot and ordered my trunk to be brought up when it should arrive, sent word to the downtown post master where to readdress my mail, then got on the train and went to

Mott Haven Canal in the early 1900s. "Summerfield looked at the poor neighborhood, the inlet of a canal some two blocks east where a series of black coal pockets were." —Theodore Dreiser. The Bronx County Historical Society Research Library.

Spuyten Duyvil, which was the next station above—about three minutes run—and entered upon the scene of my future labors.

> —Theodore Dreiser, *An Amateur Laborer*, ed. Richard W. Dowell, James L. West III, and Nada M. Westlake (Philadelphia: University of Pennsylvania Press, 1983).

Thanks to his sojourn in the bucolic Bronx, Dreiser regained his mental and physical health and began writing fiction again. He and his wife, from whom he had been separated, reunited, removed their furniture from storage, and relocated to an apartment house on Mott Avenue (now the Grand Concourse) and 144th Street in Mott Haven. In his 1915 semi-autobiographical novel, *The "Genius,"* Dreiser borrowed from his Bronx experiences to create the life of his fictional artist, Eugene Witla. Like Dreiser, Witla, a Midwesterner struggling for recognition as an artist, suffered a breakdown and worked on the railroad while living in The Bronx. Dreiser created a scene in which Witla's new employer, Daniel Summerfield, the owner of an advertising company, pays a visit to the Mott Haven apartment of the Witlas. To get there from the Third Avenue El station, they have to pass over the Mott Haven Canal, lined with coal and lumber yards.

> Eugene did not want this. He was chagrined to be compelled to take him into the very little apartment, but there was apparently no way of escaping it. . . .
>
> "I don't like you to see this place," finally he said apologetically, as they were going up the steps of the five-story apartment house. "We are going to get out of here pretty soon. I came here when I worked on the road."
>
> Summerfield looked at the poor neighborhood, the inlet of a canal some two blocks east where a series of black coal pockets were and to the north where there was flat open country and a railroad yard.
>
> —Theodore Dreiser, *The "Genius"* (Cleveland: The World Publishing Company, 1943).

While living in Mott Haven in 1905, Dreiser published a critical article stressing the sense of isolation caused by residing in one of the new Bronx urban neighborhoods.

> There are perhaps a hundred people in our apartment house, a thousand, or it may be two or three thousand, in our block. They live in small,

Mott Avenue looking south from 150th Street, March 16, 1909. Theodore Dreiser and his wife lived in the apartment house on the left-hand side at 144th Street in 1903. "There are perhaps a hundred people in our apartment house, a thousand, or it may be two or three thousand, in our block. They live in small, comfortably furnished and very convenient apartments, but they live alone." —Theodore Dreiser. The Bronx County Historical Society Research Library.

comfortably furnished and very convenient apartments, but they live alone. No one ever sees any exchange of courtesies between them. They are not interested in the progress of the lives of the people about them. You might live there for a year, or ten years, and I doubt that if your next-door neighbor would even so much as know of your existence. He is too busy. Your business might fail, your children perish. You might suffer every calamity from heartache to literal physical destruction, and I doubt whether he would ever hear of it. . . . It is all as if you really did not exist. . . . Life cannot go on without affection and tenderness—be sure of that. We cannot forever crowd into cities and forget man for mammon.

> —Theodore Dreiser, "The Loneliness of the City,"
> *Theodore Dreiser: A Selection of Uncollected Prose*,
> ed. D. Pizer (Detroit: Wayne State University Press,
> 1977).

While Dreiser was still struggling for literary acceptance, Samuel Clemens, better known as Mark Twain, was already world-famous for *The Adventures of Huckleberry Finn, The Gilded Age*, and many other works. At the age of sixty-six, Twain moved to The Bronx in an attempt to restore his wife's deteriorating physical health. In 1901, he rented the spacious and grand estate then called Holbrook House, now called Wave Hill, in Riverdale, a wealthy enclave on a hill to the west of Kingsbridge. The mansion, which overlooked the Hudson, was convenient to the Riverdale station, the New York Central stop just above the Spuyten Duyvil yards where Dreiser labored. At the time, the area consisted of large manicured estates, staffed by servants and gardeners, owned by affluent families, such as the Dodges and Delafields. At the private docks along the Hudson, millionaires anchored their yachts. Twain was looking for a substantial home befitting his status as a nationally revered man of letters. Later, he recalled:

> We drifted from room to room on our tour of inspection, always with a growing doubt as to whether we wanted that house or not; but at last, when we arrived in a dining room that was 60 feet long, 30 feet wide, and had two great fireplaces in it, that settled it.

> —Quoted by Albert Bigelow Paine, *Mark Twain*,
> vol. 3 (New York: Chelsea House, 1980).

The Bronx location proved inconvenient and remote for Twain's close friend, the noted novelist, critic, and champion of American realism William Dean Howells, who lived in Manhattan and had to use the railroad and a wagon to get to him.

Grounds of Wave Hill overlooking the Hudson River, 1911. Mark Twain lived here from 1901 to 1903. "I was at his house one afternoon and saw his Hudson and his palisades, and some of the steamboats that he delights in more." —William Dean Howells. The Bronx County Historical Society Research Library.

Manhattan was the center for writers and Howells seemed to feel that Twain should never have left. Howells wrote:

> Clemens has got so far from town as Spuyten Duyvil, and is beyond the reach of all the dinners he does not want to accept. I was at his house one afternoon and saw his Hudson and his palisades, and some of the steamboats that he delights in more. He is the only tie that binds me, here, to the old times (they *were* good, weren't they?) and I'm sorry he's got a timetable's length away.
>
> —*Life and Letters of William Dean Howells*, vol. 2, ed. Mildred Howells (New York: Russell and Russell, 1928).

In a less jocular mood, Howells reported on another visit to Twain at Riverdale.

Greyston, the mansion of the Dodge family, in 1978. "The Clemens's youngest daughter was just about the age of my sisters, and as she wanted company, she spent more of her time in summer at our house. Mark Twain loved children and became a good friend of our family." —Cleveland E. Dodge. The Bronx County Historical Society Research Library.

They kept no carriage, and there was a snowy night when I drove up to their handsome old mansion in the station carryall, which was crusted with mud as from the going down of the Deluge after transporting Noah and his family from the Ark. . . . But the good talk, the rich talk, the talk that could never suffer poverty of mind or soul was there, and we jubilantly found ourselves in our middle youth.

—Quoted by Rufus Rockwell Wilson, *New York in Literature* (Elmira, N.Y.: Primavera Press, 1947).

As a boy, Cleveland E. Dodge, heir to the Phelps Dodge copper interests, lived in Greyston, a nearby mansion. Dodge remembered the world-famous author and the Twain children:

The Clemens's youngest daughter was just about the age of my sisters, and as she wanted company, she spent most of her time in summer at our house. Mark Twain loved children and became a good friend of our family. He was just as picturesque and interesting as he has always been described. . . . One morning I went to his house with a message and found him receiving mail at his door from the postman. He was chuckling over one letter addressed to "Mark Twain, God Knows Where." He gave my mother a photograph of himself with the inscription: "Truth is the most valuable thing that we have, let us economize it."

—Cleveland E. Dodge, "Recollections of Riverdale," in *The Bronx in the Innocent Years: 1895–1925,* ed. Lloyd Ultan and Gary Hermalyn (New York: Harper & Row, 1984).

Unlike remote and relatively inaccessible Riverdale in the northern Bronx, the village of Mott Haven in the southernmost portion of the borough was in the path of rapid urbanization. Its early days were fondly recalled by Edward J. Flynn, born in 1892. Flynn, a child of Irish immigrants, later attained fame as the powerful Democratic boss of The Bronx and close advisor to President Franklin Delano Roosevelt.

The Bronx at the time my mother and father came to live there was more or less a rural community made up of many villages, or sections. I remember my father saying that when they arrived they kept cows on Willis Avenue, which is now a very busy thoroughfare. In those days, a person did not come from "The Bronx." He came from one of the small communities: Mott Haven, Melrose, West Farms, Fordham, and a great many others. Along the East River, there were many large estates, some of them there under the original grants. In the neighborhood in which I now live, Spuyten Duyvil and Riverdale, there were also mostly large estates.

In my youth the Bronx still retained a great deal of its rural or small-town atmosphere. Even at that time, when you were asked where you came from, you invariably replied that you came from Mott Haven, rather than the Bronx. There were still many farms in various sections of the Bronx. My recollection is that when I was about eighteen and was a census taker for the United States government, the district that I covered was the northern section of the Bronx, and there were at least ten farms within that area.

The people who came to settle in the Bronx were mostly immigrants who were of a better type. They were men and women who wished to bring

Willis Avenue and 136th Street, 1907. "I remember my father saying that when they arrived they kept cows on Willis Avenue, which is now a very busy thoroughfare." —Edward J. Flynn. The Bronx County Historical Society Research Library.

Townhouses on 138th Street east of Willis Avenue, March 4, 1913. "The people who came to settle in the Bronx were mostly immigrants who were of a better type. They were men and women who wished to bring their families up in an atmosphere away from the activities of a large city. As a result, they became small-home-owners." —Edward J. Flynn. The Bronx County Historical Society Research Library.

their families up in an atmosphere away from the activities of a large city. As a result, they became small-home-owners. While there were some small apartment houses in the Bronx, the small-home-owner greatly outnumbered apartment dwellers. In a neighborhood such as I was born and reared in, one knew everyone who lived within quite an area surrounding his home. There was still a neighborhood feeling. . . .

In the Bronx of my youth, people got jobs the day after they got off the boat, worked hard, reared families that were never hungry, worshipped as they pleased, earned their simple pleasures.

> —Edward J. Flynn, *You're the Boss* (New York: Collier Books, 1962).

Alongside the Irish, Germans constituted the major ethnic group on the mainland. Since their migration to the area in the mid-nineteenth century, they settled in

Morrisania, where they built Catholic and Lutheran churches. The main street of Melrose, Courtlandt Avenue, was nicknamed "Dutch Broadway" because of its concentration of German shops, saloons, beer halls, and gymnastic and singing societies. Three of the five first presidents of the new borough of The Bronx came from German stock: Louis F. Haffen, Cyrus Miller, and Henry Bruckner.

Soon, the great influx of new immigrants, largely from Italy and Eastern Europe, quickly engulfed many of the small villages, causing the small homes to be replaced with large apartment houses. Often, those of Italian background preferred to own property and to reside in their own homes in the northeastern parts of The Bronx, where farms and estates managed to linger a few decades longer. Their desire was fed by their experiences in southern Italy and Sicily where a few families owned huge estates, while ordinary peasants remained landless. In addition to their attachment to the land, many of these Bronx families kept livestock. One was the family of playwright Joan Renzetti Durant.

> There was plenty of land for those Italian immigrants who were settling in that part of The Bronx. Nobody knew who owned it, but my grandmother, Pasqualina, believed that the land belonged to those who tilled it. There we raised goats and chickens, and, on every side, dug and tilled the soil between rocks and trees, coaxing a farm to grow. Who among us would have believed that the land for which we had to fight a war back home, could be found free in America? . . .
>
> On spring and summer mornings, I was always waiting on the stoop to say goodbye as each one left for work or school. I injected my presence as if it were the instrument by which their morning departure and nightly return would be secured. They were the inhabitants of my enclosed world; the upstairs and downstairs of my grandmother's house. No matter how much yelling went on inside, the outside with its white wooden shingles and gabled rooftop preserved an air of peaceful innocence. Two cypress trees marked the entrance to the stoop. A slate sidewalk on one side of the street ran almost all the way from Boston Post Road to the El train on White Plains Road and, with woods on both sides, there were shortcuts of well-worn paths. . . .
>
> —Joan Renzetti Durant, "Old World, New World," unpublished memoir.

In the early twentieth century, even in the face of the most dire poverty, many Bronx families and individuals expressed a thirst for culture. None felt this more than Moss Hart, who later became a Pulitzer Prize–winning Broadway playwright and impresario. Despite his family's poverty, he developed an abiding interest in the theater through his remarkable Aunt Kate, who revealed its charms to him in the theaters and vaudeville houses of The Bronx and Manhattan.

> I can well remember the times we went to bed in the dark because there was no quarter to put in the gas meter; or even more vividly, some evening meals eaten by candlelight for the same reason, after which Aunt Kate would emerge from her room, attired in what she considered proper fashion, and be on her way to David Belasco's production of *The Darling of the Gods* or the equivalent hit of the moment. Incredible as it may seem, never once did she offer to forgo the theater, no matter how dire the financial crisis might be and, equally astonishing, it seems to me, was the fact that she was not expected to. In some curious way I think the answer is that we were grateful for the small patch of lunatic brightness in the unending drabness of those years. Just as she never admitted to herself the poverty in which we lived, so through her passion for the theater she made us forget it for a little while too....
>
> ... I was too young to be taken downtown to see plays, but from the time I was seven years old I was kept out of school every Thursday afternoon and taken to the Alhambra Theater—to which my aunt had a season subscription ticket each year—where I watched, sober-faced, all the great vaudeville head-liners. Then, still in conspiracy against my father, I graduated to Saturday matinées at the local stock company and a little later to touring companies at the Bronx Opera House. Not unnaturally, I lived for those wonderful Thursday and Saturday afternoons, and in between waited out the days for those evenings when my aunt returned from the greater world of Broadway....
>
> It is easy to understand how my aunt became for me a refuge against the world of reality and how the fantasy world of the theater quickly became an escape and a solace....
>
> ... My feet were embedded in the upper Bronx, but my eyes were set firmly toward Broadway.

Never quite having enough money, however, cast a shadow over Hart's boyhood. He recalled an unhappy Christmas Eve in the Bronx commercial district centered at 149th Street and Third Avenue known as the Hub, a shoppers' mecca.

> Obviously Christmas was out of the question.... On Christmas Eve my father was very silent during the evening meal. Then he surprised and startled me by turning to me and saying, "Let's take a walk.... Let's go down to a Hundred Forty-ninth Street and Westchester Avenue." My heart leapt within me. That was the section where all the big stores were, where at Christmas-

time open pushcarts full of toys stood packed end-to-end for blocks at a stretch. . . .

. . . I would merely pause before a pushcart to say, with as much control as I could muster, "Look at that chemistry set!" or "There's a stamp album!" . . . Each time my father would pause and ask the pushcart man the price. Then without a word we would move on to the next pushcart. . . . As I looked up at him I saw a look of despair and disappointment in his eyes that brought me closer to him than I had ever been in my life.

—Moss Hart, *Act One* (New York: Vintage Books, 1976).

While Hart went on to confess that he was ashamed of having to leave school early in order to go to work, author Marie Syrkin found education the center of her life. The daughter of Socialist-Zionist Nachman Syrkin, Marie grew up in poverty. However, she was surrounded by the Yiddish writers and intellectuals that formed her father's circle and met some of the leading figures of the era. Emma Goldman was an anarchist, Alexander Berkman was jailed for attempting to assassinate

Third Avenue and 149th Street looking north, with Westchester Avenue at the right, May 16, 1918. "That was the section where all the big stores were, where at Christmastime open pushcarts full of toys stood packed end-to-end for blocks at a stretch." —Moss Hart. The Bronx County Historical Society Research Library.

industrialist Henry Clay Frick, Chaim Zhitlovsky was a Yiddish writer and intellectual, and Sholem Asch was a world-renowned novelist.

Our first New York home was a four-room apartment on Charlotte Street in the Bronx. It had such improvements as gaslight in every room and central heating. Furniture, of course, was purchased on the installment plan. I was sent to a neighboring public school to begin my formal education outside the home, and life in the United States seemed hopefully launched. . . .

In some respects life was unchanged. Papa still went to the "library" and meetings. Old friends kept reappearing for the familiar hour-long discussions. Many comrades from the Berlin or Vilna days arriving in America found their way to our house. And periodically I would sleep on an improvised bed made up of four chairs while the impecunious comrade searched for living quarters. Just as in other circles it was taken for granted that relatives or "landsmen" should be housed by those who had preceded them to America, in our midst the bond was ideology. I always knew that the four chairs meant a night of long talk, much tea and obscure excitement. . . .

Wilkins Avenue looking southeast from Boston Road, March 16, 1909. To the left can be seen the rear of the apartment houses facing Charlotte Street where Marie Syrkin lived. "Our first New York home was a four-room apartment on Charlotte Street in the Bronx. It had such improvements as gaslight in every room and central heating." —Marie Syrkin. The Bronx County Historical Society Research Library.

It is hard to disentangle the mature men and women, acquaintances of my adult life from the delightful companions of my childhood years.... The brilliant, suave Zhitlovsky would be a welcome visitor, even though he and my father differed heatedly on most issues. Sholem Asch, moody and self-centered, already with an air of grandeur though not yet internationally famous, would put in an occasional appearance. The Yiddish writer Liessin lived near us.... All the active and intellectual Jewish currents in the period touched our home at some point.... One might meet Alexander Berkman and Emma Goldman unaccountably turning up at a social-democratic ball despite their anarchism. And there were endless public meetings lasting late into the night to which one had to go.... My parents felt that a bright ten-year-old should be able to appreciate political discourse at any hour.

Our family finances, despite my father's public acclaim, remained at a low ebb. Paying the rent was always postponed to the last possible day; the landlord turned out to be an admirer of my father's and was prepared to be as elastic as possible in his construction of what date constituted that last day. The grocery storekeeper was apparently a less zealous reader of the Yiddish press....

I must be careful not to leave a false impression. As a child, it would never have occurred to me to think of our family as "poor." My father's constant intellectual excitement, his marvelous exuberance, set the tone of the house.

—Marie Syrkin, *Nachman Syrkin: Socialist Zionist: A Biographical Memoir* (New York: Herzl Press and Sharon Books, 1961).

In addition to the informal education she received through contact with her father's associates, Marie Syrkin graduated from P.S. 40 in The Bronx and then attended Morris High School. The carnage of World War I, then raging in Europe, affected all the pupils and was expressed in both writing and oratory. Young Armand Hammer later became a prominent businessman with strong ties to the Soviet Union.

I remember Charlotte Street as a pleasant block of small apartment houses, walk-ups, surrounded by unlittered lots bright with dandelions in the spring. Nearby Crotona Park was a safe, green playground and a place for picnics on summer days. Morris—a good twenty minutes' walk (nobody in my block squandered five cents for a trolley ride, whatever the weather)—had pupils of ... largely immigrant background.

Morris High School around 1914. A postcard photograph. "Morris—a good twenty minutes' walk (nobody in my block squandered five cents for a trolley ride, whatever the weather)—had pupils of . . . largely immigrant background." —Marie Syrkin. Barbara Unger Collection.

The other day I came across the Annual of my graduating class. . . . Most of my classmates can be found among the rows of girls in discreet middy blouses and well-combed boys in neat suits.

. . . The writers were not strangers to the world of books. The contributions are in Latin, French, and German, in addition to English—reflecting the obligatory requirement of two foreign languages in the high school curriculum. . . . Even the average eighth grader was expected to read *Julius Caesar* (and memorize, "Friends, Romans, countrymen"), parse a sentence, spell correctly, and grapple with fractions.

. . . There was no lack of social consciousness. With the United States still at peace, the poets mourned the destruction raging in Europe. In fact, so many poems on the horrors of war had been submitted that the editor in chief had begged to be delivered from more on the theme. One sprightly prose sketch describes how two friends, close as Damon and Pythias, yet divided by conflicting sympathies for England and Germany, were patriotically reconciled by the "Proclamation of the Neutrality of the People of these United States." (The author ended up as a federal judge.) The annual oratorical contest also reflects the pervasive concern with World War I. Five of the eight contestants declaimed about the war. . . . The winner was a quiet boy none of us was sufficiently clairvoyant to pick as the most likely to succeed: Armand Hammer, whose theme was "The Last War of Mankind."

—Marie Syrkin, "Morris High School, Class of '16," *The New Republic* (November 7, 1983).

Many of the poverty-ridden and politically oppressed Russian Jews who fled persecution in the old country settled in the growing neighborhoods of The Bronx. Among them were those who penned literary works in their native Yiddish, a language based on German, Aramaic, Russian, Polish, and various Romance languages, written in Hebrew characters and spoken by Central and Eastern European Jews. While most of these Yiddish authors lived in The Bronx, their connection to the borough had seldom been noted. Since they often congregated in their favorite cafes on the Lower East Side of Manhattan, usually a "first stop" for immigrants, they became linked with that part of the city. However, in his 1948 essay, "Yiddish Literature in the United States," one of them, Joseph Opatashu, noted the arrival in The Bronx of an upstart Yiddish literary movement called the *Yunge* (Youth). Well-versed in world literature, this group experimented with newer poetic forms. The journal *De Naye Heym* (The New Home) was published from Opatashu's Bronx apartment on Crotona Avenue. Since so many of the *Yunge* lived in The Bronx, Opatashu referred to it as "the neighborhood into which the new writers gravitated." Thus, he defined the borough as one of the important centers of Yiddish literature in America.

The neighborhood into which these young writers gravitated was largely populated by Germans, who a decade earlier replaced the Scottish pioneers. The latter had entered the uninhabited section of Greater New York in the 1860's and 1870's, cut down trees and built themselves two-storied wooden homes with broad verandas. Each one had his cow, his horse and buggy, his dog. Their cows grazed where later were located Tremont Avenue, Jerome Avenue, the Grand Concourse. In time there arose a German brewery with

Washington Avenue above 169th Street looking east with Eichler's Brewery in the background, late nineteenth century. "In time there arose a German brewery with its tall chimney belching smoke day and night." —Joseph Opatashu. The Bronx County Historical Society Research Library.

its tall chimney belching smoke day and night. Others were built, and they soon served as fortresses to the German newcomers who began storming the neighborhood, establishing their beer saloons and taverns. Fifteen years later not a Scotsman remained in the vicinity.

Jews began to lay siege to this German fortress around 1903. They came from Manhattan's East Side and fought the Germans for years on end. It was at first dangerous for a Jew to pass a house occupied by a German and guarded by large vicious dogs. Blue Teutonic eyes became green with hatred for the invading Jews, but the latter persisted in their siege. Private homes were torn down and the rocky foundations were dynamited in preparation for the erection of large apartment houses. Pneumatic drills chattered deafeningly and bulldozers and tractors added to the pandemonium. But out of the hellish hubbub soon emerged the most beautiful section of the Bronx—the achievement of energetic and enterprising Jews. In this neighborhood,

Boston Road north of 169th Street in 1926. "But out of the hellish hubbub soon emerged the most beautiful section of the Bronx—the achievement of energetic and enterprising Jews." —Joseph Opatashu. The Bronx County Historical Society Research Library.

while still quite rural, young Jewish writers conceived their songs, their stories, their novels. And if they felt gratified to cleave to the soil, with its flowers and living creatures, they were even more pleased to associate with the
dynamic men who were building homes, streets, cities. This joy in nature and
this dynamism enlivened their writings. Soon Yiddish literature in the
United States, though far from its source of origin, assumed an artistic form
in many respects superior to the first masters.

> —Joseph Opatashu, "Yiddish Literature in the
> United States," trans. Shlomo Noble, in *Voices from
> the Yiddish: Essays, Memoirs, Diaries,* ed. Irving
> Howe and Eliezer Greenberg (Ann Arbor: Univer-
> sity of Michigan Press, 1972).

A 1914 rift among the *Yunge* was recalled by Yiddish writer Isaac Raboy. The
aesthetes—Zische Landau, Mani Lieb, and David Ignatov—took over one low-
circulation periodical, while I. J. Schwartz, Joseph Rolnick, and Joseph Opatashu
published another. By the middle of the decade, many Yiddish writers had house-
holds to support and worked long hours at menial jobs. Thus, they spent less time
enjoying the bohemian cafe life downtown and sought convenient meeting places
near their homes in The Bronx. At a meeting held at the Bronx apartment of poet
I. J. Schwartz, the most learned of the group, an artistic quarrel flared, the partici-
pants' dedication to controversy was affirmed, and the break became final.

> We left the house like a gang of boys, talking and shouting at the top of
> our voices, swearing to have nothing to do with the others the rest of our
> lives.
> "They have no talent among them."
> "They have no poets?"
> "Nobody with whom to put out a collection."
> "Good for them."
> "We'll finish them off."
> Such were the sounds spilling into the empty Bronx streets.
> Personally, I felt I'd wasted a day, and, bidding good night to my friends,
> went home.
> Arriving there I found my wife waiting for me. She could tell something
> was wrong.
> "So, you patched things up?"
> "No, we fought even worse."
> "What were you fighting about?"

> "I don't know myself. I don't think they knew either."
> "How can you fight over nothing?"
> "Children," I threw off with a wave of the hand.
>
> —Isaac Raboy, in *How We Lived: A Documentary History of Immigrant Jews in America 1880–1930*, ed. Irving Howe and Kenneth Libo (New York: Richard Marek Publishers, 1979).

After the meeting, friendship between the politically aloof aesthetes and the socially engaged breakaway group declined. This ideological schism foreshadowed even wider divisions to come in the ranks of the Yiddish intelligentsia.

Although most of these writers were limited by having to earn their living at humble trades, such as bootmaking and paperhanging or running a butcher shop, they were never ashamed of being workers. Beginning in 1910 or 1911, the adherents of the *Yunge* gathered in a local Bronx cleaning store owned by Isaac Bloom. The noted but improvident poet Moishe Leib Halpern, who worked briefly pressing pants there, even slept in it for several weeks. The proprietor found his business was seriously affected.

> There were fewer and fewer customers. I was forced to decide whether to take down the classic Yiddish writers from the wall, toss out their grandsons, the Bronx chapter of the Yunge, and turn my "Literary Hostel" into a real business establishment, or let things go, whatever the consequences . . . I didn't hesitate for a minute and chose the latter.
>
> —Isaac Bloom, *In Mayn Literarisher Akhsanye* [In My Literary Hostel] (Mexico City: Yiddish Cultural Center, 1964), quoted by Ruth R. Wisse in *A Little Love in Great Manhattan* (Cambridge, Mass.: Harvard University Press, 1988).

One of the aesthetes of the *Yunge* was Zische Landau, an intellectual who earned his living as a housepainter. True to his group's creed, he drew his inspiration from the rhythms and energies of the city, as well as from memories of Eastern Europe. He drew a portrait of Edgar Allan Poe's cottage, recently moved from its original location to preserve it from the danger of encroaching building construction to the newly created Poe Park across the street. A caretaker was hired and the cottage was opened to the public.

> A little park, with few trees growing;
> a wooden house sits humbly there,

on which appears a painted raven—
it all has such a childish air.

And on the wall there hangs a tablet,
and from the tablet you will know
here lived in eighteen nine and forty
the poet Edgar Allan Poe.

The name, the raven, wake within me
a memory of years before.
And since one is allowed to visit,
I let myself approach the door.

In a kimono red as scarlet
a woman's looking through the pane.
I'm so repelled by red kimonos
that in a flash I'm out again.

To stand outside suits me much better:
I clasp my hands, and focus all
my thoughts upon the roof's brown shingles,
and on the cottage's white wall.

Within my mind are mixed together
a verse of Poe's, a word, a rhyme.
Where have I heard them, come across them?
I feel they're from a distant time.

And yet, in dream and fact, they soothed me
and frightened me to my heart's core.
All this was only yesterday.
But will it come back? "Nevermore."

> —Zische Landau, "A Little Park, with Few Trees," in
> *A Century of Yiddish Poetry*, ed. and trans. Aaron
> Kramer (New York: Cornwall Books, 1989).

Landau, along with other Yiddish literati, was praised by poet I. J. Schwartz in his elegy "The Light of Summer's End." Schwartz began with the older generation and celebrated the arrival of the *Yunge*. Eliakum Zunzer was a Yiddish folk poet in whose Lower East Side print shop writers met. Poet Yehoash (Solomon Bloomgarten) was a Bronxite who, among other things, translated the Bible into Yiddish. The English translation of Morris Rosenfeld's "Songs of the Ghetto" made him internationally famous in the 1890s. In his lifetime, some aesthetes rebelled against his moralism and style, but most continued to acknowledge their debt to him. A Bronxite, Rosenfeld suffered many personal losses and was blind in his later years. Poet Abraham Liessin was the longtime editor of the literary journal *Zukunft*. Many considered the eccentric Moishe Leib Halpern the greatest poet of the circle. Writing decades later, Schwartz recalled the vigor and optimism of the *Yunge*, mourned the premature deaths of Landau and Halpern, and honored the entire group. All but Zunzer lived in The Bronx.

> A half-hour's walk from the hill on which I sit
> Lies stretched the field of spacious rest,
> Shaded by trees and covered with grasses:
> And in the elegiac light of day
> The time comes back, of building and brawn
> In the strange new world—a massive forest,
> A green uproarious forest in ascendance
> With birds and song. That era is engraved
> In my heart with charity and grace:
> I remember the old bard, Eliakum,
> As he would sit outside his printing shop
> On East Broadway in the hot summer days
> And slumber on his stool. (I here confess
> I did not read his poems myself,
> But I recollect them from my mother's lips.)
> And I recall Yehoash from nineteen-hundred-seven,
> Who radiated subtle distinction
> With his mature wisdom and young faith;
> And Rosenfeld from nineteen-hundred-nine,
> In Claremont Park in the Bronx, under a tree,
> As one infuriated, shattered by life;
> And Lyessin, man of combat and song,
> His Jewish stubbornness and consecration;
> His rebel's cry to a hostile and unfeeling world.
> A great strong generation, rooted
> In earth soaked through with our blood,
> And with heads uplifted to the skies.
> Soon there came to swell the chorus

A multitude of youth. With the great stream
That flowed here from the countless ships
Carrying refugees to our free shores,
Each ship, together with its poverty,
From the old home brought abundant tribute
To our Yiddish song. These, as the former,
Did not search for gold or pleasures—
They wanted nought and sought for nought
Except the song that burned upon their lips
And flamed within their eyes and hearts.
Each with his own countenance, this generation
Like wild young grass in an old field,
Grew up overnight with clamor,
Branches rustling and rich with fruits.
Some fell by the harsh roadside
In their most blossoming years: Moishe-Leib—
I see him now as in that youthful time
Before his head became ash gray:

Entrance to Claremont Park from Webster Avenue and Wendover Avenue, now Claremont Parkway, 1914. A postcard photograph. "And I recall . . . Rosenfeld from nineteen-hundred nine / In Claremont Park in the Bronx, under a tree." —I. J. Schwartz. Barbara Unger Collection.

A lad, a loafer, with a ruddy face
Amply sprinkled with summer freckles;
Our street drummer in the land, who
Clapped the cymbals to the moment of his death.
And Landau's princely image from that time:
A tender, graceful sprout, sprung up
"From a kingdom not of this world"
With his blue eyes and blond locks
Of wheaten gold—"the man of song."
All lie now on the field of spacious rest
Where all the generations seem as one,
Shaded by trees covered with grasses
A half-hour's walk from the hill where I now sit.

> —I. J. Schwartz, "The Light of Summer's End,"
> trans. Etta Blum, in *A Treasury of Yiddish Poetry*, ed.
> Irving Howe and Eliezer Greenberg (New York:
> Holt, Rinehart and Winston, 1969).

Of all the immigrant Russian-Jewish writers, the most famous was the Yiddish literary humorist Sholem Aleichem, born Solomon Rabinowitz, whose last home was 968 Kelly Street, one of an attached row of four-story brick houses between Westchester Avenue and East 163rd Street in The Bronx. Unlike the more esoteric work of the poets, his stories had wide popular appeal. Considered by many to have established Yiddish as a modern literary tongue, Sholem Aleichem's work has been widely translated and is internationally recognized. His stories featuring the character Tevye the milkman formed the basis for the musical *Fiddler on the Roof*.

In his short story "On America," Sholem Aleichem drily reports on an incident on a Bronx street. During the first decade of the century, street fighting and brawls were taken for granted. This American custom soon became grist for the author's comic imagination.

The author has the tale recounted by the character Berel-Ayzik, a noted bluffer, who managed to survive a few years of American life before returning to his Russian village. Of Americans, Berel-Ayzik says:

> "Hurry-up is what they call it. They do everything quickly. They even rush when they eat. They dash into a restaurant and order a glass of whiskey. I myself saw a man being served a plate which had something fresh and quivering on it. As a man lifted his knife, half of it flew off to one side, half to the other, and that put an end to that man's lunch.
>
> "But you ought to see how healthy they are. Men as strong as steel. They

have a habit of fighting in the middle of the street. Not that they want to kill you, knock your eye out, or push a few teeth down your throat like they do here. God forbid! They fight just for fun. They roll up their sleeves and they slug away to see who beats who. Boxing is what they call it. One day, while carrying some merchandise, I took a walk in the Bronx. Suddenly, two young boys started up with me. They wanted to box. 'No, sir,' I said. 'I don't box.' Well, we argued back and forth, but they wouldn't let me leave. I thought it over: if that's the way you feel about it, I'll show you a thing or two. I put my package down, took off my coat, and they beat the daylights out of me. I made it away, my life hanging by a hair. Since then, all the money in the world won't get me to box."

—Sholem Aleichem, "On America," trans. Curt Leviant, *Stories and Satires by Sholem Aleichem* (New York: Thomas Yoseloff, 1959).

N. B. Lindner, a Yiddish journalist and great devotee of Sholem Aleichem, was very close to the great writer in his last years. As a Bronx resident, Sholem Aleichem depended upon public transportation to travel from The Bronx to Manhattan. Later, in 1926, Lindner recalled:

It was a cold, wet day. Sholem Aleichem had not been feeling well and, to make matters worse, was extremely tired. He had been standing all morning, as was his custom, writing at a high table in his workroom. He had an appointment to meet someone on 42nd Street that afternoon and I was to go with him. His family was reluctant to let him go outdoors in such weather but, since the arrangements had been made some time ago, there was nothing for it but to "go to the City," as Sholem Aleichem used to say. . . .

"Never in my life have I missed so many trains as I have here in America!" exclaimed Sholem Aleichem to me once we ran

Subway entrance at Third and Melrose Avenues, 1915. "'Never in my life have I missed so many trains as I have here in America!' exclaimed Sholem Aleichem to me once we ran down the subway steps just in time to see the train pull away. I tried to explain to him that the subway trains run on a definite schedule and cannot stop at a station longer than this schedule permits." —N. B. Lindner. *The Bronx County Historical Society Research Library.*

down the subway steps just in time to see the train pull away. I tried to explain to him that the subway trains run on a definite schedule and cannot stop at a station longer than this schedule permits.

"No!" insisted Sholem Aleichem. "They are just spiteful! There are, you understand, all kinds of trains in the world, each one with its own habits and its own caprices. In Russia the trains drag along. In other countries, in Austria, for instance, they promenade. The German trains run. But the American trains—they run away! Just to spite you, they run away!"

> —N. B. Lindner, "Sholem Aleichem in New York,"
> trans. Max Rosenfeld, *Jewish Currents* (November
> 1958).

Sholem Aleichem was so well known and beloved among the Yiddish-speaking Jewish immigrants that his death caused a great outpouring of grief and the funeral became a major event. His daughter, Marie Waife-Goldberg, recalled the scene in her 1968 memoir.

He died . . . early Saturday morning, May 13, 1916. Radio being still unknown, and the morning papers already out, the Yiddish newspapers issued extras, all in black borders, the huge letters SHOLEM ALEICHEM DIED occupying most of the front page, the rest given to a picture of the sad news. Newsboys ran through the streets of the Jewish districts with their packs of extras, holding one of them unfolded over their heads, and shouting on top of their voices, "Sholem Aleichem dead," so that those inside the houses might hear and come down for an extra. Many did, congregating in the streets, shocked, grieved, gesticulating, crying. The afternoon and Sunday English papers carried the news and special feature stories about the passing of the Jewish Mark Twain.

For two days and nights the body lay in state in the living room of our apartment at 968 Kelly Street, the Bronx, with a changing guard of Jewish writers in the city, while a continuous stream of people kept passing the bier all through the night as well as during the day, the line outside, even at night, stretching for blocks around the house. They came from all boroughs of the city and from Jewish communities outside.

The funeral was possibly the largest the city had seen. While the estimates of the numbers of followers varied, the generally accepted figure was "over 100,000."

> —Marie Waife-Goldberg, *My Father, Sholem Alei-*
> *chem* (New York: Simon and Schuster, 1968).

By the end of the second decade of the twentieth century, people continued to surge northward. These newcomers were mostly Jews and Italians. The Ogden estate in Highbridge, the Varian farm in Norwood, the Astor estate in Pelham Parkway, and those of the Simpsons, Tiffanys, and Foxes of Hunts Point all went under the gavel. After several years of blasting, as streets, sewers, and sidewalks were constructed, the countrified areas of The Bronx were rapidly transformed into urban neighborhoods and homes for an upwardly mobile middle class. With increasing rapidity, the tiny Bronx villages of 1898, each separated from its neighbors by woodlands, plowed farmlands, orchards, and meadows, vanished.

4

A STEP UP

THE BRONX IN BOOM TIMES

1919–1929

THE OVERWHELMING GROWTH IN THE POPULATION OF THE BRONX continued apace into the 1920s. By 1925, over a million people lived there. Many were first- and second-generation European immigrants of middle-class Irish or Italian background, but most were of Eastern European Jewish descent. By 1930, the population of The Bronx as a whole was 49 percent Jewish, as were over 80 percent of the people living in the neighborhoods south of Tremont Avenue. Many new residents moved there from Jewish and Italian Harlem, the Lower East Side, and Brooklyn for a better life in newer, more spacious apartments with greater amenities. Parks, tree-lined boulevards, and open land provided the fresh air and greenery considered essential to raising families. The Bronx was *the* place for people who saw themselves and their children taking a step up the socio-economic ladder. In 1927, *The Jazz Singer*, the first talking motion picture, reflected this fact when Al Jolson promised his mother that they would move from the Lower East Side to The Bronx when he became a successful Broadway star. Younger Bronxites also attended neighborhood movie and vaudeville theaters. Although Bronx residents enjoyed the many nearby recreational amenities of the borough, people from Manhattan also traveled on Sundays to the vast parklands of The Bronx to escape from their congested tenements. In *Jews Without Money*, Michael Gold's proletarian novel, the author describes such an outing by a Lower East Side Jewish family. The family boards the elevated train to get to Bronx Park.

Northward to the Bronx! And at every station new mobs of frenzied sweating families loaded with lunch baskets and babies burst through the doors. There was no room for them, but they made it for themselves by standing on our feet. . . .

But my mother became happier as the train rolled on. She leaned out of the window and smiled. In the streets below, the solid palisades of tenement had disappeared. There were small houses, each set among green weedy lots, and there were trees.

"It's a pleasure to see green things again," she said. "Look, another tree! I am glad we came, Herman! When we come to Bronx Park I will take off my shoes and walk in the grass. I haven't done it for fifteen years."

"They will arrest you," snarled my father, as he glared at the fat Jewish woman standing next to him when the train lurched.

"I want to pick daisies!" cried my little sister.

"Yes, yes, my darling," said my mother, fondly, "daisies and mushrooms, too. I will show you how to find mushrooms. It is more fun than picking daisies." . . .

At last the Bronx Park! My father bought us popcorn to eat, and red balloons.

A Woodland Path, Bronx Park, New York

Photo only Copyright by R. F. Turnbull, N

A woodland path in Bronx Park in 1907. A postcard photograph. "'When we come to Bronx Park I will take off my shoes and walk in the grass.'"— Michael Gold. The Bronx County Historical Society Research Library.

Eagerly seeking the mushrooms she had known in her native Hungary, the mother takes the children into the park's woods. In her only escape from the crowded tenements of the Lower East Side, the mother achieves a transcendent moment as she finds them.

We followed her, as she poked around under the trees and bushes for her beloved mushrooms. She found many, and lifted her skirt to make a bag for them. Each new mushroom reminded her of Hungary and of things she had never told us. She talked in a low, caressing voice. She stooped to the mushrooms, and her eyes shone like a child's. . . .

Suddenly my mother flung her arms around each of us, and kissed Esther and me.

"Ach, Gott!" she said, "I'm so happy in a forest! You American children don't know what it means! I am happy!"

> —Michael Gold, *Jews Without Money* (New York: Horace Liveright, Inc., 1930).

Like the mother from the Lower East Side, many immigrants had lived near fields and woods in Europe. Thus, they found the still-countrified areas of The

Bronx both familiar and appealing. Some were able to purchase small homes in these still-rural neighborhoods. Boruch Glasman's short story "Goat in the Backyard," originally written in Yiddish, depicts such an area. A Bronx Italian street-cleaner, surveying his garden, recalls the old country.

> In Italy he had lived in wild, hilly country. In his mind he could see the light-drenched columns amidst the ruins of ancient palaces and buildings still standing in his town. He had owned a fruit-orchard and a good-sized garden. The garden hung at the edge of a cliff over a brown sea. The hills were wild and he had hunted wild goats. When he caught one he would domesticate it. It takes a lot of strength and patience to tame a wild goat.
>
> So on this particular evening the thought occurred to him—why not keep a goat here in America, too? He couldn't go out and catch a wild one, but he could still *buy* a goat. From the goat's milk he could churn his own cheese; Italians do so love cheese made out of goat-milk.
>
> Thus, one night when the weather had grown cooler and the first snow had fallen, through the bare gardens and rocky streets of the neighborhood echoed the meh-meh of a goat.
>
> —Boruch Glasman, "Goat in the Backyard," in *Pushcarts and Dreamers: Stories of Jewish Life in America*, ed. and trans. Max Rosenfeld (South Brunswick, N.J.: Thomas Yoseloff, 1967).

As more families moved into these countrified neighborhoods, apartment buildings, shops, and businesses soon followed. In 1929, the family of Cynthia Ozick, later a National Book Award winner, bought a pharmacy in Pelham Bay in the northeast corner of the borough. At the time, Pelham Bay, unlike many other Bronx neighborhoods, had lost little of its small-town atmosphere.

> Pelham Bay was at the very end of a relatively new stretch of elevated train track that extended from the subway of the true city all the way out to a small-town enclave of little houses and a single row of local shops: shoemaker's, greengrocer, drugstore, grocery, bait store. There was even a miniature five-and-ten where you could buy pots, housedresses, and thick lisle stockings for winter. Three stops down the line was the more populous Westchester Square, with its bank and post office, which the old-timers still called "the village"—Pelham Bay had once lain outside the city limits, in Westchester County.
>
> This lost little finger of the borough was named for the broad but mild

The shore of Pelham Bay Park at Pelham Bay around 1907. A postcard photograph. "All the paths of Pelham Bay Park led down to a narrow beach of rough pebbles." —Cynthia Ozick. Barbara Unger Collection.

body of water that rippled across Long Island Sound to a blurry opposite shore. All the paths of Pelham Bay Park led down to a narrow beach of rough pebbles, and all the surrounding streets led, sooner or later, to the park, wild and generally deserted. Along many of these streets there were empty lots that resembled meadows, overgrown with Queen Anne's lace and waist-high weeds glistening with what the children called "snake spit"; poison ivy crowded between the toes of clumps of sky-tall oaks. The snake spit was a sort of bubbly botanical excretion, but there were real snakes in these lots, with luminescent skins, brownish-greenish, crisscrossed with white lines. There were real meadows, too: acres of downhill grasses, in the middle of which you might suddenly come on a set of rusty old swings—wooden slats on chains—or a broken red brick wall left over from some ruined and forgotten Westchester estate.

—Cynthia Ozick, "A Drugstore Eden," *The New Yorker* (September 16, 1996).

Many families came to The Bronx for a brighter future for their children. During the 1920s, they also hoped ethnic and class differences would, in time, yield to money and social mobility. Higher incomes, opportunity, and a growing economy lent credence to their hopes. Immigrant parents often sacrificed to accelerate their children's assimilation into the American mainstream and their family's rise on the socioeconomic ladder. Material luxuries were also available. After World War I, a symbol of upward mobility was the purchase of an automobile, which still remained a comparatively rare luxury in a borough so well served by public transportation. Nevertheless, the appearance of cars accelerated the demand for paving the remaining dirt roads in The Bronx. In her memoir, Joan Renzetti Durant recalls the stern reaction of her Italian-American grandfather when her uncle, Nicola, bought a car.

"The automobile will destroy the city and eventually the whole country," prophesied my grandfather Vittorio. Our more progressive neighbors in the Northeast Bronx had to compromise with Vittorio on neighborhood improvements and ended up with no more than a strip paved down the center of the road because Vittorio insisted upon keeping the old dirt road on either side for the horses.

The reaction to the coming of the automobile, as part of the rapid pace of technological and social change, not only created a division in attitude between the generations, but also between the sexes. Manners and morals were undergoing a revolution in the 1920s. Necklines plunged, hemlines rose, and Bronx women were experiencing their first taste of freedom. Some, however, were still ambivalent about it.

Even before he bought his first automobile, my aunt's husband Bertrando let his wife Maria know that driving was not for women. This anarchist admirer of Emma Goldman and supporter of the vote for women, liked to quote some saying . . . to the effect that no woman was physically fit enough to run an automobile. Most men agreed. At the movies, the very sight of a female behind the wheel of a car was cause for general laughter and the sight of a woman cranking up the motor turned the laughter to tears, unstitching every row of buttons on male trousers.

The women in the family saw the automobile as an extension of the man's world. Zia Maglia, Pasqualina's favorite sister, nicknamed "The Suffragette," was the authority among her sisters on the monumental issues of war and peace and the working conditions of women. Of the automobile, she said, "It's a man's toy."

"*Un altra moda* . . . another way to kill himself," added Pasqualina, always happy to agree.

However, the chief avenue of upward mobility for many Bronx immigrant families was education for their sons and daughters. For some, this meant a high school diploma. Others dreamed of a college education and even advanced preparation for the professions. Not until the relatively affluent 1920s did this dream become attainable for many Italian Americans.

> Giorgio was Vittorio's favorite son and on him, his last descendant, he pinned his hopes. Despite the fact that he had worked two jobs while Pasqualina farmed in the summer and preserved fruit and vegetables for winter, he had been unable to provide an education for his sons. Not Nicola, not Franco, not Gugliemo. Nor had it helped to hang the American flag in front of his house on Washington's birthday. He even named his youngest son, Giorgio, after George Washington. But over the years, Vittorio had grown bitter.
>
> Now, after many years, there was reason to hope. Nicola, the eldest, promised to help pay Giorgio's tuition through university and medical school. Even at age three, Giorgio had been fascinated by his grandfather's medical books. It was all the proof Vittorio needed. It little mattered what the child had perceived in those anatomical drawings. He had learned to identify *fegato, pulmone, reni . . . curoe* and *cervello*. His whims and impulses were treated like new growth. Every step Giorgio took enlarged his father's hopes.
>
> —Joan Renzetti Durant, "Old World, New World,"
> unpublished memoir.

Many working-class Jewish immigrant families also grasped at education as the way to make further steps up, and increasing numbers of Bronx women attended high school and college. Nevertheless, some Old World attitudes persisted. In her memoir *Bronx Primitive*, travel writer Kate Simon, who grew up in an apartment on Lafontaine Avenue in the Tremont area north of Crotona Park, noted that her father exhorted her to quit school when she was thirteen so she could earn money for the family. Her mother, however, stressed the value of education and a career.

> My mother didn't accept her fate as a forever thing. She began to work during our school hours after her English classes had taught her as much as they could, and while I was still young, certainly no more than ten, I began to get her lecture on being a woman. It ended with extraordinary statements, shocking in view of the street mores. "Study. Learn. Go to college. Be a

schoolteacher," then a respected, privileged breed, "and don't get married until you have a profession. With a profession you can have men friends and even children, if you want. You're free. But don't get married, at least not until you can support yourself and make a careful choice. Or don't get married at all, better still." This never got into "My mother said" conversations with my friends. I sensed it to be too outrageous. . . . In the community fabric . . . was the conviction that girls were to marry as early as possible, the earlier the more triumphant.

—Kate Simon, *Bronx Primitive: Portraits in a Childhood* (New York: The Viking Press, 1982).

Although young Kate Simon was not religiously observant, she was still surrounded and shaped by her immigrant milieu. In *Inside, Outside*, his novelized memoir, Pulitzer Prize–winner Herman Wouk, too, showed that assimilation into the American mainstream did not require the abandonment of his Jewish roots. The family dressed for the Sabbath and lit candles.

We ate Friday supper and Saturday dinner at the oval dining table in the parlor; otherwise we ate in the kitchen. With this shift in setting went different talk. The incessant weekly laundry chatter—what Brodofsky said, what Gross did, the repairs to the boiler, the threat of a strike, the troubles with Jake the drunk—all this endless, endless business drivel—was shut off. My parents told stories of their Minsk childhoods, sang old songs of the old country, played little table games, games as simple as trying to slap a hand before it was snatched away, or they asked us about our Jewish studies, Lee's at an afternoon Yiddishist school, mine with a Hebrew tutor. After supper Pop would read Sholem Aleichem aloud, and Lee and I would roll around on the davenport screaming with laughter, tears streaming down our cheeks, while Mama too laughed like a fool.

—Herman Wouk, *Inside, Outside* (Boston: Little, Brown & Company, 1985).

For most Bronx immigrant children, the New York City public school was the center of existence. Sometimes, Bronx schools of the era uncritically placed pressure on these children to adopt the beliefs of mainstream American culture. In the case of Jewish schoolchildren, that meant celebrating Christmas and Easter, Christian holidays, alongside their non-Jewish classmates. Short story writer, poet, and essayist Grace Paley, in her short story "The Loudest Voice," recounts a Jewish family's reaction to the news that their daughter had been given a leading role in her public elementary school's Christmas play because of her loud, clear voice. Their Jewish neighbors chime in with their own opinions, too. The mother speaks:

> "Listen," she said sadly, "I'm surprised to see my neighbors making tra-la-la for Christmas."
>
> My father couldn't think of what to say to that. Then he decided: "You're in America! Clara, you wanted to come here. In Palestine the Arabs would be eating you alive. Europe you had pogroms. Argentina is full of Indians. Here you got Christmas. . . . Some joke, ha?"
>
> "Very funny, Misha. What is becoming of you? If we come to a new country a long time ago to run away from tyrants, and instead we fall into a creeping pogrom, that our children learn a lot of lies, so what's the joke? Ach, Misha, your idealism is going away."
>
> "So is your sense of humor."
>
> "That I never had, but idealism you had a lot of."
>
> "I'm the same Misha Abramovitch, I didn't change an iota. Ask anyone."
>
> "Only ask me," says my mama, may she rest in peace. "I got the answer." Meanwhile the neighbors had to think of what to say too.
>
> Marty's father said: "You know, he has a very important part, my boy."
>
> "Mine also," said Mr. Sauerfeld.
>
> "Not my boy!" said Mrs. Klieg. "I said to him no. The answer is no. When I say no! I mean no!"
>
> The rabbi's wife said, "It's disgusting!" But no one listened to her.

The bilingual daughter, Shirley, successfully acts her role in the play with her father's approval. After the performance, the family has tea in the kitchen with neighbors, sharing their differing opinions over the kitchen table.

> They debated a little in Yiddish, then fell in a puddle of Russian and Polish. What I understood next was my father who said, "Still and all, it was certainly a beautiful affair, you have to admit, introducing us to the beliefs of a different culture."
>
> "Well, yes," said Mrs. Kornbluh. "The only thing . . . you know Charlie Turner—that cute boy in Celia's class—a couple of others? They got very small parts or no part at all. In very bad taste, it seemed to me. After all, it's their religion."
>
> "Ach," explained my mother, "what could Mr. Hilton do? They got very small voices; after all, why should they holler? The English language they know from the beginning by heart. They're blond like angels. You think it's

so important they should get in the play? Christmas . . . the whole piece of goods . . . they own it."

> —Grace Paley, "The Loudest Voice," *The Little Disturbances of Man* (New York: Doubleday & Company, Inc., 1959).

In addition to school, the neighborhood was an important influence on Bronx residents. Playwright, novelist, and poet William Gibson, who later wrote *The Miracle Worker*, recalled when his family returned to reside in the Irish Highbridge neighborhood. In Gibson's boyhood, the neighborhood provided opportunities for a variety of children's pastimes. In the summer, children dove off the banks into the Harlem River to swim. In the fall, roasted potatoes, called "mickies," were popular. The neighborhood's hills were ideal for sledding in winter. In the springtime, however, the entire neighborhood came to life.

> In spring, when we were digging dirtholes with our heels for immies— marbles, imitations—our fathers were in view digging with spades, until the field next to the end house was a crazy quilt of little vegetable gardens; here in the evenings the grown-ups would cluster in twos and threes, the mothers in aprons talking, the men on their knees in old pants coaxing along their tomatoes and stringbeans. In the untended afternoons these garden squares, staked and roped off, made ideal sites for their sons to stage mock prizefights in, a sport which resulted in some baffling crop failures. The true sport was baseball on the plateau of our hill, a trodden diamond in the rough, alive all day with a scatter of players, the gang I was in and the teen-age giants who chased us off and after supper the young fathers in collarless shirts, home from the bondage of offices. At a bottom corner of the hill was a dell with the communal oak, where in late spring the "strawberry festival" with its free ice cream was sponsored by our wardheelers for a pandemonium of neighborhood children and our mothers, who had recently received the vote; their purity was expected to redeem the world, a hope which was not quite realized, it succumbed under my eyes to free strawberry ice cream.
>
> —William Gibson, *A Mass for the Dead* (New York: Atheneum, 1968).

In the Hunts Point neighborhood of the early 1920s, parents showed their aspirations for higher social status by dressing themselves and their children on weekends and holidays in the best new clothes they could afford. Good times demanded good clothing. This did not deter boys from having fun, as do the fictional Herbie Bookbinder and his cousin, Clifford Block, as they amble toward the Bronx River in

City Boy, an early novel by Herman Wouk. Wouk modeled Herbie's apartment house on the one on Longfellow Avenue in which he resided as an adolescent. While some streets in that area do commemorate noted authors, the streets named for Byron, Shakespeare, Tennyson, and Homer are fictional.

Both boys were dressed from head to foot in those articles of wardrobe which, being most recently purchased, had exclusive Sunday status. They were the customary boys' costume of the time: black shoes, long stockings, "knickers," short jackets, white shirts with four-in-hand ties (askew five minutes after tying), and soft round felt hats, jeered at by boys too small to wear them as "cake-eaters." They carried their finery with mixed feelings, disgust at the constraint of it struggling with the bit of peacock that is not absent from a boy's heart. Their parents would not send them into the street on Sunday except in this gala state, especially so soon after Passover, when their new clothes were really so new. . . .

Herbie and Cliff found the vacant lots along Homer Avenue too commonplace to still the restlessness of the first warm Sunday in May. They had gone down the long hill of Westchester Avenue past Byron, past Shakespeare, past Tennyson Avenues, to the creek which they avoided all year round, partly in obedience to the sternest sort of orders from their parents, but more because of the legend that the river bank was the haunt of a pack of boyish cutthroats known as the "creek gang." . . .

The thought that they might encounter these desperadoes lent an edge of pleasure to the excursion of Herbie and his cousin, for today they were in a mood for braving the unknown. To reach the bank of the stream they had to cross the railroad tracks, another tremendous taboo. They slid carefully down a gravel embankment and picked their way across the cinder bed on which the tracks rested. Of course they avoided the rails, which were supposed to have a power of suction that could hold unwary treaders fast until the next train destroyed them, and they leaped anxiously over the death-dealing third rail, along which they both averred they could hear the hum of the fatal electric current. These hazards passed at last, the boys reached the side of the creek and lolled on the fresh grass and spiky weeds that covered the narrow strip of wasteland between the railroad bed and the river mud. The sun was high; the ground was warm; the smell of the mud and the slime of the inlet at low tide was pungent and interesting. The boys were alone in a new place, lying on the ground in Sunday clothes, successfully defiant of their parents' orders and their own fears.

—Herman Wouk, *City Boy* (New York: Simon and Schuster, 1948).

While Wouk's Herbie Bookbinder ruined his best clothes on the banks of the Bronx River, Kate Simon, in her Tremont neighborhood, enjoyed excursions to theaters, libraries, and nearby Crotona Park.

To the west of Lafontaine was Arthur Avenue, a mixture of Jewish tenements and frame houses in which lived Italian families and a number of Irish. Beyond was Belmont, whose only significance was that it held, at its meeting with Tremont, the movie house we all trooped to on Saturday after lunch. The other movie house, which offered a combination of films and vaudeville, was a rare pleasure; it cost more and was saved for special occasions, or a report card that said A for work, A for effort, A for conduct.

This theater for celebrations was also on Tremont, toward the west, not far from Webster Avenue, beyond Bathgate and Washington. Bathgate, moving southward from Tremont toward Claremont Parkway was the market street. . . . On the next block, Washington, was the public library. . . .

Our suburbs, our summer country homes, our camps, our banks and braes, our America the Beautiful, our fields of gaming and dalliance and voyeurism, were in Crotona Park, whose northern border fronted on Tremont Avenue.

The New York Public Library's Tremont Branch on Washington Avenue in 1912. A postcard photograph. "On the next block, Washington, was the public library." —Kate Simon. The Bronx County Historical Society Research Library.

The northern edge of Crotona Park at Tremont Avenue in 1922. A postcard photograph. "Our suburbs, our summer country homes, our camps, our banks and braes, our America the Beautiful, our fields of gaming and dalliance and voyeurism, were in Crotona Park, whose northern border fronted on Tremont Avenue." —Kate Simon. Barbara Unger Collection.

Immigrant families brought with them a variety of traditional musical favorites. Their sounds filled the apartment house courtyard, along with those of itinerant street singers.

The afternoon sounds were "Practice. Go practice. Now I say," and the assembled pianos cranked out the wobbling sounds of an immense broken merry-go-round. . . . The "Ole Close" men called as the sun began to pale, never doing a brisk trade. Old clothes were sent to relatives in the Old Country. The yard singers did better with their mixed repertoire of "O Sole Mio," "Eli Eli," "Delia oh Delia," and "Daisy, Daisy." It wasn't only the singing and the romantic presence of the street singer but the luxury of giving away money for something intangible that spurred us kids to hop around the mothers nagging for two pennies, three. We wrapped them securely in large wads of newspaper and flung them down, feeling like lords. . . . The later hours were parents' time, a rich tapestry—if one could stay awake long enough—of Victrola horns, spilling jigs and reels, Alma Gluck, Yosele Rosenblatt, Caruso, "When You and I Were Young, Maggie," Sousa marches, flowing through over and around the banging of doors and chairs, the weeping and shouting of adult quarrels.

—Kate Simon, *Bronx Primitive: Portraits in a Childhood* (New York: The Viking Press, 1982).

Generally, the neighborhoods to the south and east, then called the East Bronx, were considered less desirable than those to the north and west. In Thomas Bell's proletarian novel *All Brides Are Beautiful*, young Peter Cummings and his new wife, Susan, lived in the newer western part of The Bronx, whereas Martha Beasley, Susan's married sister, lived in the older East Bronx, where her mother-in-law owned an apartment house on Union Avenue. Peter and Susan, like many young couples of the era, dream of leaving The Bronx in a few years and of buying their own home. Bell opens the novel with a tongue-in-cheek description of The Bronx.

The Bronx may be identified as that one of New York City's five boroughs which is on the mainland of the North American continent, the others being distributed over three islands off its coast. It has a population of one and a half millions; it is cold in winter, tropically hot in summer, and on a Jewish holiday indistinguishable from a city stricken with a completely successful general strike. A zoo, a cocktail, and a derisory cheer have been named after it. Most of its employed residents earn—receive—twenty-five dollars or less per week and pay an average monthly rental of ten dollars per room. The customary price of a glass of beer is ten cents, of admission to a picture theater twenty-five cents. . . .

Martha Beasley receives an invitation to a wedding, which proves to be bad news to her mother-in-law. The elder Mrs. Beasley had rented an apartment in her less-than-fashionable building to the reliable McGonigles for many years. She had no idea that her tenants aspired to purchase a home of their own.

In June Martha and Mrs. Beasley attended the wedding; in July, the blow fell. The McGonigles had bought a two-family house in Throgg's Neck; the elder McGonigles and their unmarried son Frankie—a helper in a service station on Boston Road, studying for night school downtown and languidly mad about aviation—were going to live on the ground floor, and Joseph, Jr. and his bride on the second floor. There were—after the first, embarrassed shocks had faded—discussions of the advantages of owning one's own home, of Throgg's Neck as a place to raise children, of real estate as an investment. . . .

> —Thomas Bell, *All Brides Are Beautiful* (Boston: Little, Brown and Company, 1937).

Although a two-family house in countrified Throggs Neck represented a step up for the fictional McGonigles, other, more densely populated areas, especially in the western part of the borough, were considered far more prestigious. Perhaps the most prominent of all was the Grand Concourse, home to well-to-do professional and business people. This wide, elegant, tree-lined boulevard, flanked by six-story apartment houses with elevators, lavish lobbies, and uniformed doormen, emerged as the borough's answer to Park and Fifth Avenues in Manhattan. It was designed after the Champs Elysées in the 1890s and completed in 1909. For Jews of the era following World War I, a Grand Concourse address was a symbol of having achieved economic and social success. Humorist Arthur Kober, later a Hollywood screenwriter and contributor to *The New Yorker*, tells the tale of a young man, Mortimer Aarons, trying to make a date with a young woman, Bella Gross, on a Grand Concourse bus. The characters use the dialect that became known as the Bronx accent, but they observe all the social proprieties expected of residents of that elegant boulevard.

> Bella waited at McClellan Street on the Grand Concourse for the Mosholu Parkway bus. She could have taken the Grand Concourse subway to get to Jennie's, but it was a warm and beautiful Saturday afternoon, and she felt the bus ride would do her good.
>
> She was unaware of the snappily dressed young man with the black, toothbrush mustache when he sat down beside her. She therefore gave a violent start when he addressed her. . . .
>
> "I don't meanna bother you, Miss." Toothbrush Mustache seemed genuinely apologetic. "But might I ast don't you work in the Berger Building on the sixth floor?"
>
> Bella looked at him in surprise. "Yeah," she replied, "but hoddeya know?"
>
> The young man smiled again, and Bella's eye caught a flash of gold. "I knew you looked familiar. I musta seen you in the elevator at lease a dozen times. I got an account on the sixth floor. L. Spiegelgass & Son, the account."
>
> He was busy removing his card from his card case. A wisp of tissue paper deserted the card and fell to the floor. "I'm with Jaffe & Sackheim," the young man said. "I represent their gloves."

The northern end of the Grand Concourse at Mosholu Parkway, July 26, 1932. This is where the Concourse bus line ended its run. Note the double-decker bus on the right, southbound lane of the Concourse beginning its ride. "Bella waited at McClellan Street on the Grand Concourse for the Mosholu Parkway bus." —Arthur Kober. The Bronx County Historical Society Research Library.

Bella hesitated a moment, and then diffidently took the card. . . . In the lower left-hand corner she saw the name, Mortimer Aarons.

Mr. Aarons watched Bella study the card. "I knew I'd seen you before," he said triumphantly. "With me, once I see a face I never forget it." Then, raising his hat, he said, "Might I ast your name, please?"

Bella, aware of the unorthodox manner of this meeting, again held out for the proprieties. "I'm not in the habit of talking to people I haven't been formerly innaduced to."

Mr. Aarons, not to be outdone, countered with "And I'm not the type man who goes arounn picking up young ladies. Y'know something?" He paused significantly. "I got absolutely no use fa the fresh type person who goes arounn picking up young ladies. Jail is too good fa them fellas!"

The two then introduce themselves, and Mortimer informs Bella of his destination.

"I'm gonna visit a frienda mine on the Concourse. Mr. Feldman, his name. He's in ladies' gomments, wholesale oney. Y'know, this Mr. Feldman, I don't know how much he knocks out a year, it must be in the heavy thousands, but with him it's the best of evveything. With him, nothing is too good."

"Well, that's O.K. if you can afford it," said Bella, philosophically. "The oney time it's not O.K. is when you can't afford it."

"With him, regella like clockwork, evvey year he and the Missus must knock off and go to Europe. That's where I met him. On the S.S. De Grasse. French boat, y'know."

"I never get seasick," said Bella. "Me and my bunch we took three-four excursions to Bear Mountain and not once did I get seasick."

> —Arthur Kober, "The Daring Young Man on a Bus," *Thunder over The Bronx* (New York: Simon and Schuster, 1935).

After further conversation, Bella gives Mr. Aarons her telephone number. This action reflected the changing manners and morals of the 1920s as more young people dated without parental consent and supervision.

While many readers snickered at Kober's Jewish characters, lovers of the Yiddish language cringed. For a small but devoted group, Yiddish formed the center of their lives. They read Yiddish newspapers, novels, poems, and stories, and attended the Yiddish theater. Many gravitated to what was then called the East Bronx where they formed a community. There, Yiddish writers continued to seek suitable meeting places to share work and ideas, such as in the large six-room apartment of poet Berthe Kling, whose husband, a doctor, was also a devotee of Yiddish literature. There, on a weekend or a holiday, she made a buffet meal, put out chairs, and invited members of the local Yiddish intelligentsia. This Bronx "literary salon," which endured through the 1930s, was so popular that often not an empty seat could be found. Another group, nicknamed "The Crotona Park Gang," met at a rock outcropping on the northern end of Crotona Park in good weather. Evening in the park inspired flamboyant Bronx Yiddish poet Anna Margolin to write "Girls in Crotona Park."

> Into the autumn evening
> girls have woven themselves
> like a fading painting.
> Their eyes are chilled,
> their smiles unkempt and thin.

The color of their dresses, lavender,
antique rose and apple green.
Dew flows in their veins.
Their words are light and vacuous.
It is they Botticelli once loved in
a dream.

> —Anna Margolin, "Girls in Crotona Park," *Lider*
> (New York: N.p., 1929). Unpublished translation
> from the Yiddish by Norma Fain Pratt.

Crotona Park also inspired Aaron Glanz-Leyeles, leader of the Introspectivists, who favored complex free verse in Yiddish. His poem "November" suggests the gradual aging of Yiddish culture in the East Bronx.

Melancholy green of November,
How juicy is your browning in the early morning
    in Crotona Park.
How you move me today, Crotona Park,

Crotona Park in July 1934. In November, the trees would be bare. "How you move me today, Crotona Park." —Aaron Glanz-Leyeles. The Bronx County Historical Society Research Library.

In your damp tulle of November,
In your foggy detachment
Smiling through tears.
Memories of better days
Gleam white in your sad experienced smile,
The smile of a fifty-year-old
Bespectacled lady
Leaving over a novel of young life,
In the corners of her eyes
Glisten humid pearls. . . .

—Aaron Glanz-Leyeles, "November," *Rondeaux and Other Poems* (1929), in *American Yiddish Poetry*, ed. Benjamin and Barbara Harshav (Berkeley and Los Angeles: University of California Press, 1986).

While some Bronxites appreciated the arts, making money seemed the primary interest. The 1920s were marked by a strong entrepreneurial spirit among all the new arrivals in The Bronx. New shops and businesses sprang up in the rapidly urbanizing borough. Poet w r rodriguez memorialized his feisty Italian grandfather's circuitous and difficult climb up the economic ladder. The shoeshine parlor, at Brook Avenue just off the corner of 138th Street, was purchased in 1924.

his father was an exporter
so it wasn't hard for him to leave italy
as it was for a lot of others   & work
his way up the coast   florida to phillie
bought land there with his brothers-in-law
had a barber shop   & a store   on main street too
but he left it   all in a family argument
returned only for funerals   & weddings
the old fashioned kind   with buffets   home pressed wine
virgin brides

he made it to new york   with his wife
& the children they had on the boat   & in various other states
then in manhattan   my mother   the ninth & last
not counting the two who died of pneumonia & tb
all living in a cold water flat by the polo grounds
then in the south bronx   right around the corner

from the shoe shine parlor he bought
in the early 20's

                 worked it with his sons
swept streets   & speak easies on the side
bartended after the repeal   had as much fun
as anyone during the depression   went fishing & crabbing
in pelham bay before it was polluted   & sometimes
on sundays   treated ma to a ride on the third avenue el
& once a year   took the whole family for a picnic
sailing the dayliner to bear mountain

                 but mostly he worked
ten or twelve hours a day   came home   took a short nap
woke   went for a walk   returned with the paper
read it & made sure his daughters were home by nine. . . .

—w r rodriguez, "grandfather," *the shoe shine parlor poems et al.* (Madison, Wisc.: Ghost Pony Press, 1984).

The significant increase in Italian residents, along with the already-established Irish population of the borough, led to a growth in the number of Catholic parishioners in The Bronx. This also gave rise to businesses that catered to Bronx Catholics. The fictional John Scanlan in Pulitzer Prize–winning author Anna Quindlen's novel, *Object Lessons,* was an Irish-American entrepreneur who, at the age of twenty-one, launched a communion wafer business that later became a successful Bronx business empire.

For a week after he quit school John had thought about growth industries and then he had rented a pressing machine and space in a garage on a back street in the South Bronx and begun to stamp out little wafers of unleavened bread. The Jews who rented him the place thought he was crazy. Two years later he had his own factory and twenty-two employees.

He began to make holy cards, vestments, and assorted communion veils and confirmation robes.

—Anna Quindlen, *Object Lessons* (New York: Random House, 1991).

Another aspect of upward social mobility in The Bronx was the ability of housewives to pay for services, such as professional laundering, formerly labori-

The shoeshine parlor at Brook Avenue just off the corner of 138th Street about 1930. "the shoe shine parlor he bought / in the early 20's / worked it with his sons." —w r rodriguez. The Bronx County Historical Society Research Library, William R. Rodriguez Collection.

ously performed in the home. In *Inside, Outside*, Herman Wouk, whose father owned the Fox Square Laundry, relates the ascent of the fictional Isaac Goodkind's Russian Jewish immigrant father from laundryman to owner of a prosperous Bronx business. Wouk stresses the father's loyalty to those who helped him when he had nothing.

> Reuben Brodofsky founded the Fairy Laundry, by supplying the hundred fifty dollars for the down payment on a washing machine, a mangle, and a press. That is undeniable. A hundred he had saved; the fat Newark girl's dowry furnished the other fifty. That cleaned out Brodofsky. Sidney Gross from his savings paid the rent on the little store on Attorney Street for the first year. My father was taken in as a partner, though he had no money. In lieu of capital investment, he worked for nothing....
>
> By the time the business moved to the Bronx, Papa was boss man. I don't write this out of fondness or pride. That he burned out his bright brief candle in the laundry business is a tragedy about which I prefer to be silent.

He would have been good at anything. Given his rudimentary schooling, his uprooting, the chance that threw him in with Brodofsky and Gross, and the financial pressure on immigrants, he lived and died a laundryman. Investors often begged him to drop the partners, leave the Fairy Laundry, and start a new large-scale plant. I heard Mama urging him to accept one of these offers.

"What would Brodofsky and Gross do?" he said. "They would starve."

—Herman Wouk, *Inside, Outside* (Boston: Little, Brown & Company, 1985).

Some new entrepreneurs displayed less gratitude to those who had helped them climb the ladder of success. One of these was the narrator's mother in Jerome Weidman's semi-autobiographical novel *Tiffany Street*. She experienced culture shock in adapting to the isolation of her quiet Bronx neighborhood. Weidman, who later won a Pulitzer Prize for his musical play *Fiorello!*, shows a woman's journey from housewife to piece-worker to business entrepreneur.

On East Fourth Street my mother had been on intimate terms with all our neighbors. On Tiffany Street she did not know the names of our neighbors. Neither did I. The Tiffany Street tenements were smaller than the monstrous gray stone buildings in which I had been raised on East Fourth Street. The toilets were indoors. We even had a bathtub. The sidewalks were cleaner. But they were deserted. People did not sit out on the stoops in the evening eating Indian nuts and gossiping. In fact, there did not seem to be any people. It was my first experience with a neighborhood that was essentially a bedroom for people who worked in other parts of the city. . . .

All of her years in America my mother had dreamed of "improving" herself. Escaping from the slums. Moving her life uptown. Now she had done it. And what did she have? In her own Yiddish words: "A great big fat empty day with nothing to do except cook for Papa and stare out at the trees."

But it was the trees that eased her fears and enabled her to turn her back on what I see now was a disappointment. A street with trees on it was what America was all about, and she finally made it to a street with trees. They were pretty terrible trees. Once, when I discovered that I was worrying about my mother and our new home, I made it a point to find out what these scruffy trees were called.

Ailanthus. . . .

Since the mother still needs to work to make ends meet, she gladly gives up the boredom of staying home and goes to work for Mr. Lebenbaum.

Philip Lebenbaum was an entrepreneur who operated what my economics textbook in Thomas Jefferson High School called a cottage industry. Mr. Lebenbaum was a manufacturer of men's neckwear. Not the sort of neckwear that requires knotting. Mr. Lebenbaum manufactured what we used to call on East Fourth Street "jazz bows." Permanently knotted bow ties with elastic neckbands that snapped into place. He operated out of a store on Intervale Avenue, around the corner from our home on Tiffany Street. In this store Mr. and Mrs. Lebenbaum performed the groundwork functions, so to speak, that enabled the women of the neighborhood, my mother included, to produce the completed jazz bows.

Like many who began as workers, the mother soon establishes her own Bronx-based business, modeled upon similar operations on Manhattan's Lower East Side. Inspired by the entrepreneurial spirit of the 1920s, she begins to manufacture her own jazz bows in her Tiffany Street apartment. She is backed financially by a new friend and salesman, Sebastian Roon, a young Jewish immigrant from England. The family's work necessitates an adjustment involving Jewish religious traditions, such as lighting the Friday night Sabbath candles. At the Sabbath table in the dining room, now converted into a cutting table, the mother discusses how to craft jazz bows with her reluctant, wheelchair-bound husband, whom she has enlisted in the new enterprise.

> "It's easy," my mother said, "You cut. I sew."
> My father looked around the room.
> "Yesterday it was a place to eat on Friday night," he said. "Today it's a factory."
> "From eating on Friday night," my mother said, "you don't get rich."
> My father looked down at the ugly knife in his lap. When his head came up, his cheeks looked a little more shrunken. When he spoke, he sounded a little weaker.
> "On Friday night," he said. "The candles. Where will you *bentsh licht*?"
> "It doesn't say in the Torah God will throw you out of heaven if you light the *Shabbes* candles in the kitchen," my mother said. An edge came into her voice. "On East Fourth Street I once had a chance for a life, and I lost it. Now here on Tiffany Street I have something I thought I'd never have again. I have a second chance. I'm not going to lose it. You hear me? I'm not going to lose it. Not a second time. You'll cut silk, or you won't eat. You hear?"

Increasingly successful, the ambitious mother employs the neighborhood women who had formerly worked for Mr. Lebenbaum, offering them better wages and working conditions, thus ruthlessly undercutting his business. On the day when her new employees are lined up to receive their wages, he bursts into the apartment.

> "You're killing me!" Mr. Lebenbaum screamed. "You're throwing me out of business!"
>
> My mother shrugged. "That's America," she said.
>
> "You dirty rotten—!"
>
> "Here now," Sebastian Roon said. He stood up and grabbed Mr. Lebenbaum in two places: the small man's collar and the seat of his pants. "That will be enough of that, my good man."
>
> He hustled Mr. Lebenbaum out of the kitchen.
>
> "Next!" my mother said.
>
> —Jerome Weidman, *Tiffany Street* (New York: Random House, 1974).

This "rags to riches" story had an even seamier side. In the 1920s, business had become a national obsession. As people spent avidly, the economy spiraled upward. Most thought prosperity would never end. Many Bronx Italians and Jews toiled in New York's garment district. The fictional Bronxite Harry Bogen, in Jerome Weidman's earlier controversial novel, *I Can Get It for You Wholesale*, also wants to rise on the economic and social ladder. His mother arranges an advantageous marriage between Harry and a neighborhood East Bronx girl. She remains unaware that her son, a labor thug and strikebreaker, and now a partner in a Seventh Avenue garment firm, has clawed his way to the top by exploiting and robbing the workers he claimed to represent.

> "All right," Mother said. "Now that you're so smart, and you talked so much, so I'll tell you something. It wouldn't hurt you or that new business of yours if you should go out with Ruthie Rivkin. Now what do you think of that?"
>
> "What do you mean?" I asked.
>
> "Nothing," Mother said with exaggerated casualness. "Only Mrs. Rivkin told me that the boy that marries her Ruthie, that boy gets ten thousand dollars to go in business with, that's all."
>
> He ought to get a medal, too.
>
> "Stop kidding me, Ma," I said. "No grocer on Fox Street is giving away ten thousand dollars with a daughter."
>
> "So maybe you know better than the whole world," she said. "But I'm telling you one thing. The boy that marries Ruthie —". . . .

"... That boy who marries Ruthie Rivkin, he gets ten thousand dollars to go in business. Now what do you think of that?"

She'd never forgive me, if I told her.

"What's the matter?" I said, "Is she so hard to get rid of?"

However, his mother does not know that the greedy Harry has set his cap for Broadway singer Martha Mills. Caught up in the dizzy world of drinking, jazz, and late-night parties, he dips into his firm's till to buy her extravagant gifts. When a criminal investigation into the firm's bankruptcy threatens, the wily Harry schemes to pin the blame on his innocent partner, Babushkin. As his partner is jailed, Harry buys Martha a diamond bracelet and then admires himself in a mirror.

"Boy," I said out loud to the face in the mirror, "is that Harry Bogen, or am I nuts? Two years ago I was just another poor slob from the Bronx. And to-night I'm going to sleep with an actress."

—Jerome Weidman, *I Can Get It for You Wholesale*
(New York: The Modern Library, 1937).

As abhorrent as Bogen's cutthroat business practices were, the most extreme expression of ruthless capitalism in the period was gangsterism. The era of Prohibition, 1919–1933, when the manufacture and sale of alcoholic beverages were illegal, never decreased the public's demand for beer and liquor. Organized crime arose to meet this demand. In The Bronx, the business was tightly controlled by the infamous mobster Dutch Schultz, who aroused the admiration and awe of Bronx street boys. In his novel *Billy Bathgate*, E. L. Doctorow, National Book Award winner, has the orphan of the book's title narrate the story of his first meeting with the "Bronx Beer Baron" on the Bronx's Park Avenue. The street was flanked by warehouses, and New York Central trains ran on tracks in an open trench in the middle of the thoroughfare.

All the time that we hung out there for a glimpse of the beer trucks, the other guys pitched pennies against the wall, or played skelly on the sidewalk with bottle caps, or smoked the cigarettes they bought three for a cent at the candy store on Washington Avenue, or generally wasted their time speculating what they would do if Mr. Schultz ever noticed them, how they would prove themselves as gang members, how they would catch on and toss the crisp one-hundred-dollar bills on kitchen tables of their mothers who had yelled at them and the fathers who had beat their ass—all this time I practiced my juggling. . . .

The Park Avenue warehouse was one of several maintained by the Schultz gang for the storage of the green beer they trucked over from Union City, New Jersey and points west. When a truck arrived it didn't even have to blow its horn the warehouse doors would fold open and receive it as if they had an intelligence of their own. The trucks were from the Great War, and still the original army khaki color, with beveled hoods and double rear wheels and chain-wheel drives that sounded like bones being ground up; the beds had stakes around the sides to which homemade slats were affixed, and tarpaulin was lashed down with peculiar and even gallant discretion over the cargo as if nobody would know then what it was. But when a truck came around the corner the whole street reeked of beer, they carried their gamy smell like the elephants in the Bronx Zoo. . . .

. . . And then one day, I remember it was particularly steamy, so hot in July that the weeds along the spear fence pointed to the ground and visible heat waves rose from the cobblestone, all the boys were sitting in an indolent row along the warehouse wall and I stood across the narrow street in the weeds and rocks overlooking the tracks and demonstrated my latest accomplishment, the juggling of a set of objects of unequal weight. . . . I . . . had no mind for the rest of the world as for instance the LaSalle coupé that came around the corner of 177th Street and Park Avenue and immediately pulled up to the curb in front of the hydrant and sat there with its motor running, nor of the Buick Roadmaster with three men that came next around the corner and drove past the warehouse doors and pulled up at the corner of 178th Street nor finally of the big Packard that came around the corner and rolled to a stop directly in front of the warehouse to block my view, if I had been looking, all the boys slowly standing now and brushing the backs of their pants, while a man got out from the front right-hand door and then opened, from the outside, the right rear door, through which emerged in a white linen double-breasted suit somewhat wilted, with the jacket misbuttoned, and a tie pulled down from his shirt collar and a big handkerchief in his hand mopping his face, once a boy known to the neighborhood as Arthur Flegenheimer, the man known to the world as Dutch Schultz.

—E. L. Doctorow, *Billy Bathgate* (New York: Random House, 1989).

During this era, crime and prostitution often seemed the easiest way to "strike it rich," especially for the children of impoverished immigrants. In *Bronx Primitive*, Kate Simon described two such youngsters, Frankie and Carol Polanski, the janitor's children. *Nafka* is Yiddish for a woman of ill repute.

We hadn't seen Frankie at all for some time when the boys' admiring grapevine reported that he had been arrested along with a couple of his gang for stealing—what, where, we didn't know—and was in prison. Those days Mrs. Polanski sat in our kitchen—only after the stairs had been cleaned and the landings shined—crying and questioning, all in Polish. Nor was the report to our father when he came home helpful, also recounted in Polish. We gathered slowly, bit by bit, that my mother had told Mrs. P. to go downtown on the El to where many Polish people lived, on First and Second avenues, around 7th and 8th streets, and to ask them to take her to the Polish immigrant center. There she would find advice and maybe a lawyer. Mrs. Polanski had never, once she came to Lafontaine, been more than two blocks from her house and was sure she would get lost on the El and the downtown streets. She didn't go and Mr. Polanski was reported to have said when his wife suggested he make the trip, "Let him rot in prison.". . .

. . . No practical Buster Brown haircut for Carol, as she now called herself. Her light hair was waved in deep curves, spitcurls pasted on her forehead and around her face, almost into her long green eyes and pointing up her high cheekbones. She always had something remarkable to show: a new red patent-leather pocketbook, shining high heeled shoes, and real money, dollars. When we asked where she had gotten her spenders, she gestured languidly. "Oh, I have a lot of friends, rich friends, who give me presents." We had no idea that such friends could be acquired, but I got some inkling from my father and his indignation when he caught a glimpse of her one Sunday afternoon, strolling vampishly, eyeing the bench sitters in the park. He didn't bother with the tact of Polish, his Yiddish fury obviously was meant for me to understand, to take warning. See, he was right. Carola had started as a "street girl," a girl who didn't go to school, who could hardly read and write, who stayed out late and hung around with boys, and now, as he knew she would, had turned into a full-fledged *nafka*. At sixteen, with beauty-parlor hair, silk stockings, and her cheap, vulgar pocketbook (his expertise extended to bags as well as shoes), what was she looking forward to? A good job? A decent husband and children? No, of course not. But in a few years she wouldn't be pretty, she would have to go into a house of *nafkas* and serve men who would beat her. And then would come the diseases and the hospitals like Bellevue where the crazy people were kept also, and finally out in the street, wrinkled and ugly, to beg at thirty.

—Kate Simon, *Bronx Primitive: Portraits in a Childhood* (New York: The Viking Press, 1982).

For most Bronxites, however, bootlegging, prostitution, and crime remained remote. Despite the daring clothes, scandalous dances, and sensual jazz music of the era, most young residents were too busy earning a living or getting an education to become immersed in the excesses of "flaming youth."

Baseball's New York Yankees moved to The Bronx and became a symbol of excellence. Their new Yankee Stadium at 161st Street and River Avenue opened on April 23, 1923, and was immediately christened "The House That Ruth Built," after Babe Ruth, whose spectacular home runs attracted millions of fans to the ball park. In 1927, when Ruth hit a then-record sixty home runs, he became one of the most popular celebrities in the world. Bronx-born and -bred amateur naturalist John Kieran, a noted sportswriter of the time and later a radio quiz-show personality, was moved to write some verse about this man who best symbolized the era.

Yankee Stadium just before its first opening day, April 1923. The owners of the New York Yankees were able to afford to build the structure because of the popularity of the team's slugger, Babe Ruth. The stadium is still called "The House That Ruth Built." "But I'll stand and shout till the last man's out / There never was a guy like Ruth." —John Kieran. The Bronx County Historical Society Research Library.

My voice may be loud above the crowd
And my words a bit uncouth
But I'll stand and shout till the last man's out
There never was a guy like Ruth.

> —John Kieran, untitled poem, reprinted in *This Fabulous Century* (New York: Time-Life Books, 1988).

The Bronx was also catapulted into the spotlight by a popular radio show, *The Goldbergs*, starring Gertrude Berg as a Bronx housewife. She brought the warmth and humor of Jewish family life and the colorful Bronx argot into millions of homes around the nation. The show would stay on the air well into the 1950s, when it made a brief transition to television. The era also produced a bumper crop of local authors who would eventually make their mark on American letters and literature.

The euphoria that marked the 1920s, and which seemed would never end, came to a shocking halt on Black Tuesday, October 29, 1929, when the stock market collapsed. The effect of this sudden economic disaster soon engulfed the nation in a period of hard times when the struggle to survive led many people in The Bronx to question traditional institutions and values.

5

A STEP LEFT

THE BRONX IN THE GREAT DEPRESSION

1929–1940

With the onset of the Great Depression, many businesses in The Bronx, metropolitan New York City, and throughout the nation shut their doors, causing widespread unemployment. Many apartment house tenants, finding it increasingly difficult to meet the rent, lived in fear of eviction. Proud families were forced to accept charity and, later, home relief, the term used for what is today called welfare. Thanks to the powerful Democratic boss of The Bronx, Edward J. Flynn, who had close connections with President Franklin D. Roosevelt, government works projects rose in The Bronx, providing jobs for some. These included the Bronx Central Post Office, the Bronx County Jail, the Triborough and Bronx-Whitestone Bridges, and expansions and improvements in parks, schools, and streets. Under Flynn's leadership, local Democratic clubs became sounding boards for the people they served. Such attention to patronage and jobs delivered landslide victories to the borough's Democrats.

One of the new public works projects, largely funded with federal money, was the new Orchard Beach in Pelham Bay Park. Unlike the garish and noisy carnival atmosphere of Brooklyn's Coney Island, Orchard Beach was a smooth crescent of imported sand on the shores of Long Island Sound with elegant bathhouses. The president of the Bronx Chamber of Commerce dubbed it "The Riviera of The Bronx." Starting with its opening in the mid-1930s, many families, including Kate Simon's, made great efforts to get there. The method of transportation, the trolley, also offered special pleasures to a young mind.

> My mother carrying the baby, my brother with the rolled blanket, and I with the shopping bag went to Tremont Avenue to wait for the summer trolley, a chariot of the gods served by Mercury. It clanged, it swayed, it screeched, and when its delicate wand slipped the wires of the sky, it shot

little lightnings. Mercury got down from his daring ledge that ran the length of the trolley and coaxed its capricious wand that bent and quivered back to its wire. When he wasn't mastering electricity (at times, I thought, like a young, graceful Ben Franklin, without the spectacles and the moral wise-cracks), our hero swung from open row to row, collecting fares, tapping change from the coin-shaped tubes on his chest, ripping transfers off a pad, one foot on his narrow ledge, one swinging in the air behind him, like Mercury, like a bird taking off.

We transferred to another trolley and yet another, riding into a place that had lawns around houses and trees to screen them from the trolley tracks. We got off where the tracks were gritty and pulled our feet through the hot sand toward the water. It was never as crowded as Coney Island nor as interesting. We couldn't go into the water over our heads, we didn't eat hot dogs, only wholesome everyday food, we couldn't throw sand at each other because it might get into the baby's face. The sailboats in the distance were pretty to watch, dipping and straightening like ice skaters, and we argued about cloud shapes, was it a giant or a rhinoceros.

—Kate Simon, *Bronx Primitive: Portraits in a Childhood* (New York: The Viking Press, 1982).

Even an extensive public works program in the borough could not provide enough jobs. Other forms of public employment were possible, including teaching. Sarah L. Delany, a black woman who held a master's degree in education from Columbia and resided in the Sugar Hill area of Harlem, recalled how she obtained a high school teaching position in The Bronx in *Having Our Say*, a memoir co-written with her sister, later made into a play.

I had wanted to teach at a high school because it was considered a promotion, and it paid better. But I had to be a little clever—Bessie would say sneaky—to find ways to get around these brick walls they set up for colored folks. So I asked around quietly for some advice. A friend of my brother Hubert's who worked for the Board of Education suggested a plan, which I followed.

This is what I did: I applied for a high school position, and when I reached the top of the seniority list after three years, I received a letter in the mail saying they wished to meet with me in person. At the appointment, they would have seen I was colored and found some excuse to bounce me down the list. So I skipped the appointment and sent them a letter, acting like there was a mix-up. Then I just showed up on the first day of classes. It was risky, but I knew what a bureaucracy it was, and that in a bureaucracy it's easier to keep people out than to push them back down.

Child, when I showed up that day—at Theodore Roosevelt High School, a white high school—they just about died when they saw me. A colored woman! But my name was on the list to teach there, and it was too late for them to send me someplace else. The plan had worked! Once I was in, they couldn't figure out how to get rid of me.

So I became the first colored teacher in the New York City system to teach domestic science on the high school level. I spent the rest of my career teaching at excellent high schools! Between 1930 and 1960, when I retired, I taught at Theodore Roosevelt High School, which is on Fordham Road in the Bronx, then at Girls' High School in Brooklyn, and finally at Evander Childs High School, which is on Gun Hill Road in the Bronx.

—Sarah L. Delany and A. Elizabeth Delany with Amy Hill Hearth, *Having Our Say: The Delany Sisters' First 100 Years* (New York: Dell, 1994).

In Thomas Bell's novel *All Brides Are Beautiful*, the dreams of Peter and his wife, Susan, collapse when Peter loses his job and is unable to find another. Only Susan's continued employment keeps them from going on relief. Now economically strapped and unable to leave The Bronx, as the couple had hoped, the proud but realistic Peter suffers. His situation gnaws at his conscience.

His misfortune was no personal disgrace, certainly not unique. This was the Bronx; unemployment was a familiar hell. "Man, there's people been out of work years. No money, no furniture, no nothing. You're lucky." . . . Susan went out into the morning's rain or snow, the smells and crowds of the subway, a day's work; . . . when he turned from watching her out of sight down the stairs to confront her breakfast dishes; unmade beds. . . . Hunger, even injustice, one could endure, but this piecemeal disintegration of one's pride, one's self-assurance, was a slow death. There were times when he found it hard to meet Susan's eyes.

When he was not actively seeking any type of work in the union hiring halls downtown, all Peter could do was walk about the largely Irish Highbridge section of The Bronx to pass the empty time.

This part of Sedgwick Avenue was like a road on the shabby outskirts of a city. Somewhere in the blackness beyond the railroad tracks was the river, and beyond that the solid wall of Washington Heights with little houses and lights and the water tower on its crest; the world ended there. Beside them the Bronx was a weedy slope that climbed abruptly to the yellow-windowed apartment houses on University Avenue—the southernmost, undistinguished part; from there the arches of High Bridge, like a Roman aqueduct, marched across the valley. Farther north Peter glimpsed a segment of the 181st Street Bridge, and the tiny moving lights of a trolley; under that slight burden the bridge seemed preposterously huge.

At one point, Peter finds a job and, to celebrate, takes Susan to a dance at the fictional Ironquill Club, the local Democratic political organization, on Southern Boulevard. The show consisted of vaudeville entertainment of the era and was designed to appeal to the ethnic diversity of the people of the district.

> . . . two young Jews who tap-danced themselves breathless; a Negro girl in red shorts and a beaded brassiere who screamed a song about Harlem and writhed in a manner which should have brought a visceral collapse; an Irish tenor who bellowed, "When Irish Eyes Are Smiling"; a Jewish tenor who wailed, "Eli, Eli"; a child prodigy who sang about love and wriggled her little torso suggestively; and finally Mr. Tim Bagley himself, who paraded his shirt front and waved a cigar through a speech praising the good old U.S.A., our President, the solid homely virtues of the Bronx, and the unique distinctiveness of the Ironquill Club which existed solely to do good for the residents of the district, which, as it happened, Mr. Bagley represented in the councils of Tammany Hall.

But Peter once more loses his job and he gradually begins to identify with the plight of other unemployed working-class people of The Bronx. He believes that unionization is the only solution for the working man. Naively, like many Americans at the time, he turns to the Communists for answers. He develops a growing kinship with the ideas of 1930s radical thinkers, most of which were ultimately accepted by the American mainstream and are now embodied in law.

> So you joined a union and fought for the right to organize, for better wages and security in your job; yes, and for clean toilets and hot water to wash with. You fought for unemployment insurance, for decent housing, for the right of your children to grow up strong and healthy. You fought for free speech, the equality of women, the freedom of the Negro, for recognition of the principle—a constitutional amendment might be necessary—that the

Bill of Rights be applied to poor people . . . things were stirring and changing. . . . America was stirring, the ordinary men and women of its streets and
farms and shops.

—Thomas Bell, All Brides Are Beautiful (Boston:
Little, Brown and Company, 1937).

Although radical ideas, such as Peter's, were related to the frustration of sudden
enforced unemployment, radicalism was not new to The Bronx in the 1930s. Even
during the 1920s, the entrepreneurial spirit was countered by the left-wing ideas of
some Eastern European Jews who had fled from oppression in czarist Russia (where
socialist ideas had been rife), and those of other immigrant groups. While mastering the ways of American society, they sought to improve it through their political
passions. These radicals, however, were splintered into many warring factions ranging from communism, Trotskyism, and socialism to democratic trade unionism.

One offshoot of Marxist thought was the Jewish-led workers' cooperative
movement, which sparked the construction of cooperative housing developments
in The Bronx. In each apartment complex, the laborer-tenants owned the buildings
collectively and paid monthly rent to cover the costs. The development was operated by a board of directors elected by the tenant-owners. In effect, the tenants
owned their own buildings and apartments. Journalist Calvin Trillin explained the
ideological diversity in this movement.

In the late twenties, a Jewish garment worker who wanted to move his
family from the squalor of the lower East Side to the relatively sylvan north
Bronx could select an apartment on the basis of ideology. It was a period in
New York when workers seemed interested in banding together in cooperative ventures—not just cooperative housing but cooperative cafeterias and
even cooperative hat shops—and which cooperative a worker joined could
be considered part of his political identity. (It was a period when everyone
seemed interested in political identity.) Someone who happened to be an
active supporter of the Social Democratic wing of the Jewish labor movement—the wing whose views were reflected by Abraham Cahan in the Jewish Daily Forward, the wing that had, after a ferocious struggle with the
radicals, retained control of the largest clothing unions—would probably try
to obtain an apartment in the Bronx cooperative project sponsored by the
Amalgamated Clothing Workers. . . . A follower of Hayim Zhitlovsky, the
leader of a movement absorbed with the preservation of secular Jewish culture, could live in a cooperative called the Sholem Aleichem Houses. A radical—someone who continued to defend the Soviet revolution after other
Socialists had turned against it, someone who subscribed to the Morgen Frei-

heit, a Yiddish daily that was then faithfully pro-Soviet, and read the *Forward* only to see what the enemy was up to—could move into the Workers Cooperative Colony, shortened by everyone to two syllables: the Coops.

—Calvin Trillin, "U.S. Journal: The Bronx: The Coops," *The New Yorker* (August 1, 1977).

A rich cultural life in and around the Coops at Bronx Park East and Allerton Avenue was recalled by Sophie Paul.

The Coops were apartment buildings for working class people of all ethnicities, a grand experiment in cooperative living, built by the Union. It was *the* gathering place—I'd go from working all day to dance, to Jewish chorus with my papa, and later participated in my children's Yiddish education there. There was even a restaurant with a section especially for single people. It was where I met my husband.

My parents, my husband and our children lived together in a five-room apartment near the Coops. Our lives were communal and politically active. . . . My husband's work was with the Fur Workers' Union in Manhattan.

Our social life and political life were connected. At night we'd gather

The interior court of the Amalgamated Houses on Van Cortlandt Park South and Dickinson Avenue, built in 1927. A postcard photograph. "Someone who happened to be an active supporter of the Social Democratic wing of the Jewish Labor Movement . . . would probably try to obtain an apartment in the Bronx cooperative project sponsored by the Amalgamated Clothing Workers." —Calvin Trillin. Barbara Unger Collection.

with friends to plan, to eat and to sing. Although I had friends not involved
in the politics of the day, for me the Bronx was vibrant with progressive
activity.

> —Sophie Paul, "I Remember the Bronx," unpub-
> lished essay.

At the Sholem Aleichem Houses at Sedgwick Avenue and Giles Place, another
cooperative development, the accent was on the preservation of Yiddish culture.
Bess Myerson, who later became a Miss America, grew up there and told Susan
Dworkin of her experiences. The WPA, the Works Progress Administration, a New
Deal program, was formed to provide jobs for the unemployed, including out-of-
work writers, artists, and musicians.

> In addition to mutually held social ideals, Sholem Aleichem residents
> shared an overriding belief in education. They expected their children to
> attend college. They had given up their interest in religion.... However, their
> cooperative in particular was inspired by a love of *Yiddishkeit*, the Yiddish
> language and the wit and wisdom of its literature and more generally by a
> dedication to *Kultur*—the arts.
>
> From their inception, the buildings included a large auditorium where
> a musical ensemble or drama group could perform and where dances and
> other festivities could be held. Special studios were built to encourage the
> membership of artists in the cooperative. Bess remembered Aaron Goodel-
> man, a sculptor; Abraham Maniewich, a painter; a poetess named Malka Lee;
> and Isaac Raboy, who wrote Jewish cowboy stories. "I loved the artists," Bess
> said. "I would hang around their studios hoping they would invite me in to
> see a painting in progress, or hear a new poem. They enchanted and inspired
> me. They never made me feel I was intruding."...
>
> The artists in the Sholem Aleichem complex . . . were only working
> thanks to the dole of such agencies as the WPA.

> —Susan Dworkin, *Miss America, 1945: Bess Myer-
> son's Own Story* (New York: Newmarket Press,
> 1987).

Poet Joseph Rolnick and novelist Isaac Raboy, who wrote in Yiddish and had
been associated with the *Yunge* in their youth, were drawn to the Sholem Aleichem
Houses because of its stated mission to preserve Yiddish culture. Although they held
different political beliefs, they remained good friends. In his poem "Neighbors,"
Rolnick, a moderate, reminisced about his long association with the Marxist Raboy.

I and the poet Isaac Raboy
are next-door neighbors.
Maybe I drop in at his place,
or he comes over to me.

Between us—me and him—
only plaster over some lath.
Each one hears the other walking—
I on the right, Isaac on the left.

We go back twenty-five years
together—to Henry Street.
Like one family then. And now
they call us "the old timers."

I work in a word stable,
and he at marten and mink.
I lean a little to the right,
and he is thoroughly left.

We talk like good old friends,
we talk plainly and honestly,
though he's just left through and through
and I—just a bit to the right.

And when we remember Levine's Cafe
those five steps down,
a soft warm dew starts
to melt through our limbs.

And when we remember home,
Mir is mine, his Rishkan,
I'm no longer a little bit right
and he's not left anymore.

My father owned a flour mill,
his father, horses and wagons.
Our wheel turned in the water
and his ran over the earth.

We talk of Sabbath and weekdays,
about all kinds of foods,
what we prepared for the holidays,
what they were cooking in Rishkan.

We talk like old, good friends,
we speak from the heart and honestly —
though he is left through and through
and I just a bit on the right.

—Joseph Rolnick, "Neighbors," trans. Irving Feldman, in *The Penguin Book of Modern Yiddish Verse*,
ed. Irving Howe, Ruth Wisse, and Khone Shmeruk
(New York: Viking Penguin, Inc., 1987).

Abraham Reisen, another Yiddish writer who moved to the Sholem Aleichem
Houses, also managed to rise above the political divisiveness that wracked the
Yiddish-speaking community. The most popular Yiddish writer of the time, a
socialist and influential editor, Reisen taught in Bronx and Lower East Side Yiddish
schools. He became a cultural hero and many of his poems portraying Jewish Eastern European life were set to music. Yiddish poet Louis Goldberg captured Reisen's
place in the heart of the immigrant community he served in Manhattan and The
Bronx in "Abraham Reisen in New York."

He goes walking through the Bronx,
Through Second Avenue and East Broadway,
Where no one wonders hearing Yiddish,
Hearing children use Yiddish in their play.

He walks there as in Minsk or Warsaw
Or Kaidanov, his native town.
The people look to him for comfort,
He brings on weekdays their Sabbath down.

He walks through a business street,
Happy to see so many people there.
His books are in the bookshop windows.
His Yiddish tongue rings in the air.

You see him in a Yiddish school,
Often till late at night,

Slim-bodied, white-haired,
Teaching, explaining, bringing light.

He pats a child's head like a father.
And the child quotes his own poem to him,
We no longer "sleep eight in a bed,"
Like sardines, limb to limb.

A tear glistens in his eye,
Thinking how times are better to-day.
He walks through the streets of the Bronx,
Through Second Avenue and East Broadway.

> —Louis Goldberg, "Abraham Reisen in New York,"
> in *The Golden Peacock: A Worldwide Treasury of
> Yiddish Poetry*, trans. and ed. Joseph Leftwich (New
> York: Thomas Yoseloff, 1961).

Despite Abraham Reisen's prominence and the presence of Yiddish schools in The Bronx, the impact of the language continued to diminish as the children of the immigrant generation assimilated into the larger society. Indeed, the older immigrants rushed to learn English, used it, and encouraged their children to speak it exclusively. Even Abraham Liessin, a noted Yiddish poet, paid homage to the work of the famed American writer Edgar Allan Poe in his poem "At the Poe Cottage in Fordham" only five days before his own death at the age of sixty-five in 1938.

Tall buildings glower in arrogant mood,
And on the side a white cottage sleeping,
Away from the turmoil secluded,
As it would an old fable tell; peeping
Heedless, a thousand windows view
As it's deafened by the street's cry and hue.

... With a slanting sun ray—darkly twinkled,
And all tattered, a dream lay in the wind
On the cherry tree and the little white shrine.

I see him upright, as I close my eyes
Embittered, near a cloud of luminous lace,
Choked with pride, his heart agonized
Staring forlornly at the cold fireplace;

Lethargic he pines, galled in fever—
A phantom disheveled, aquiver.

Awake in stillness; the "child-wife" spiritless
Lies stretched on the same narrow bed;
And white her body, black as the raven her tresses,
And like pearls her luminous eyes glistened;
His beloved, when the "winged seraphs coveted"—
His Annabel Lee. . . .

Dying, she lies upon the straw mattress,
In his old soldier's coat enveloped;
And with its body a cat warms her breast;
And to warm her hands so icy cold
He breathes on them and breathes; and as a refrain
On the roof there beats a blinding rain.

Unmoved, there peer a thousand windows
From the houses tall upon the drama concluded

Poe Cottage in Poe Park on the Grand Concourse and Kingsbridge Road in the 1940s. A postcard photograph. "Tall buildings glower in arrogant mood, / And on the side a white cottage sleeping." —Abraham Walt Liessen. Barbara Unger Collection.

As in the grayness of the noisy street below
The little white cottage nestles, secluded....

> —Abraham Walt Liessin, "At Poe Cottage in Fordham," in *America in Yiddish Poetry*, ed. and trans. Jehiel B. Cooperman and Sarah H. Cooperman (New York: Exposition Press, 1967).

Like the Leftists who established cooperative houses in the borough, many other Bronxites felt a strong passion for social justice. Most hoped it could be achieved peacefully through the elective process. Poet, short story writer, and essayist Grace Paley recalled the time when the prosperity of the 1920s in The Bronx turned into the despair of the 1930s. She begins with the 1928 presidential candidacy of New York Governor Alfred E. Smith, Democrat, the first Catholic nominated for the office. Many Jews saw Smith as a champion against intolerance.

The greatest shock to me after Smith failed was the sight from my middle-class window of my friends' family furniture out on the street, the beloved couch, the dining-room table upon which no one in the immediate family had ever been allowed to eat—all draped in old curtains, cloths, a blanket, no sure cover from the rain, no safety from thieves.

The neighbors, as I remember, then went from apartment to apartment gathering nickels and dimes that would enable the evicted family to find a new place to live. This was usually only a couple of blocks away, where, because landlords were also in trouble, they might get three months' concession. So there was a kind of vagabondage even within the neighborhood. Families moved six or seven times before home relief appeared, before Hoover, the man who beat Smith, was beaten himself....

The 1928 election was not the end of my contact with large events. My kindergarten and other classes were invited by Mayor Jimmy Walker to meet him on East 174th Street. Clusters of children, with an occasional stalk of large person sticking up, waited silently, tired, having walked long from Public School 50 on Vyse Avenue....

What was Mayor Walker inviting us to? The grand opening of the East 174th Street steel bridge. It didn't seem so then, but this bridge could have become important to the Bronx in a modest way. All roads, all bridges connect and lead us away or to. This bridge poured the Bronx eastward into little booms of real estate, little houses and short tenements. If 1929 and its crash hadn't arrived so precipitously, more and bigger tenements could have come of it.

Paley describes the impact of Franklin Delano Roosevelt's reelection campaign visit to The Bronx in the midst of the Great Depression. Roosevelt was soon almost unanimously regarded as a savior by the people of the borough.

> One nice, mid 1930's day, my mother asked me to take a folding chair and go to Southern Boulevard and sit. In about two hours, President Franklin D. Roosevelt would drive by. She wanted a reserved front-row sight of him. In an hour and a half, she came for her seat under the IRT elevated-subway tracks. Thunder above and hurrays in Yiddish, Russian, Polish and English below. He arrived, waved to my mother and, in a slow minute, passed. It turns out that Roosevelt was the President my neighborhood had come to this country for.
>
> —Grace Paley, "Tough Times for a City of Tenants," *New York Times* (January 25, 1998).

Although Paley's neighborhood was heavily Jewish, other ethnic groups were represented. The liberal ideology of Paley's family led to ready acceptance of this diversity and humanity.

> In school I met my friend Adele, who together with her mother and father were not Jewish. Despite this, they often seemed to be in a good mood. There was the janitor in charge of coal, and my father, unusually smart, spoke Italian to him. They talked about Italian literature, because the janitor was equally smart. Down the hill under the Southern Boulevard El, families lived, people in lovely shades of light and darkest brown. My mother and sister explained that they were treated unkindly; that they had in fact been slaves in another part of the country in another time.
>
> —Grace Paley, "Introduction to a Haggadah," *Just as I Thought* (New York: Farrar, Straus and Giroux, 1998).

Some Bronx Leftists took to soapboxes, organizing people to rectify social injustice. This was recorded by Vivian Gornick in *Fierce Attachments*, her memoir of life in what was then called the East Bronx. She recounts her radical mother's opposition to tenant evictions.

> I had known since early childhood that my parents were fellow travelers of the Communist Party, and that of the two my mother had been the more politically active. By the time I was born she had stood on soapboxes in the Bronx pleading for economic and social justice. It was, in fact, part of her

deprivation litany that if it hadn't been for the children she would have developed into a talented public speaker.

During the Depression the Communist Party sponsored and ran the Tenants' Councils, organizations formed to fight evictions for nonpayment of rent. My mother became head of Tenants' Council Number 29 in the Bronx ("I was the only woman in the building who could speak English without an accent, so automatically I was voted head"), and continued to act as head until shortly after I was born, when my father made her "stop everything" to stay home with the baby. Until then, she said, she ran the council. Mama running the council was a childhood classic. "Every Saturday morning," she would tell me, the way others told their children Mary had a little lamb, "I would go down to Communist Party headquarters in Union Square and receive my instructions for the week. Then we would organize, and carry on." How she loved saying, "Then we would organize and carry on." There was more uncomplicated pleasure in her voice when she repeated those words than in any others I ever heard her speak.

Tenants' Council Number 29 was made up of most of the women in the building my parents were then living in.

—Vivian Gornick, *Fierce Attachments* (New York: Farrar, Straus and Giroux, 1987).

Clifford Odets, author of *Waiting for Lefty* and *Golden Boy*, dramatized the era's social problems. In this earlier play, *Awake and Sing*, he depicted the moral chaos he saw around him as a result of the Great Depression and perceived flaws in the capitalist system. He set the play in the area of The Bronx where he had been raised—Longwood Avenue and Beck Street. The Berger family, including Myron the father and Bessie the mother, sit in the dining room of their apartment with the Berger's daughter, Hennie:

MYRON: You can buy a ticket for fifty cents and win fortunes. A man came in
    the store—it's the Irish Sweepstakes.
BESSIE: What?
MYRON: Like a raffle, only different. A man came in—
BESSIE: Who spends fifty-cent pieces for Irish raffles? They threw out a family on Dawson Street today. All the furniture on the sidewalk. A fine old
    woman with gray hair. . . .
MYRON: A butcher on Beck Street won eighty thousand dollars.
BESSIE: Eighty thousand dollars! You'll excuse my expression, you're bughouse!

MYRON: I seen it in the paper—on one ticket—765 Beck Street.

BESSIE: Impossible!

MYRON: He did . . . yes he did. He says he'll take his old mother to Europe . . . an Austrian!

HENNIE: Europe . . .

MYRON: Six percent on eighty thousand—forty-eight hundred a year.

BESSIE: I'll give you money. Buy a ticket in Hennie's name. Say, you can't tell—lightning never struck us yet. If they win on Beck Street we could win on Longwood Avenue.

> —Clifford Odets, *Awake and Sing*, produced in 1935, in *The Literature of American Jews*, ed. Theodore L. Gross (New York: The Free Press, 1973).

During the very real hardships of the Great Depression, even children could see the anguish in their parents' faces as they struggled to get by. Bronx families worked long hours and made small economies in order to survive and to keep their children from realizing how tenuous their situation really was. Yet, young Cynthia Ozick did notice, perhaps without fully comprehending it, some of the grim reality of the time.

This is Pelham Bay, the Bronx, in the middle of the Depression, all cattails and weeds, such a lovely place and a tender hour! Even though my mother takes me on the subway far, far downtown to buy my winter coat in the frenzy of Klein's on Fourteenth Street, and even though I can recognize the heavy power of a quarter, I don't know it's the Depression. On the trolley on the way to Westchester Square, I see the children who live in the boxcar strangely set down in an empty lot some distance from the Spy Oak (where a Revolutionary traitor was hanged—served him right for siding with the redcoats); the lucky boxcar children dangle their stick legs from their train house maw and wave. . . . My mother and father are in trouble, and I don't know it. I am too happy. I feel the secret center of eternity, nothing will ever alter, no one will ever die.

> —Cynthia Ozick, "A Drugstore in Winter," *Art and Ardor* (New York: E. P. Dutton, 1984).

She also witnessed the desperation that affected the rest of the nation.

It was the trough of the Great Depression. In the comics, Pete the Tramp was swiping freshly baked pies set out to cool on windowsills; and in real life tramps (as the homeless were then called) were turning up in the Park View nearly every day. Sometimes they were city drunks—"Bowery bums"—who had fallen asleep on the subway and ended up in Pelham Bay. Sometimes they were exhausted Midwesterners who had been riding the railroads and had rolled off into the cattails of the Baychester marsh. But always my father set them down at the fountain and fed them a sandwich and soup. They smelled bad, and their eyes were red and rheumy; often, they were very polite. They never left without a meal and a nickel for carfare.

No one was worse off than the tramps, or more desolate than the family that lived in an old freight car on the way to Westchester Square, but no one escaped the Depression.

> —Cynthia Ozick, "A Drugstore Eden," *The New Yorker* (September 16, 1996).

The economic hardships of the Great Depression often produced a lasting effect upon children who grew up in The Bronx in that era. Looking back, poet Naomi Replansky recalled those times.

> "Five dollars, four dollars, three dollars, two,
> One, and none, and what do we do?"

Westchester Square in the late 1920s. "I don't know it's the Depression. On the trolley on the way to Westchester Square ... I feel the secret center of eternity, nothing will ever alter, no one will ever die." —Cynthia Ozick. *The Bronx County Historical Society Research Library.*

This is the worry that never got said
But ran so often in my mother's head

And showed so plain in my father's frown
That to us kids it drifted down.

It drifted down like soot, like snow,
In the dream-tossed Bronx, in the long ago.

I shook it off with a shake of the head.
I bounced my ball, I ate warm bread,

I skated down the steepest hill.
But I must have listened, against my will:

When the wind blows wrong, I can hear it today.
Then my mother's worry stops all play

And, as if in its rightful place,
My father's frown divides my face.

> —Naomi Replansky, "An Inheritance," *The Dangerous World: New and Selected Poems, 1934–1994* (Chicago: Another Chicago Press, 1994).

Literary and social critic Irving Howe, like Naomi Replansky, came from a Bronx Jewish background. However, he felt that the Depression had a less marked effect on The Bronx than it did on other parts of the city. The rigors of the Depression led him to join actively Leftist causes in his teens. In "A Memoir of the Thirties," this former editor of *Dissent* and *The Partisan Review*, anthologizer of Yiddish literature, and author of *World of Our Fathers* looked back on those hard years and The Bronx he had known while in his teens and twenties as a student at the City College of New York.

While Howe was aware of the hunger and suffering caused by the Depression, he felt that such sights as the Hooverville shacks and evicted tenants with their children sitting atop piles of furniture in the streets were far more common in Manhattan than in The Bronx. There, Howe felt that the effects of the Depression were mitigated by cultural factors.

> I knew . . . idle men standing . . . near the rowboats of Crotona Park. But while the east Bronx was a place of poverty, it kept an inner discipline: Jews

felt obligated to look after each other, they fought desperately to avoid going on relief.

The Bronx during the Depression was unique in other respects, according to Howe. Firstly, many young Bronxites turned to the Left but, to the chagrin of the hard-liners, a sizable number, including Howe, remained staunchly anti-communist. Secondly, young Leftist Bronx Jews never relinquished their identity as Jews. Thus, they were tolerated within their communities, where they were often not taken as seriously as they might have liked. Thirdly, the camaraderie among young Bronx Jewish radicals, including those in Howe's circle, more than compensated for the pain of the Depression.

At the age of fourteen I wandered into the ranks of socialist youth and from then on, all through my teens and twenties, the Movement was my home and passion, the Movement as it ranged through the various left-wing, anti-communist groups.

. . . In the thirties the ordinary New York Jew realized that Jewishness was not something one had much choice about, and in this respect his instincts were sounder, both morally and practically, than that of the radicals who chose for their "party names" almost anything that did not sound Jewish. You might be shouting at the top of your lungs against reformism or Stalin's betrayals, but for the middle-aged garment worker strolling along Southern Boulevard you were just a bright and cocky Jewish boy, a talkative little *pisher.* . . .

. . . In the winter, when the Bronx is gray and icy, there were cafeterias in which the older comrades, those who had jobs or were on WPA, bought coffee while the rest of us filled the chairs. In the summer, after meetings, we would parade across the middle bulge of the Bronx from the tenements on Wilkins Avenue in the East to the forbidding apartment houses of the Grand Concourse on the West.

—Irving Howe, "A Memoir of the Thirties," *Steady Work: Essays in the Politics of Democratic Radicalism 1953–1966* (New York: Harcourt, Brace & World, Inc., 1966).

While Howe and his student friends philosophized and agitated, other Bronxites lost their businesses to the Great Depression. Young Edgar, the narrator of E. L. Doctorow's novel-memoir *World's Fair*, and his Jewish family lived in a private house on Eastburn Avenue near Mount Eden Avenue. The Depression began to affect Edgar when his father lost his musical instrument and sheet music store.

Money was tight. Edgar's older brother, Donald, dropped out of City College to take a job in Philadelphia.

> And then I was told that we would be moving out of our house. The reasoning was that with Donald not living at home anymore, the three of us didn't need such a large place. The landlord was intending to raise the rent when the lease was up, and it just wasn't worth the money. My mother had found just the apartment for us and she took me to see it while it was being painted. It was up on the Grand Concourse. She met me after school. North of 174th Street, Eastburn Avenue becomes a hill. We trudged up Eastburn past apartment houses of the walk-up variety, four or six stories around small courtyards and with dingy front halls. Our new house was at the top of the hill where Eastburn met with the Concourse and also 175th Street—to a six-story edifice of ocher brick. . . .
> I had never lived anywhere but in a private house near the park. The Concourse was a wide six-lane thoroughfare with pedestrian islands to help one cross, the outer lanes being for local traffic, the four inner lanes for express traffic. The pedestrian islands were planted with trees. Way over on the far side was an unbroken bank of apartment houses, north and south, as far as the eye could see.

As the family's financial situation worsened, Edgar enters a World's Fair essay contest on the theme of the Typical American Boy. He desperately wants to see all of the fair at Flushing Meadow in the borough of Queens, but the family's finances will not permit it. When his essay wins honorable mention, he is awarded free admission to the fair and all its attractions for himself and his family. Upon hearing the news, the proud family goes out to celebrate at a popular ice cream parlor.

> Krum's was up near Fordham Road. At the fountain were devised the best ice cream sodas in the Bronx. Perhaps the world. The evening was balmy, the sun had set but the sky was still blue. The Concourse was alive with cars and people strolling in the early evening. The trees on the road dividers were in full leaf. The streetlamps had come on. . . . My father strode along as he did when he felt good.
>
> —E. L. Doctorow, *World's Fair* (New York: Fawcett Crest, 1985).

Unlike Edgar, some Bronx children living in immigrant neighborhoods were hardly aware that the Depression existed. For them, it was an untroubled place.

Vito A. Merola recalled conditions at the time in his Tremont neighborhood in his memoir, "Memories of a One Way Passage."

> The Bronx was made up of tightly knit neighborhoods composed mainly of middle-class working people. The sociologists of the day would have labeled it Middle-middle. At that time, The Bronx was the place you learned to ice skate with your sisters on Indian Lake in Crotona Park, and to swim in the pool there. You learned to ski and ride sleds in one season and to play baseball and football on the same fields in another. The park was also the place where you learned to roll "Bull Durham" behind the rocks, which were behind the comfort stations at the corner of Tremont and Third. And, finally, it was a place where your parents walked on a summer evening because it was the only place around where trees could be found. It was the place we called home.
>
> At this point, you're probably thinking that the hackneyed tales of growing up poor in an Italian Bronx neighborhood would be better left unsaid. No fear. We weren't and it wasn't. As a matter of fact, I have no recollection at all of anyone standing on a food line or selling apples on a street corner in the early 1930s. I do recall a free milk station across the street from where we lived that opened and closed shortly thereafter, probably because no one used it.
>
> —Vito A. Merola, "Memories of a One Way Passage," *The Bronx County Historical Society Journal* (Spring 1990).

Ironically, a few Bronx families actually prospered in the Great Depression. Herman Wouk chronicled the progress of the fictional Morgenstern family from The Bronx to Manhattan's fashionable Central Park West in his novel *Marjorie Morningstar*, which was later made into a motion picture. The daughter, snobbish and spoiled Marjorie, aspires to be an actress leading a bohemian life. Soon after moving to Manhattan, she returns to The Bronx on a date with her boyfriend. Because of her family's new-found prosperity and her overweaning ambition, she looks upon the sights, sounds, and smells of her former life with disdain.

> From the start, everything about the evening depressed Marjorie; the all-too-familiar Bronx apartment house, one of an unbroken line of gray houses along a dirty narrow street, the dark stairway of the fourth floor, with its memory-wakening smells of immigrant cooking and baby-breeding, of stale paint and fresh wet laundry, the cramped apartment blazing with

electric bulbs, the cheap furniture, the paintings that were copies of copies, the worn best sellers on the shelves . . . the loud voices, the barbarous pronunciation (awfice, yeah, daance, lor stoodent, idear, tawk); the singsong cadence which jarred on her more because she was still trying to free her own speech of it, the unvarying cream soda, the sponge cake, and sugary purple wine; the inexorable vanilla ice cream rushed in paper boxes from the drugstore by a small brother to climax the party; the proud fat parents, the proud fat bride in a red evening dress from Klein's, with a bunch of tea roses in a huge silver ribbon on her shoulder. . . .

—Herman Wouk, *Marjorie Morningstar* (Garden City, N.Y.: Doubleday and Company, 1955).

Despite the economic hardships that affected most Bronxites, they retained fond memories of the borough in the 1930s. To them, it was still "the beautiful Bronx," when family life seemed stable and neighbors were friendly. In 1930, humorist and poet Ogden Nash wrote the now oft-quoted lines,

The Bronx?
No, thonx!

—Odgen Nash "Random Reflections: Geographical," *The New Yorker* (July 12, 1930).

Bronxites chuckled along with the rest of the country at the quip. It was then taken to be merely an amusing comment on the sound of the borough's name, written in the same vein as Arthur Guiterman's 1920 poem, "The Legend of The Bronx." Chaim Potok, who grew up in the borough and who was to become the author of *My Name Is Ascher Lev* and other books about New York Jews, saw The Bronx in the same light as Huckleberry Finn's Mississippi River and its valley.

The Bronx of the Thirties and Forties was my Mississippi River Valley. Yes, I saw poverty and despair, and I remember to this day the ashen pallor on my father's face that night in the late Thirties when he told us we would have to go on welfare. And, yes, the streets were on occasion dark with gang violence and with the hate that had made the sea journey from the anti-Semitic underbelly of Europe. But there were books and classes and teachers; there were friends with whom I invented street games limited only by the bounds of the imagination. And alone, on a concrete and asphalt Mississippi, I journeyed repeatedly through the crowded sidewalks and paved-over backyards, the hallways of the brick apartment houses, the hushed public libraries, dark movie houses, candy stores, grocery stores, Chinese laundries, Italian shoe-repair shops, the neighborhoods of Irish, Italians, blacks, Poles—journeys impelled by eager curiosity and a hunger to discover my sense of self, my place in the tumult of the world. I was an urban sailor on the raft of my own two feet.

I had little quarrel with my Jewish world. I was deep inside it, with a child's slowly increasing awareness of his own culture's richness and short-comings. But beyond the tiny Hannibal of our apartment, there was an echo-ing world that I longed to embrace; it streamed in upon me, its books, movies, music, appealing not only to the mind but also to the senses. Faintly redolent of potential corruptions of the flesh, dark with the specter of con-quest by assimilation, it seemed to hold out at the same time the promise of worldly wisdom, of tolerance, of reward for merit and achievement, and—the most precious promise of all—the creations of the great minds of man.

I was one of millions, millions, making that concrete Mississippi jour-ney. We were the children and grandchildren of the last great tribal migra-tion of our species on this planet, the east-west wandering of the frightened, the persecuted, the hungry, the poor, the seekers after new wealth and power—the movement around the turn of the century from Europe that inundated this land. . . .

—Chaim Potok, "Culture Confrontation in Urban America: A Writer's Beginnings," in *Literature and the Urban Experience*, ed. Michael C. Jaye and Ann Chalmera Watts (New Brunswick, N.J.: Rutgers University Press, 1981).

Like Potok, many who wrote about The Bronx of this era created their works in later years, driven by an urge to preserve memories before they were lost forever. Indeed, early Bronx memories inspired poet Allen Ginsberg to write "White Shroud." A native of Paterson, New Jersey, the poet laureate of the Beatniks lived briefly with his mother's family in The Bronx in 1929 when he was three years of age. Ginsberg frequently visited The Bronx both as a child and as a young man. His poem is written in the form of a mystical hallucination.

. . . I found myself again in the Great Eastern Metropolis,
wandering under Elevated Transport's iron struts—
many windowed apartments walled the crowded Bronx road-way
under old theater roofs, masses of poor women shopping
in black shawls past candy store news-stands, children skipped beside

Davidson Avenue and 183rd Street, June 7, 1932. The 183rd Street station of the elevated Jerome Avenue IRT subway is to the right. "I found myself . . . / wandering under Elevated Transport's iron struts— / many windowed apartments walled the crowded Bronx road-way." —Allen Ginsberg. The Bronx County Historical Society Research Library.

grandfathers bent tottering on their canes. I'd descended
to this same street from blackened subways Sundays long ago,
tea and lox with my aunt and dentist cousin when I was ten. . . .
Surprised, I passed the open Chamber where my Russian Jewish
Grandmother lay in her bed and sighed eating a little Chicken
soup or borscht, potato latkes, crumbs on her blankets, talking
Yiddish, complaining solitude abandoned in Old Folks House.
I realized I could find a place to sleep in the neighborhood, what
relief, the family together again, first time in decades!—
Now vigorous middle aged I climbed hillside streets in West Bronx
looking for my own hot-water furnished flat to settle in,
close to visit my grandmother, read Sunday newspapers
in vast glassy Cafeterias, smoke over pencils & paper,
poetry desk, happy with books father'd left in the attic,
peaceful encyclopedia and a radio in the kitchen.

An old black janitor swept the gutter, street dogs sniffed red hydrants,
nurses pushed baby carriages past silent house fronts.
Anxious I be settled with money in my own place before
nightfall, I wandered tenement embankments overlooking
the pillared subway trestles by the bridge crossing Bronx River. . . .

> —Allen Ginsberg, "White Shroud," *Poems: 1980–1985*
> (New York: Harper & Row, 1985).

Despite the deprivation and anxiety of the Depression, for most Bronxites, the era was a time when streets were safe and close-knit families struggled to attain the American Dream. Poet w r rodriguez captured this nostalgic mood of "the beautiful Bronx" a half a century later in "roosevelt's bust."

the windup clock
ticks away the present
amid depression blue ashtrays
what a time it was
before i was born
in the beautiful bronx
pristine tenements
beflowered parks
free glassware at five cent
double feature movies
five cent trolleys
through well swept cobblestones
everything cost the nickel
no one had
neighbors thin the stew
and share
all night unlocked doors
at christmas santa leaves
love and best wishes
nothing to fear but hunger
and fascism spreading across the old countries
these are the good old days
so fondly remembered
strikeouts forgotten
home runs sail forever
into happy bleachers

The filled bleacher section of Yankee Stadium in the early 1930s. A postcard photograph. "home runs sail forever / into happy bleachers." —w r rodriguez. Barbara Unger Collection.

Franklin D. Roosevelt campaigning for his third term in a motorcade on 138th Street and Brook Avenue, October 28, 1940. "the crowds cheer / roosevelt rides triumphant through the bronx." —w r rodriguez. The Bronx County Historical Society Research Library.

prohibition prohibited
dutch schultz dead
all that beer and no money for drink
the family endures
gathers together
the radio warm as a hearth
never lost never sold
fireside chats
sound effects serials
yankee slugfests
baseball transcends history
for a while and the crowds cheer
roosevelt rides triumphant through the bronx
all are immigrants and the immigrants are
fellow americans
compassion is nourished by despair

—w r rodriguez, "roosevelt's bust," unpublished
poem.

6

THE BRONX HOME FRONT

THE WAR YEARS

1936–1950

THE EVENTS LEADING UP TO WORLD WAR II HAD A POWERFUL impact on the people of The Bronx. When Bronx Jewish families realized that the Nazis threatened the very survival of their kin who still resided across the Atlantic, the fight began on the Bronx home front. For a time, Father Coughlin and other anti-Semites divided some Bronxites from others, but once the war began most residents hoped Britain would hang on. After the United States entered the conflict in 1941 with the Japanese bombing of Pearl Harbor, all Bronxites united to support the war effort. Even the New York Yankees baseball hero Joe DiMaggio, who had set a record hitting in fifty-six consecutive games in 1941, joined the service. As youths were drafted and went overseas in uniform, fear was mingled with patriotism.

The rise of Hitler in Germany in the 1930s found an echo in some parts of The Bronx, especially in those neighborhoods where the Jewish residents were in a distinct minority. One of these places was Pelham Bay, where Cynthia Ozick recalled being tormented for being Jewish.

> In P.S. 71 I carry weighty as a cloak the ineradicable knowledge of my scandal—I am cross-eyed, dumb, an imbecile at arithmetic; in P.S. 71 I am publicly shamed in Assembly because I am caught not singing Christmas carols; in P.S. 71 I am repeatedly accused of deicide.
>
> —Cynthia Ozick, "A Drugstore in Winter," *Art and Ardor* (New York: E. P. Dutton, 1984).

In E. L. Doctorow's novel *World's Fair*, young Edgar, fascinated with airships, has the overwhelming desire to see the German zeppelin the *Hindenburg* on its maiden flight over the Atlantic to New Jersey. The giant airship was seen by many people as it passed over The Bronx on its way to Lakehurst, New Jersey.

I didn't think of the Bronx as a place where anything happened. The Bronx was a big place with miles of streets and six-story apartment houses ..., up hills and down hills it went, every neighborhood had its school like my school, its movie, its street of shops built into the sides of the apartment houses; it was tunneled with subways and bound together by trolley lines, and elevated lines; but for all that, and for all of those who lived here, myself included, it was not important. It was not famous. It was not central to the world. I thought the *Hindenburg* would more naturally fly over Manhattan, which was central to the world....

I went to the small park, the Oval, in the middle of Mt. Eden Avenue. Here, as it happened, one had a clear view of a good deal of sky. I don't remember doing much of anything. Perhaps I bought a Bungalow Bar. Perhaps I was looking for Meg, who sometimes came to the Oval with her mother. Over the roofs of the private houses that bordered the north side of Mt. Eden Avenue, across the street from the park, the nose of the great silver *Hindenburg* appeared. My mouth dropped open. She sailed incredibly over the housetops, and came right toward me, just a few hundred feet in the air, and kept coming and kept coming and still no sight of the tail of her. She was tilted toward me as if she were an enormous animal leaping from the sky in monumental slow motion. . . . The *Hindenburg* was headed over Claremont Park now, toward Morris Avenue. . . . Everyone was looking at her.

Soon afterward, Edgar learns about the explosion and crash of the *Hindenburg* in New Jersey.

My mother had said she was a German ship, sent over by Hitler for his own glory, and that if those people had to die she hoped they were Nazis.

—E. L. Doctorow, *World's Fair* (New York: Fawcett Crest, 1985).

However, during the 1939 Hitler-Stalin Nonaggression Pact, most pro-Stalin Leftists believed there would be no war between fascism and communism and that politics and neighborhood life would go on as before. In the area of Bronx Park East between Allerton Avenue and Pelham Parkway, where the radically inclined Coops were located, it was still possible to discern a person's politics from the Yiddish-language newspaper he or she read. *Freiheit* was the most radical newspaper, while the *Forward* was centrist. Poet Myra Shapiro captured life from her perspective while growing up in this neighborhood during the war in her poem "Across from

The left-hand side of the balcony of the Loew's Paradise Theatre on the Grand Concourse near Fordham Road in 1971. "the Loew's Paradise / on the Grand Concourse / the height of all going / no dreams went beyond." —Myra Shapiro. The Bronx County Historical Society Research Library.

Bronx Park." The opulent movie palace, Loew's Paradise, was located on the Grand Concourse near Fordham Road.

> We lived near the elephants
> and a garden of roses
> our parents arrived at
> from work in sweatshops.
> We climbed in the playground
> and wandered like gypsies
> on land not yet cleared
> of forests and streams.
> Women leaning out windows
> watched as we left them—
> they'd shout directions
> for crossing the street.
> From above they could see
> both sides of the parkway

traffic had parted—
GONOWWATCHOUT!
Sitting on benches neighbors
argued for hours—*Freiheit!*
Forward!—from opposite camps.
When we finished playing
we'd ask and they'd watch us
cross Bronx Park East
back home again.
I'd get my friend Lola
who lived near me in 6C
to meet after supper
up on the roof—
and as we grew older
we'd scheme how to meet boys
at the Loew's Paradise
on the Grand Concourse
the height of all going
no dreams went beyond.

> —Myra Shapiro, "Across from Bronx Park,"
> unpublished poem.

At the outbreak of the war in Europe, many Bronx residents with families there had heightened fear for their relatives' safety. The few avenues of escape were rapidly closing. Cynthia Ozick recalled the reaction of her family in the northeast Bronx in her memoir.

> German tanks were biting into Europe. Weeping, my grandmother pounded her breast with her fist: The British White Paper of 1939 had declared that ships packed with Jewish refugees would be barred from the beaches of Haifa and Tel Aviv and returned to a Nazi doom. In P.S. 71, our neighborhood school, the boys were drawing cannons and warplanes.

> —Cynthia Ozick, "A Drugstore Eden," *The New Yorker* (September 16, 1996).

As the war raged in Europe, young Edgar, the Bronx lad narrating E. L. Doctorow's novel *World's Fair*, made drawings for his own amusement. Even in his boyish imagination, he knew what was at stake. His hero, Daring Dave, was modeled after the newspaper comic strip *Smilin' Jack*.

But now that World War Two had come to Europe I decided to get Dave into a fighter plane. I put him in a Spitfire flying over London for the Royal Air Force. The English insignia was a bull's eye colored red, white and blue.... I showed Nazi Messerschmitts going down in smoke.

—E. L. Doctorow, *World's Fair* (New York: Fawcett Crest, 1985).

Before the entrance of the United States into the war, Bronxites experienced the conflict only through newsreels shown between double features in neighborhood movie theaters. But the war became tangible, and even closer, as some Bronx young men were subjected to the first peacetime draft in 1940. In Eliot Wagner's novel *Grand Concourse*, Julie Margulies, who lived on Tiffany Street in Hunts Point, and Dr. Mario Vito, the son of a Bronx barber and resident of the Italian Bronx neighborhood of Belmont, fell in love. The young couple attended the Excelsior, modeled on the genuine Loew's Paradise. The newsreels not only depicted battle scenes but also showed how prominent isolationists supported America's neutrality. The aviation ace Charles Lindbergh was one of these.

One night in the Excelsior ..., Julie could take no more of the newsreel: draftees charging a hillock, teeth and bayonets fixed; tanks being derricked to a freighter; London ablaze; guns near Benghazi; Lindbergh at a Senate table—*"I'm against appeasement, but I am more opposed to an unnecessary war.... We are not changing the trend of the war by sending Britain aid—we're just prolonging it.... I don't believe the Germans think they can come over, but if they tried, I believe in war to the uttermost."*

They dressed themselves for outdoors in the great hall of the theater. Huge posters slanted over oriental rugs. The sluggish goldfish in the fountain were unmoved by war exploding intermittently from the sound track inside.

Julie tilted to Mario a face as ingenuous as a child's. "Will they take you?" she asked.

Mario drew himself to full height, his chest and shoulders wide, very impressive. "What do *you* think?"

"I think you should marry me. We could have a child right away."

Even though Mario is drafted into the army, he and Julie become engaged. Unfortunately, he dies even before war is declared when his army truck and a train collide. Leon Eisler, the son of a wealthy family in the Riverdale section of The Bronx, tries to woo Julie, with whom he had been in love even before her engagement. Then comes December 7, 1941.

The Margulieses had been an hour around the radio. Even Mr. Margulies . . . excited at the first news of the bombing, sat apathetically. Radios barked throughout the building, an unharmonious counterpoint. Bulletins, rehashings; sailors killed; ships destroyed; Secretary of State said. . . .

The radio continued, not loud, but the floor vibrated from the one downstairs. Nobody talked. Mrs. Margulies, terrified, didn't dare to look at anyone. Gerald slouched expressionless on the sofa, his chin sunk to his chest. Julie's mouth turned down; a tear she had been unable to hold back had dried on her cheek. . . .

Leon was let in . . . when he called. Late to bed and risen late, he had heard no radio; he knew nothing of it. His eyes moved from Julie to Gerald, from Mr. Margulies to his wife.

"Somebody die?" he asked.

"A lot of people died in Pearl Harbor," said Gerald.

"We're in the war," Julie said.

"What? What?"

Mr. Margulies began incoherently to bring Leon up to date.

Julie and Leon then decide to go for a walk in the neighborhood.

. . . Crotona Park too had its sitters and walkers in the sun. And a few riders, pedaling the bicycle oval. Elderly men dressed heavily talked in Yiddish: shivering, gesticulating, they were interested only in the war. Hitler would soon learn, they said.

The trees were dark and brittle, the tan earth yellow-patched with sere grass.

Julie and Leon followed the park's concrete meanderings. "Will they take you?" she suddenly asked.

It all at once struck him that they might, so her concern gave him only mingled pleasure. But, outwardly composed, he answered, "They already turned me down." . . .

She said, "But mightn't they call you again?"

Leon felt persecuted. "So?" he said. "If they call me, I'll go."

Julie shuddered, reminded of another time: Mario—the same question, the same answer. And though she felt Leon's irritation, she exclaimed, "No, no, don't say that!" and gripped his arm so fervently that she released it almost at once. "I'm sorry," she said, abashed. . . .

Leon wanted to blurt, "Marry me, Julie." But he hesitated, and as her hand dropped and she walked from him to a bench near by, he merely followed, wondering how to retrieve the lost moment.

*The Concourse Plaza Hotel on the Grand Concourse and 161st Street about 1939. "Gerald observed
... the fantastic preparation for the wedding. The grand ballroom at the Concourse Plaza, no less...!"
—Eliot Wagner. The Bronx County Historical Society Research Library.*

The American entry into the war had some far-ranging effects on many Bronx
residents. In many cases it led to hasty marriages caused by a mixture of love, anxiety, fear, and foolishness. Thus, Julie decides to marry the wealthy Leon Eisler. Her
brother, Gerald, watches the event unfold.

> Gerald observed with passive disbelief the fantastic preparation for the
> wedding. The grand ballroom at the Concourse Plaza, no less—that's where
> it was supposed to take place! Papa ... engaged the room with all the pride of
> Leon's money. And subsidiary rooms to dress in!
>
> —Eliot Wagner, *Grand Concourse* (Indianapolis:
> The Bobbs-Merrill Company, Inc., 1954).

Vito A. Merola, in his memoir, "Memories of a One Way Passage," records how
the effect of the war and its first casualty suddenly burst upon his quiet section of
The Bronx along Tremont Avenue north of Crotona Park.

> My first realization (I guess you could say "our" first realization) that a
> war was being waged occurred when we were told that Johnny Lee was killed

in action. He was what a modernist would today call an Amerasian (the term
had not yet been invented), being the offspring of an Irish-American mother
and a Chinese father. To us, in those days, he was our big brother who lived
in the apartment under us and everybody liked him. He was friendly, always
immaculately dressed, and seemed always to be around without ever hanging around with us because he was much older. The last time I saw Johnny
was when he came home on his first leave before going overseas. He wore his
uniform well, and as he told us war stories, we had our example of strength.
He was, I suppose, the role-model we needed to emulate *in absentia* later on.

—Vito A. Merola, "Memories of a One Way Passage," *The Bronx County Historical Society Journal*
(Spring 1990).

The war also transformed many Bronx women. They became economically
emancipated by entering the work force to take the place of drafted men. Some even
entered the armed forces. The recently built campus of Hunter College in The
Bronx, later Lehman College, just to the east of the Jerome Park Reservoir was taken
over by the government as a training base for the WAVES, the womens' branch of
the navy. Their presence influenced one young teenage girl who saw new horizons
opening up for females beyond the previously circumscribed and expected future
of marriage and homemaking. Barbara Unger recounts this in her poem "The Fog
of the Forties." After the war, the Bronx campus admitted men.

> O blue ladies of The Bronx, the Waves,
> my borough-loyal mizzens, for you
> I would have lashed myself to the prow
> as I watched your legs on well-oiled hinges
> strut past Jerome Reservoir to Hunter College,
> home of brainy women philosophers.
>
> A high command of daughters,
> You were ready to ride destroyers
> Carrying aircraft to the landlocked infantry.
>
> I envied your invulnerable Kotex,
> your jaunty smiles like medals
> pinned to an Admiral's chest.
>
> O blue ladies of The Bronx,
> you'd never get bumped by boys

WAVES march on Goulden Avenue about 1943. The Jerome Park Reservoir is to the left and the buildings of Hunter College, now Lehman College, are to the right. "O blue ladies of the Bronx, the Waves, / . . . I watched your legs on well-oiled hinges / strut past Jerome Reservoir to Hunter College." —Barbara Unger. Lehman College Archives.

destined for coeducation
or have the wind knocked
out of your sails,
stricken by shyness.

Your virginity was a treasure
painstakingly built
like a boat inside a bottle,
out of matchbooks
and swizzle sticks,
a mixed blessing,
sent out to sea
with a message,
nautical but nice.

I would wait for you in violet twilight
to anoint me with a smile.

Instead, each day I'd sail
at dawn's earliest light
into swarms of pimply girls
at junior high, discontented
with the world. I wanted to walk
to the end of the dock
and jump off into my life. . . .

> —Barbara Unger, "The Fog of the Forties," *Blue Depression Glass* (Winnetka, Ill.: Thorntree Press, 1991).

Those who remained in The Bronx mobilized to aid the war effort. Home front work included planting vegetables for home consumption in empty lots turned into Victory Gardens so that more food could be sent to beleaguered Britain and the troops abroad. Children collected funds for America's other ally, the Soviet Union, which was responsible for turning the tide of war against the Nazis at the Battle of Stalingrad. Periodically, sirens would sound all over the city for an air raid drill. All these experiences are found in Barbara Unger's poem "Mosholu Parkway."

Wearing my plastic disc
in case of death by air raid
I enter the wire gate,

weed my leafy Victory Garden
on 208th Street,

find my way home
skipping over pavement cracks
for good luck,

eat all the food on my plate
for the starving children.

In the collection can
clink of pennies
for our Red brothers,
smiling heroes of
Stalingrad.

> —Barbara Unger, "Mosholu Parkway," *Inside the Wind* (Decatur, Ga.: Linwood Publishers, 1986).

Cynthia Ozick's uncle in her Pelham Bay neighborhood also cultivated a garden during the war.

> In Europe the German death factories were pumping out smoke and human ash from a poisoned orchard of chimneys. In Pelham Bay, among bees and white-wing flutterings, the sweet brown earth pumped ears of corn.
>
> —Cynthia Ozick, "A Drugstore Eden," *The New Yorker* (September 16, 1996).

Some people who lived outside of The Bronx came to the more open areas of the borough to find a plot to plant a Victory Garden. Sisters Sadie and Bessie Delany, two black professional women living at Edgecomb Avenue in northern Manhattan's Sugar Hill, recalled this experience in their joint memoir, *Having Our Say.*

> But there was really no room to grow a substantial garden on the grounds of 80 Edgecomb. So our cousins in the Bronx said it would be OK to use a vacant lot next to their property. We went up there as often as we could, and grew the best Victory garden in the neighborhood. . . .
>
> After the war was over, we didn't want to give up our Victory garden. We started thinking about moving from Harlem to the Bronx. Why, wouldn't it be nice to live where Mama could have a garden? Wouldn't it be nice to get Mama out of an apartment?
>
> Well, that's exactly what we did. We bought a little cottage in the North Bronx, next to where we had our Victory garden. There was lots of vacant land there, then, and trees and shrubs. It was like the country.
>
> —Sarah L. Delany and A. Elizabeth Delany with Amy Hill Hearth, *Having Our Say: The Delany Sisters' First 100 Years* (New York: Dell, 1994).

Scrap drives, war bond drives, and rationing were constant reminders of the war at the Bronx home front. They were methods by which people far from the fighting felt they could contribute to the war effort. In the leftist strongholds of the cooperative housing developments, women knitted socks for the troops as the men, steeped in left-wing politics, debated the fate of the predicted post-revolutionary Marxist world. Barbara Unger captured this in her poem "Near Sholem Aleichem Houses."

> Needles chirp like an army of mad crickets
> as nimble fingers transform balls of wool
> into comforters, socks, sweaters.

The women knit,
full of "live and let live,"
blame and forgive.

I help card wool as
unanswered questions droop
from my wrist,

as if I could cover
millions of graves in Europe
with warm woolen squares,

as the men debate how to
save the world,
divide the wealth.

Ghosts of Veblen, Marx
swirl among Yiddish voices
in tobacco smoke,

someone hums a revolutionary
anthem, a man in a French beret,

as I watch their dreams die
as borders fold over each other,
then disappear.

—Barbara Unger, "Near Sholem Aleichem Houses,"
Wordsmith (Spring 1992).

During the war, the lack of a letter from a son or brother in the service, or from a family member in or near the European war zones, raised the level of anxiety for those at home in The Bronx. This fear is recounted by Jerome Charyn in his comic memoir, *The Dark Lady from Belorusse*.

We weren't on a pleasure stroll. It was our daily trip to the post office, where my mother was expecting a letter from Mogilev, in White Russia, where her brother lived, a schoolteacher who'd raised her after her own mother had died. I'm not sure why this letter couldn't have been delivered to the mailbox in our building. Had the Germans seized Mogilev, and my uncle could only write via some secret system in the Soviet underground?

The postmaster would always come out from behind his window when my mother appeared. He was a cranky little man who wore slippers and liked to shout at his clerks. But he was kind to the dark lady's little boy. He would take me through his side of the wall and show me the "graveyard," a gigantic sack where all the dead letters lay, sad undeliverable things, with postmarks from all over the planet. I would sift through the pile, look at the pictures on the stamps, smell the glue, while the postmaster squeezed my mother's hand. But not even this wizard of the mail could produce a letter from Mogilev.

She would tremble on the journey home as we climbed hill after hill. She walked like a drunken lady. It was from my mother that I learned how memory could kill. She could survive as long as she had word from Mogilev. But there was no word in the middle of a war, only mountains of dead-letter boxes between Belorusse and the Bronx.

—Jerome Charyn, *The Dark Lady from Belorusse*
(New York: St. Martin's Press, 1997).

In an echo of Nazi anti-Semitism, some Bronx Jewish children found themselves the target of local prejudice. Arlene Gross, in her short story "What Does Holloween Have to Do with It?" told of a spunky Bronx girl's calculated effort to obtain revenge on a gang of neighborhood youths who had hurled an anti-Semitic remark at her. Hawthorne and Wordsworth Avenues are fictional names for genuine streets in the Hunts Point area named after different authors. "Program" stands for pogrom, and Halloween is deliberately misspelled to capture the Bronx accent. In the story, young Rita dirties her middy blouse while spying on the boys near the Bronx River through opera glasses taken from her mother's drawer. When her mother questions her, Rita uses Halloween as an excuse.

"So, it's Holloween? What does Holloween have to do with it? We don't celebrate Holloween."

"Everyone in America celebrates Holloween," the learned daughter now plays teacher to the ignorant mother. But the mother isn't really listening, doesn't buy this. To her this is no explanation at all, just a stall. Blue-eyed darts from mother into daughter's blue-eyed targets. "Spill it," the mother demands.

And she gets some sort of an answer, which if you believe it, makes sense. It goes something like this. When you are a fifth grader and Holloween comes, the boys from Wordsworth Avenue descend the hill to Hawthorne and write all over you in colored chalk, pounding you with socks filled with flour and rocks. And you run while they call you things like Hawthorne

Hebes and Sheenies. You get very messy but lucky it is too hot and no one is wearing a sweater.

Rita's mother doesn't hear the part about the sweater. Her eyes are wide, filled with tears and she's shouting, "*Gotenyu*, a progrom, a regular progrom." And, now she encircles her tall, skinny girl in her arms and kisses her face fervently but the girl squirms out of the hold. "Nah. It's just a bunch of squirts thinking they're so smart. Don't worry. Beside, Holloween is over tonight. Finished. Squirts. Squirts. Squirts.". . .

So when her mother leaves, Holloween isn't over for her. She has work to do. . . .

Rita takes her mother's red cape, buys a devil's mask, draws pentagrams on her body with lipstick, and dresses for her revenge.

Her school clothes into the laundry hamper and she tosses a light summer dress over herself to hide not quite her shame but her nakedness, at least. Shoes without socks because she won't be needing socks. Oh, three cheers for the weatherman, she thinks. He keeps his promise. It's hot. Hot as *Hell*. She whispers to herself the forbidden word, hears it with nothing but her own inner ear, giggles on the way to the private drawer. The glasses are there where her mother put them yesterday. Next hurry to the window and train the glasses in the direction of The Creek. They are there. The enemy. Just starting to undress which is fine with her. She's off with her knapsack filled with a red satin cape, a red wool hat and a devil's mask, she's off to regain honor for Hawthorne Avenue from Wordsworth. . . .

And, at long last, they climb up to the very top of the rock pile and jump in, splash, crash, diving under the mucky water, throwing foam suds into each other's eyes. Advantage to Rita now who scoots behind the rock pile with the old clothes, strips off her dress and shoes, opens the knapsack, puts on the mask, the cape and the red wool hat and ascends to the very peak of the mountain of rubble, spreading her arms wide. The red cape ripples on the light breezes rising from the water. It catches the glow of the late afternoon sun on this first day of November. She is indeed a visitation, a demon unleashed by the fury of her street defeat of the day before.

"Skeeeeeeeedoooooooo! Skeeeeeeeedoooooooo! Skeeeeeeeedooooooooo!"

A banshee's shriek. A call to arms. The girl exists no longer. No. No. This is the girl transformed, the heroine, beyond Wonder Woman, beyond Joan of Arc. To the enemies this guise is horrific. To these astonished frogs, these turtles, these insignificant toads, the woman warrior has come. They see her when they look up and begin shoving and yowling. . . .

They hurl themselves out of The Creek, scared minnows, all dithery with the spunk sucked from their bones, skittering away so fast they never gather up their clothes heaped behind the rock pile.

But Rita, the Avenger does. Gathers those clothes and flings every last stitch—worn trousers, frayed shirts, soiled underpants, dirty socks, smudged and torn sneakers—right into The Creek. Watches the smelly things float on the current, sins cast upon the water. Rita, the avenger, prays out loud that their stuff should wash up in Germany, along with the orange peels, old shoes, dead fish and those funny white balloons. And shouts in exaltation, "Skeeeeeeeedooooooooo. Skeeeeeeeeedooooooooo. Skeeeeeeeeedooooooooo."

> —Arlene C. Gross, "What Does Holloween Have to Do with It?: A Story about People in the 1940s Who Call Halloween 'Holloween,'" unpublished story.

If fear of anti-Semitism lingered among some Bronx Jews, people of varied ethnic groups also emerged from their enclaves during the war and got to know members of other groups. Young James Baldwin, who was later to become a major black author, traveled from Harlem to attend the all-male DeWitt Clinton High School in The Bronx. At the school, he became editor-in-chief of the school's literary publication and published his first stories, thus launching his writing career. While at Clinton, Baldwin formed close friendships with Jewish boys who had interests similar to his. These friendships led him to question the teachings of his stepfather's Harlem church and, later, give up his aspirations as a preacher to become a writer.

The Jewish boys in high school were troubling because I could find no point of connection between them and the Jewish pawnbrokers and landlords and grocery-store owners in Harlem. . . .

. . . My best friend in high school was a Jew. He came to our house once, and afterward my father asked, as he asked about everyone, "Is he a Christian?"—by which he meant "Is he saved?" I really do not know whether my answer came out of innocence or venom, but I said coldly, "No. He's Jewish." My father slapped me across the face with his great palm, and in that moment everything flooded back—all the hatred and all the fear, and the depth of a merciless resolve to kill my father than allow my father to kill me—and I knew that all those sermons and tears and all that repentance and rejoicing had changed nothing. I wondered if I was expected to be glad that a friend of mine, or anyone, was to be tormented forever in Hell, and I also thought, suddenly, of the Jews in another Christian nation, Germany. They were not so far from the fiery furnace after all, and my best friend might have been one of them. I told my father, "He's a better Christian than you are," and walked out of the house. The battle between us was in the open, but that was all right; it was almost a relief. A more deadly struggle had begun.

—James Baldwin, *The Fire Next Time* (New York: Dell, 1963).

Another future author who attended school in The Bronx was Jack Kerouac, who later became a major writer of the Beat Generation. In his book *Vanity of Duluoz*, Kerouac looked back on his youth when he left his hometown, Lowell, Massachusetts, to attend Horace Mann High School in the Riverdale section of The Bronx on a football scholarship. Kerouac erred in thinking it was in upper Manhattan. He recalls his first brush with New York and the insularity of prep school life.

The prep school was really an advanced high school called Horace Mann School for Boys, founded I s'pose by odd old Horace Mann, and a fine school it was, with ivy on granite walls, swards, running tracks, tennis courts, gyms, jolly principals and teachers, all on a hill overlooking Van Cortlandt Park in New York City upper Manhattan. Well, since you've never been there why bother with the details except to say, it was at 246th Street in New York City and I was living with my stepgrandmother in Brooklyn New York, a daily trip of two hours and a half by subway each way.

Nothing deters young punk kids, not even today....

By the time we're at Times Square, or maybe Penn Station at 34th just before that, most people rush out, to midtown work, and Ah, I get the usual corner seat and start in on the physics studies. Now it's easy sailing. At 72nd Street we pick up another slue of workers headed for uptown Manhattan and Bronx work but I dont care anymore: I've got a seat.... Now you'd think I'm close to school but from 96th Street we go past Columbia College, we go up into Harlem, past Harlem, way up, another hour, till the subway emerges from the tunnel (as tho by nature it was impossible for it to go underground so long) and goes soaring to the very end of the line in Yonkers practically.

Near school? No, because there I have to go down the elevated steps and then start up a steep hill about as steep as 45 degrees or a little less, a tremendous climb. By now all the other kids are with me, puffing, blowing steam of morning, so that from 6 A.M. when I got up in Brooklyn, till now, 8.30, it's been two and a half hours of negotiating my way to actual class....

I don't understand why, except it must be an exceptional school; but 96 percent of the students are Jewish kids, and most of them are very rich: sons of furriers, famous realtors, thissa and thatta and here come mobs of them in big black limousines driven by chauffeurs in visored hats, carrying large lunchboxes full of turkey sandwiches and Napoleons and chocolate milk in thermos bottles. Some of them, like students of the first form, are only ten years old and 4 feet tall; some of them are funny little fat tubs of lard, I guess because they didnt have to climb that hill. But most of the rich Jewish kids took the subway from apartments on Central Park West, Park Avenue, Riverside Drive. The other 4 percent or so of the students were from prominent Irish and other families, such as Mike Hennessey whose father was the basketball coach of Columbia, or Bing Rohr a German boy whose father had been a contractor connected with building the gym. Then came the 1 percent to which I belonged, called ringers, B or A average students who were also athletes, from all over, New Jersey, Massachusetts, Connecticut, Pennsy, who had been given partial financial scholarship arrangements to come to Horace Mann, get their credits for college, and make the joint the Number One high school football team in New York City, which we did that year.

But first, 8.45 or so, we all had to sit in the auditorium and be led in the singing of 'Onward Christian Soldiers' by English Professor Christopher Smart, followed by 'Lord Jeffrey Amherst' which was a song no more appropriate for me to sing (as descendant of French and Indian) than it was appropriate for the Jewish kids to sing 'Onward Christian Soldiers.' It was fun no less.

—Jack Kerouac, *Vanity of Duluoz: An Adventurous Education, 1935–46* (London: Paladin, 1990).

While Baldwin felt empathy with the Jews, and Kerouac, disdain, the fictional Kathleen Lynch in Elizabeth Cullinan's short story "Dreaming" develops an inferiority complex toward her Jewish peers, which she finally overcomes. Kathleen's mother enrolls her two daughters, Kathleen and Eileen, in a Bronx settlement house music school, which she has selected because she wants hem to have the best instruction available. They are the only two non-Jews in a class of 150 students. Kathleen falls to the bottom of her class, while her older sister, Eileen, oblivious to the cultural differences, excels.

One cause of Kathleen's low self-esteem is the constant criticism that the bookish child endures at the hands of the nuns at Holy Family School, the Catholic institution she attends. The nuns command:

"Pay attention." "Keep your head where it belongs." "An idle mind is the devil's workshop." The nuns spoke to Mrs. Lynch and told her, "Kathleen is a dreamer. She's always off in the clouds."

Kathleen observes the differences between the settlement house music school, modeled upon Bronx House, and Holy Family, modeled upon St. Raymond's in the Parkchester area of The Bronx. The settlement house is a noisy, chaotic place, its walls decorated with colorful abstract art exhibits, and its hallways filled with dancing students in tights practicing their movements.

> It was all very different from Holy Family where silence and restraint were drummed in so constantly as to seem to prevail. . . . Noises heard in the corridor of Holy Family were faint, like the step of a solitary child on stone stairs or on the wooden floor. . . . Or there were solid, heavy sounds—a whole class tramping up or down stairs, or reciting the times table or a spelling lesson, or learning a hymn; bodies moving and voices being raised in unison—another kind of silence.

Since the Lynch sisters have to leave Holy Family early in order to take music lessons, they are still dressed in their school uniforms when they arrive. Kathleen feels different from the Jewish children, who are more casually dressed. She sometimes feels ashamed when her classmates ask her what the emblem on the pocket of her uniform stands for, although she knows that she is supposed to be proud of her faith. She often feels self-conscious about her background. Kathleen's parents take the sisters to Radio City Music Hall for a treat, while the Jewish children attend classical music concerts at Carnegie Hall, where they hear the greats such as Vladimir Horowitz, Artur Rubenstein, and Jascha Heifetz, who were Jewish. For Kathleen, the music school is a deviation from everything she knows.

Recognizing Kathleen's struggle, Miss Rosen, her music teacher, tries to help her. She assigns Schumann's *Träumerei* as one of two pieces Kathleen will play at a recital, hoping it will bring out the best in her. As the day of the recital arrives, Kathleen feels great anxiety. Her first piece does not go well. As Kathleen then begins playing *Träumerei*, voices in her head begin to guide her.

> "'*Träumerei*' means a kind of dreaming," Miss Rosen had said, "and I think you like to dream." The nuns said, "Come down to earth." "Keep your mind where it belongs." "Stop dreaming." . . . Dreams were her sin and her salvation, her fall and redemption. She offered them now, note by note.

Miss Rosen's plan works. Kathleen now feels a part of the music. In the audience, Kathleen's proud mother sits beside an esteemed listener, who offers his praise of Kathleen's performance.

The rabbi turned to Mrs. Lynch. "Dear lady," he said, "your child is a musician."

—Elizabeth Cullinan, "Dreaming," in *Yellow Roses*
(New York: Viking Press, 1977).

Bronx men and women in the service often found themselves far from home during the war years. In 1943, for instance, Vito A. Merola from the Tremont neighborhood joined the navy. As in the case of many Bronxites in the service, it was his first experience away from home, and enabled him to mingle with people from diverse localities and social backgrounds.

While eating dinner with my buddies in the mess hall at the Naval Shipyards in Portmouth, Virginia—fresh out of The Bronx for the first time in my life—I heard a loud voice from across the table. In an accent reminiscent of New Jersey nothing and Pennsylvania twang, I heard the sailor say, "Ah, ha, there's a New York bread folder. What part of The Bronx do you come from?"

It was unmistakable. The voice was directed at me. I became something short of hysterical with laughter. I couldn't believe what I was hearing. I let out a real guffaw.

"How do you know?" I asked, finding it difficult to contain myself.

"I just told you," was the answer. "You buttered your bread, then folded it."

"No, I mean how do you know I'm from The Bronx?" I yelled down the table and over the din of the chow hall.

"I didn't until tonight," he hollered back through cupped hands.

"Last night I watched you fold the bread. Tonight, I heard you talk!"

—Vito A. Merola, "Memories of a One Way Passage," *The Bronx County Historical Society Journal* (Spring 1990).

Eventually, many Bronxites in the service crossed the ocean and were posted in foreign countries. In his novel *Tiffany Street*, Jerome Weidman reunited two former Bronx sweethearts, Hannah Halpern and Benny Kramer, in 1942 in Hannah's villa in Islington Crescent, Blackpool, England, where they tried to find shelter during a German air raid. Now happily married to an Englishman, Hannah explains to Benny why she decided not to marry him in the past, long before the war broke out. Leslie Howard and Greer Garson were movie stars of the era.

"It's like this," Hannah said. "For a Bronx girl in nineteen thirty, I was sitting pretty. I had this cockamamy job at Gold-Mark-Zweig, Inc., on Mosholu

Apartment houses on Walton Avenue north of 161st Street in the mid-1930s. "'Our first home? Walton Avenue, natch. Sure, it's the Bronx. But the classy Bronx.'" —Jerome Weidman. The Bronx County Historical Society Research Library

Parkway. A living. I had a steady boyfriend. A delight. I could read the future more clearly than that dame in the *Daily News* with the horoscope. All I had to do was wait. You would graduate from law school. You would get a job with some good solid Rock of Gibraltar firm with one of those names. You know. White & Case. Sullivan & Cromwell. Weil, Gattschal & Manges. You know what I mean. The lads who sail in the summer on Martha's Vineyard and hire boys from East Fourth Street and Tiffany Street to win the cases that pay for the mizzenmasts. The One Twenty Broadway gang. And pretty soon you'd be earning enough to move your father and mother from Tiffany Street in the Bronx to like say Central Park West or West End Avenue. Then you'd get the old *noodge* from your mother: Benny, it's time you should think about a wife. Well, for God's sake, who was there to think about? Who but Hannah Halpern, from the balcony in Loew's One Hundred and Eightieth Street with the Gabillas's knishes? The wedding? Concourse Plaza. What else? Our first home? Walton Avenue, natch. Sure, it's the Bronx. But the classy Bronx. On Saturdays and Sundays you could go up on the roof with the other young lawyers and their wives and eat Eskimo pies while you looked down into the Yankee Stadium for free and watched Babe Ruth and Lou Gehrig belt Wait Hoyt out of the park. This is bad? Think about it, Benny. Think!"

I did. And in 1942, in a neat little semidetached villa on Islington

Crescent in Blackpool, in the middle of a war and an increasingly nervous-making air raid, my thoughts were astonishingly simple. The answer to Hannah's question was: No, it is not bad. But the answer was upsetting. If it was not bad, how come Hannah and I had not achieved it? . . .

I thought about it, and I could feel my face grow hot. The truth was brutal. All I had ever thought about Hannah Halpern in those days was getting up into the balcony of Loew's 180th Street with a couple of hot knishes.

"Hannah," I said, "this is nineteen forty-two and I'm almost thirty years old. I no longer remember what I thought about when I was seventeen in nineteen thirty."

Hannah gave me one of those over-the-glasses looks, although she did not wear glasses.

"I could refresh your recollection," she said. "But the point is all the Bronx girls I knew were like me. They wanted to get out of the Bronx. And most of them had a sort of rough plan. Like me. Then one night you went and loused it all up by introducing me to an English boy named Sebastian Roon. Never mind that it later turned out to be Seymour Rubin. That night he was Sebastian Roon, and boy did he look it. That marvelous profile. That tweed suit with those three jazzy buttons down the front. That beautiful dark brown hair. Those manners. And my God, Benny, that accent! Can you imagine what it's like to a girl from the Bronx who has secret dreams of becoming Greer Garson to meet Leslie Howard in the flesh? On Vyse Avenue yet?"

"No, I can't," I said. "Because my friends in the theater tell me Leslie Howard was also Jewish."

"Who cares?" Hannah said. "If you look like Leslie Howard, and you talk like Leslie Howard, and you have that slinky smile, and you turn it on a girl from the Bronx, you've got her, boy, you've got her."

—Jerome Weidman, *Tiffany Street* (New York: Random House, 1974).

At home during the war years, the political power of Bronx Democrat boss Edward J. Flynn grew stronger. In 1940, he became the Democratic party's national chairman and his relationship with President Franklin Delano Roosevelt deepened. Jerome Charyn in *The Dark Lady from Belorusse* satirizes the patronage practices that solidified Flynn's political base. The Bronx Borough president in the novel is called Fred R. Lions, but the borough president at the time was really named James J. Lyons.

America had two wartime capitals: the Bronx and Washington, D.C. FDR ruled the country from his wheelchair at the White House, but it was

Boss Flynn who kept him there, who brought out the voters, and held the other bosses in line. "Manhattan?" Lions loved to growl, like Boss Flynn's private little parrot. "Ain't that where the Republicans live?"

Manhattan had a Republican mayor, La Guardia, but Flynn had banished him from the Bronx. He boycotted City Hall, treated the Bronx like his own enclave. He didn't require any largesse from Fiorello La Guardia. He had FDR on his side, and he had his own army. Policemen, firemen, and garbagemen in the Bronx were loyal to Flynn. How many people would dare oppose a man who had his own bed at the White House, who played poker with FDR? Even La Guardia listened to Flynn, and stayed out of the Bronx . . . leaving it to Mr. Lions.

—Jerome Charyn, *The Dark Lady from Belorusse*
(New York: St. Martin's Press, 1997).

As the war drew toward a close, Bronxites, as well as other Americans, experienced to two major events: the death of President Franklin D. Roosevelt on April 12, 1945, and the dropping of the atomic bomb on Hiroshima and Nagasaki in Japan that ended the war in August of that year. The reactions of one Bronx family are recorded by Gerald Rosen in his humorous memoir, *Growing Up Bronx.*

It began to rain harder. The news came on the radio. Eleanor Roosevelt was speaking about freedom and the prairies and the mountains of America. My mother, who was the consummate American dreamer, was carried along on the waves of glorious rhetoric. Tears came into her eyes as always when she heard someone intone the majesties of America. . . . My aunt Rose began to laugh and to mimic Eleanor Roosevelt, parading around the room with a stern expression and spouting out in a falsetto voice, "Boy Scouts of Amur-rikkka. . . ."

And yet, one day, in 1945, I would come home to find both of them in the kitchen, crying.

"What happened, Mommy? What's wrong?"

"President Roosevelt died, Danny. President Roosevelt died," and she burst into sobs as she said it. She wiped her eyes with a hankie. Blew her nose. Tried to control herself. "He was good to the Jews, Danny. He was good to the Jews."

My aunt slumped there on a chair in the corner, weeping.

A few months later, the larger world interposed on the small circle of my life once again. My Cousin Herbie, who was a year older than I, came up to me in front of our building and told me there was some new kind of bomb we had dropped. Something like a "Tom Mix" bomb.

When Herbie's father, my Uncle Lenny, split off from a group of men who had been talking animatedly on the corner and walked toward our building, we intercepted him.

"That's right, boys," he replied to our question. "They call it an atomic bomb. That's what everyone's talkin' about. It can blow up a whole city."

"In one shot?" Herbie said.

"You know it, boys," Lenny said buoyantly. "The war's gonna be over now. You watch and see."

"It is, Uncle Lenny?"

"That's right. And boys, I want you to remember this day. They said on the radio this is going to be the turning point in history. God, I only wish I was your age."

"Why is that, Pop?" Herbie said.

"Because, boys, this bomb is made out of the power of the sun. And that power can do anything." My uncle was filled with the fire of exuberance and grand feeling. "When you grow up, boys, you'll have all kinds of new things. Airplanes. Everything."

"I'll have my own airplane?" I said.

"Why not? Then you can live in the country and fly to work. And listen, boys, one teaspoon of this atomic stuff is so powerful it can air-condition the whole city of New York. Believe me, when you boys grow up, you won't be sitting on hot fire escapes in the middle of the night because your house is like a sweatbox and it's drivin' you crazy."

"Hey, no one's gonna mess with us now!" Herbie said. "If the Nazis or the Japs try anything now—WHAMMO!"

"That's right, boys. That's the best part of it. There'll be no more wars now. There's only three people who can even understand this bomb. Einstein and two other scientists. And they're not gonna tell anyone how to make it." He nodded to my grandfather who passed us on the sidewalk. "I only wish they had it a few years sooner. Then Phil Blumenthal, my friend who lived up in 4C, would still be alive." My uncle was somber suddenly. "Listen. boys, don't ever underestimate the power of America. The Germans and the Japs underestimated us, but we showed 'em. This is a great country and we can do anything if we put our minds to it."

When I went into my apartment, I told my mother and my Aunt Rose about the new bomb.

"... and Uncle Lenny says it can blow up a whole city in one shot!"

"In one shot?" my mother said.

"That's what Uncle Lenny said."

My Aunt Rose giggled and said, "Hey, maybe we can get them to drop it on Rifkin, across the air shaft, when he sings off key with his window open."

—Gerald Rosen, *Growing Up Bronx* (Berkeley, Calif.: North Atlantic Books, 1984).

After the war, The Bronx became a haven where some refugees could once again pick up the lives that had been shattered by the war. Many, however, were unable to do so. In the novel *Enemies, A Love Story*, Nobel Prize–winning Yiddish writer Isaac Bashevis Singer tells the story of Herman, a Holocaust survivor, who was entangled with three women. None of the three knew of the others' existence. Thoughts of the Holocaust years invade his mind on a subway trip to The Bronx to see his mistress, Masha, also called Mushy, and again at the Bronx Zoo.

Herman didn't have to go to his office. Masha was through at noon and he went to the cafeteria to meet her. She was to get her first vacation this summer—one week. She was anxious to go somewhere with him, but where? Herman walked down Tremont Avenue toward the cafeteria. He passed shops selling factory goods, ladies' wear, stationery. Salesmen and saleswomen sat and waited for customers just as in Tzivkev. Chain stores had driven many of the small businesses into bankruptcy. Here and there a for-rent sign hung on the door. There was always someone ready to try his luck again.

Herman entered the cafeteria through the revolving door and saw Masha. There she stood, the daughter of Shifrah Puah, accepting checks, counting money, selling chewing gum and cigarettes. She caught sight of him and smiled. According to the cafeteria clock, Masha had twenty minutes more to work, so Herman sat down at a table. He preferred a table next to the wall or, if possible, in a corner between two walls, so that no one could come up behind him. Despite the big meal he had just eaten, he bought a cup of coffee and some rice pudding at the counter. It seemed impossible for him to put on weight. It was as if a fire in him consumed everything. From a distance, he watched Masha. Although the sun shone through the windows, the electric lights were on. At neighboring tables men were openly reading Yiddish newspapers. They didn't need to hide from anyone. It always seemed like a miracle to Herman. "How long can this last?" he would ask himself.

One of the customers was reading a Communist paper. He probably felt dissatisfied with America, hoped for a revolution, for the masses to swarm into the street, to break the store windows Herman had just passed, and drag the salespeople off to prison or to slave-labor camps. . . .

Mushy finished her work at the cash register, gave the money and the checks to the cashier who was relieving her, and came over to Herman's table with her lunch on a tray. She had slept very little the night before and had awakened early, but she didn't look tired. The usual cigarette hung between her lips, and she had already had quite a few cups of coffee. . . .

"When is your vacation?"

"I'm not sure yet. Come, let's get out of here! You promised to take me to the zoo."

Both Mushy and Herman could walk for miles. Mushy stopped often at store windows. She belittled American luxuries, but she had a keen interest in bargains. Businesses that were closing down might be selling goods at great reductions—sometimes less than half price. For pennies Mushy would buy remnants of fabric from which she made clothes for herself and her mother. She also sewed bedspreads, curtains, even slipcovers for the furniture. But who came to visit her? And where did she go? She had alienated her refugee friends. . . .

They stopped at the Botanical Gardens to look at the flowers, palms, cactuses, the innumerable plants grown in the synthetic climate of hothouses. The thought occurred to Herman that Jewry was a hothouse growth—it was kept thriving in an alien environment nourished by the belief in a Messiah, the hope of justice to come, the promises of the Bible—the book that had hypnotized them forever.

After a while Herman and Mushy continued on to the Bronx Zoo. Its reputation had reached them even in Warsaw. Two polar bears dozed in the shadow of an overhanging ledge by a pool of water, undoubtedly dreaming of snow and icebergs. Each animal and bird conveyed something in its own wordless language, a story handed down from prehistoric times, both revealing and concealing the patterns of continuous creation. The lion slept, and from time to time lazily opened his golden eyes, which expressed the despondency of those who are allowed neither to live nor to die, and with his mighty tail swept away the flies. The wolf paced to and fro, circling his own madness. The tiger sniffed at the flooring, seeking a spot on which to lie down. Two camels stood immobile and proud, a pair of Oriental princes. Herman often compared the zoo to a concentration camp. The air here was full of longing—for deserts, hills, valleys, families. Like the Jews, the animals had been dragged here from all parts of the world, condemned to isolation and boredom. Some of them cried out their woes; others remained mute. Parrots demanded their rights with raucous screeching. A bird with a banana-shaped beak turned its head from right to left as if looking for the culprit who had played this trick on him. Chance? Darwinism? No, there was a plan—or

Polar bear at the Bronx Zoo. A postcard photograph. "Herman and Mushy continued on to the Bronx Zoo. Its reputation had reached them even in Warsaw. Two polar bears dozed in the shadow of an overhanging ledge by a pool of water, undoubtedly dreaming of snow and icebergs." —Isaac Bashevis Singer. The Bronx County Historical Society Research Library.

at least a game played by conscious powers. Herman was reminded by Masha's words about the Nazis in heaven. Wasn't it possible that a Hitler presided on high and inflicted suffering on imprisoned souls? He had equipped them with flesh, blood, teeth, claws, horns, anger. They had either to commit evil or to perish.

—Isaac Bashevis Singer, Enemies, A Love Story
(New York: Doubleday, 1972).

Sadly, most Jewish Bronxites lost loved ones in the Holocaust. They, like other Bronxites, were proud of the country's eventual victory over her enemies in World War II, and were particularly relieved to witness the liberation of Hitler's death camps and release of the survivors, some of whom made new homes in the predominantly Jewish neighborhoods of The Bronx. As the period of peacetime began, most Bronx residents looked forward to the future with eager anticipation. Hunter College finally returned to claim its campus, but even then change was evident. So many servicemen had returned from the war demanding an education that Hunter opened its Bronx campus to males. At the end of the 1940s a new period of prosperity washed over the borough.

7

THE PERILS OF PROSPERITY

THE BRONX IN THE POSTWAR YEARS

1946–1961

FOR MOST AMERICANS, THE POSTWAR YEARS WERE A PERIOD OF unprecedented prosperity. The American Dream for young adults was to get married, have children, buy a car, and move to the suburbs. Like their parents who moved up from the Lower East Side to The Bronx, the postwar generation left the borough. Even those who wanted to stay faced a housing shortage that forced them into other parts of the city and the suburbs.

For youngsters whose families stayed and prospered, the era seemed like the Golden Age of The Bronx as the borough retained its aura of middle-class stability. As in the past, a good education, often free at one of the city colleges or available with tuition paid through the new G.I. Bill, was seen as the route to economic security, and more young Bronxites than ever before availed themselves of it.

Wide-ranging changes occurred during the era. The Marshall Plan rebuilt Europe, the Cold War started, American boys were sent to fight in Korea, Senator Joseph McCarthy of Wisconsin waged a war on Communist spies, a popular Republican, Dwight D. Eisenhower, was twice elected president, and the civil rights movement was born. In The Bronx, Robert Moses, the city's "Master Builder," condemned wide areas to construct "projects," new high-rise, low-income housing developments for the poor, and to build superhighways for the increasing numbers of motorists. With this, even more Bronxites began to move out of the borough. At the same time, large numbers of blacks from the South and Harlem and Puerto Ricans from East Harlem and the island migrated to The Bronx. Despite signs of impending change, the Democratic political clique led by Irish and working-class Jews maintained its grip on the governmental and business life of The Bronx.

The number of black families in The Bronx remained relatively small until the mid-1940s. Sadie Delany recalled relocating to the North Bronx with her sister, Bessie, in their joint memoir, *Having Our Say.*

The first thing we did was to hire a man to put a porch on our little cottage. He laughed at us. He said, "You're going to put a porch on that little old two-room cottage?" And we were very annoyed at him. We said, "Mister, we're from North Carolina and we've been cooped up in apartments since the First World War. Now we've got this cottage out in the country, and where we're from, a house ain't a home unless it got itself a porch!"

The Delany sisters' mother died in 1956 at the age of ninety-five, leaving Sadie as the head of the family. Sadie continues their story. The housing project she mentions is the Gun Hill Houses.

Bessie and I just figured that we should keep on living at the cottage in the Bronx. We didn't have any other plans. But the neighborhood there was not what it had been. Even before Mama died, things had gone downhill.

You see, they put this housing project in. Why, the city had wanted to tear down our little cottage, and put the housing project there. But Bessie and I filed a lawsuit. We asked that they salvage our little cottage, move it across the street. . . .

Anyway, they went and built this silly housing project, with us living right across the street from it. Some of the children from the housing project got into trouble. You can't just take people who don't have anything, don't know what they're doing, pack them in a bunch of buildings, and expect it's going to all work out somehow. No, it brought the neighborhood down.

—Sarah L. Delany and A. Elizabeth Delany with Amy Hill Hearth, *Having Our Say: The Delany Sisters' First 100 Years* (New York: Dell, 1994).

A far larger number of black families relocated to the southern part of the borough. Colin Powell, the future chairman of the Joint Chiefs of Staff, moved with his parents and his sister, Marilyn, from Harlem. They settled in the Hunts Point area of The Bronx in the mid-1940s.

After early years in Harlem and at a couple of other addresses, I grew up largely at 952 Kelly Street in the Hunts Point section of the South Bronx, where my family moved in 1943, when I was six. The 1981 movie *Fort Apache, The Bronx*, starring Paul Newman, takes place in the police precinct where I lived. In the movie, the neighborhood is depicted as an urban sinkhole, block after block of burned-out tenements, garbage-strewn streets, and weed-choked lots, populated by gangs, junkies, pimps, hookers, maniacs, cop killers, and third-generation welfare families—America's inner city nightmare come true. That is not quite the Hunts Point I was raised in, although it was hardly elm trees and picket fences. We kept our doors and windows locked. I remember a steel rod running from the back of our front door to a brace on the floor, so that no one could push open the door. Burglaries were common. Drug use was on the rise. Street fights and knifings occurred. Gangs armed with clubs, bottles, bricks, and homemade .22 caliber zip guns waged turf wars. Yet, crime and violence in those days did not begin to suggest the social breakdown depicted in *Fort Apache, The Bronx*. That was yet to come. When I was growing up in Hunts Point, a certain rough-edged racial tolerance prevailed. And, critically, most families were intact and secure.

We lived in a four-bedroom apartment on the third floor of a four-story brick tenement, two families on each floor, eight families in all. When I stepped out of the door onto Kelly Street, I saw my whole world. You went left three blocks to my grade school, one more block to my junior high school; between the two was a sliver of land where stood St. Margaret's Episcopal Church, our church. A few blocks in the opposite direction was the high school I would later attend. Across the street from us, at number 957, lived my Aunt Gytha and Uncle Alfred Coote. On my way to school, I passed 935 Kelly, where Aunt Lurice and Uncle Vic and their children lived. Farther down, at 932, my godmother, Mable Evadne Brash, called Aunt Vads, and her family lived. And at 867 were Amy and Norman Brash, friends so close they were considered relatives. "Mammale and Pappale" we called them. Don't ask me why the Jewish diminutives, since they were also Jamaicans. Most black families I knew had their roots in Jamaica, Trinidad, or Barbados, or other islands of the West Indies.

The Brashes' nicknames may have reflected the fact that in those days Hunts Point was heavily Jewish, mixed with Irish, Polish, Italian, black, and Hispanic families. The block of Kelly Street next to ours was slightly curved, and the neighborhood had been known for years as "Banana Kelly." We never used the word "ghetto." Ghettos were somewhere in Europe. We lived in tenements. Outsiders often have a sense of New York as big, overwhelming, impersonal, anonymous. Actually, even now it's a collection of neighborhoods where everybody knows everybody's business, the same as in a small town. Banana Kelly was like that. . . .

The South Bronx was an exciting place when I was growing up, and I have never longed for those elms and picket fences. . . .

I have been asked when I first felt a sense of racial identity, when I first understood that I belonged to a minority. In those early years, I had no such sense, because on Banana Kelly there was no majority. Everybody was either a Jew, an Italian, a Pole, a Greek, a Puerto Rican, or, as we said in those days, a Negro. Among my boyhood friends were Victor Ramirez, Walter Schwartz, Manny Garcia, Melvin Klein. The Kleins were the first family in my building to have a television set. Every Tuesday night, we crowded into Mel's living room to watch Milton Berle. On Thursdays we watched *Amos 'n' Andy*. We thought the show was marvelous, the best thing on television. It was another age, and we did not know that we were not supposed to like *Amos 'n' Andy*.

Racial epithets were hurled around Kelly Street. Sometimes they led to fistfights. But it was not "You're inferior—I'm better." The fighting was more like avenging an insult to your team. I was eventually to taste the poison of bigotry, but much later, and far from Banana Kelly.

—Colin L. Powell with Joseph Persico, *My American Journey* (New York: Random House, 1995).

Families from Puerto Rico had been trickling into The Bronx since the early twentieth century. However, cheaper air fares and the availability of well-paying jobs on the mainland during World War II, and the ensuing postwar prosperity, encouraged large numbers of Puerto Ricans to migrate to the mainland. In 1953, Puerto Rican migration peaked. The new migrants vied with blacks for apartments in the Mott Haven and Hunts Point neighborhoods. As in the case of earlier ethnic groups, the hope of a better life in The Bronx clashed with the actuality of poverty. Many Puerto Ricans, arriving from a tropical agricultural society, faced an added burden of having to adjust to the realities of continental urban life. This is shown by award-winning author Nicholasa Mohr, who is of Puerto Rican descent and who grew up in The Bronx, in her short story "A Very Special Pet." It is a tale of the Fernández family, their pet hen, Joncrofo, and their cat, Marilu.

Graciela and Eugenio Fernández had come to the Bronx six years ago and moved into the small apartment. Except for a trip once before to the seaport city of Mayagüez in Puerto Rico, they had never left their tiny village in the mountains. To finance their voyage to New York, Mr. and Mrs. Fernández had sold their small plot of land, the little livestock they had, and their wooden cabin. The sale had provided the fare and expenses for them and their five children. Since then, three more children had been born. City life was foreign to them, and they had to learn everything, even how to get on a subway and travel. Graciela Fernández had been terribly frightened at first of the underground trains, traffic, and large crowds of people. Although she finally adjusted, she still confined herself to the apartment and seldom went out.

She would never complain; she would pray at the small altar she had set up in the kitchen, light her candles and murmur that God would provide and not forget her and her family. She was proud of the fact that they did not have to ask for welfare or home relief, as so many other families did.

"Papi provides for us. We are lucky and we have to thank Jesus Christ," she would say, making the sign of the cross.

Eugenio Fernández had found a job as a porter in one of the large buildings in the garment center in Manhattan. He still held the same job, but he hoped to be promoted someday to freight-elevator operator. In the meantime, he sold newspapers and coffee on the side, ran errands for people in the building, and was always available for extra work. Still, the money he brought home was barely enough to support ten people.

"Someday I'm gonna get that job. I got my eye on it, and Mr. Friedlander, he likes me . . . so we gotta be patient. Besides the increase in salary, my God!—I could do a million things on the side, and we could make a lotta money. Why I could . . ." Mr. Fernández would tell his family this story several times a week.

"Oh, wow! Papi, we are gonna be rich when you get that job!" the children would shriek.

"Can we get a television when we get rich, Papi?" Pablito, the oldest boy, would ask. Nellie, Carmen, and Linda wanted a telephone.

"Everybody on the block got a telephone but us." Nellie, the oldest girl, would speak for them.

The younger children, William, Olgita, and Freddie, would request lots of toys and treats. Baby Nancy would smile and babble happily with everybody.

"We gonna get everything and we gonna leave El Bronx," Mr. Fernández would assure them. "We even gonna save enough to buy our own farm in Puerto Rico—a big one! With lots of land, maybe a hundred acres, and a chicken house, pigs, goats, even a cow. We can plant coffee and some sugar, and have all the fruit trees—mangoes, sweet oranges, everything!" Mr. Fernández would pause and tell the children all about the wonderful food they would eat back home in his village. "All you need to get the farm is a good start."

"We gonna take Joncrofo, right?" the kids would ask. "And Marilu? Her, too?"

"Sure," Mr. Fernández would say good-naturedly, "even Raúl, her husband, when she finds him, eh?" He would wink, laughing. "And Joncrofo don't have to be tied up like a prisoner no more—she could run loose."

It was a dream of Graciela and Eugenio Fernández to go back to their village as owners of their own farm, with the faith that the land would provide for them.

But times were hard. They had not saved a penny for their farm and were deeply in debt. Mrs. Fernández even considered slaughtering the beloved hen, Joncrofo, for dinner, but relented and went back to her daydreams about returning home to Puerto Rico.

—Nicholasa Mohr, "A Very Special Pet," *El Bronx Remembered: A Novella and Stories* (Houston: Arte Público Press, 1986).

Unlike the Fernández family, many Puerto Rican newcomers intended to stay and put down solid roots in The Bronx. In another story by Nicholasa Mohr, "Mr. Mendelsohn," the large Suárez family of Prospect Avenue prospers and begins to climb the socioeconomic ladder as earlier Bronx residents had done. Like many Puerto Ricans, they become friends with their Jewish neighbors. One of them, the elderly Mr. Mendelsohn, first asked Mrs. Suárez to light his stove on the Jewish Sabbath. As their friendship grew, Mr. Mendelsohn became a regular guest at the Suárez Sunday dinner. He frequently falls asleep in their comfortable armchair. He also likes to play the card game War with the children and tells them about how the neighborhood looked when he first arrived in the early years of the century.

"The Bronx has changed. Then, it was the country. That's right! Why, look out the window. You see the elevated trains on Westchester Avenue? Well, there were no trains then. That was once a dirt road. They used to bring cows through there."

"Oh, man!" Georgie and Yvonne both gasped.

"Sure. These buildings were among the first apartment houses to go up. Four stories high, and that used to be a big accomplishment in them days. All that was here was mostly little houses, like you still see here and there. Small farms, woodlands . . . like that."

"Did you see any Indians?" asked Georgie.

"What do you mean Indians?" laughed the old man. "I'm not that old, and this here was not the Wild West." Mr. Mendelsohn saw that the children were disappointed. He added quickly, "But we did have carriages with horses. No cars and lots of horses."

"That's what Mami says they have in Puerto Rico—not like here in El Bronx," said Yvonne.

"Yeah," Georgie agreed. "Papi says he rode a horse when he was a little kid in Puerto Rico. They had goats and pigs and all them things. Man, he was lucky."

"Lucky?" Mr. Mendelsohn shook his head. "You—you are the lucky one today! You got school and a good home and clothes. You don't have to go out to work and support a family like your papa and I had to do, and miss an education. You can learn and be somebody someday."

"Someday," said Yvonne, "we are gonna get a house with a yard and all. Mami says that when Ralphy gets discharged from the Army, he'll get a loan from the government and we can pay to buy a house. You know, instead of rent."

Later, both the Suárez family and Mr. Mendelsohn leave Prospect Avenue, but still maintain contact. The upwardly mobile Suárez family, using Ralphy's G.I. loan, purchase a house in the North Bronx. Mr. Mendelsohn's stand-offish sisters, Jennie and Sarah, place the elderly man in an old-age home. As he unpacks, he looks at a photograph of Tato, the youngest and his favorite of the Suárez children.

They had a nice house around Gun Hill Road someplace, and they had taken him there once. He recalled how exhausted he had been after the long trip. No one had a car, and they had to take a train and buses. Anyway, he was glad he remembered. Now he could let them know he had moved, and tell them all about what happened to the old neighborhood. That's right, they had a telephone now. Yes, he said to himself, let me finish here, then I'll go call them. He continued to put the rest of his belongings away.

Later, the Suárez family swallows a discriminatory remark when they pick up Mr. Mendelsohn at the old-age home to take him for another visit.

Mr. Mendelsohn sat in the lobby holding on to his cane and a cake box. He had told the nurse at the desk that his friends were coming to pick him up this Sunday. He looked eagerly toward the revolving doors. After a short while, he saw Ralphy, Julio, and Georgie walk through into the lobby.

"Deliveries are made in the rear of the building," he heard the nurse at the desk say as they walked toward him.

"These are my friends, Mrs. Read," Mr. Mendelsohn said, standing. "They are here to take me out."

"Oh, well," said the nurse. "All right; I didn't realize. Here he is then. He's been talking about nothing else but this visit." Mrs. Read smiled.

Ralphy nodded, then spoke to Georgie. "Get Mr. Mendelsohn's overcoat."

—Nicholasa Mohr, "Mr. Mendelsohn," *El Bronx Remembered: A Novella and Stories* (Houston: Arte Público Press, 1986).

Sculptures on and around the Mario Merola Bronx County Building, summer 1978. "Public buildings were supported by semi-nude figures, wearing New Deal chitons." —Laura Cunningham. The Bronx County Historical Society Research Library.

For many, postwar relocation to The Bronx led to improved living conditions. This was certainly true of the fictional child Lily and her struggling single mother, Rosie, in Laura Cunningham's novel *Sleeping Arrangements*. After living with relatives, they arrive one day in The Bronx near Yankee Stadium in an area consisting of block upon block of five- and six-story brick apartment houses constructed in the 1920s and 1930s reflecting many styles that had originated in the Old World—Moorish, Tudor, Spanish, Baroque, and Art Deco. Lily falls in love with the "exotic" Bronx and her new and improved sleeping arrangements in apartment 3M.

3M, I saw by hard daylight, was set into a building of schizoid design. While the exterior was blandly modern white brick, the interior was decorated in a style that might be called Babylonian Bronx. In the lobby, murals depicted scenes of Dionysian excess, and mosaic maidens walked a deluded diagonal along the walls toward the mailboxes. The mood and the maidens came to a dead halt at the elevator door. From there, it was a short ride from Babylonia-in-the-Bronx to seven stories of "worker" housing cubicles that could easily fit into Stalingrad. The housewives of AnaMor Towers pushed their wire grocery carts across marble lobby floors, rode the "ionic" elevator up to "junior fours."

. . . I soon discovered the other little girls in AnaMor Towers were deeply indebted to pagan ritual for routine play. How could we avoid it? Every AnaMorite had to pass a frieze of Pompeii on the way to the incinerator.

AnaMor Towers did not stand alone. The entire neighborhood was a cross-section of ersatz bygone cultures. In the park, marble mermaids lounged, with rust running down their navels. Public buildings were supported by semi-nude figures, wearing New Deal chitons. Many of the apartment buildings were modern Towers of Babel, mixing details from Ancient Rome, Syria, Greece. (In retrospect, one wonders if the Jews who designed these edifices were paying some delayed tribute to ancient enemies.)

On my way to kindergarten, I saw that the neighborhood became increasingly extraordinary. There was something inhuman in the scale of the streets. The avenues seemed overly wide, suitable only for mass invasion. The main thoroughfare, Grand Concourse, was a reproduction of the Champs Élysées, with the substitution of Yankee Stadium for the Arc de Triomphe.

The old stadium dominated the area in more than a merely physical way. Built for ritual on a major scale, the arena cast a spiritual net that extended for at least ten blocks. (My mother and I soon discovered that AnaMor Towers, a few streets from the stadium, stood on a baseball fault zone. The building reverberated with collective roars of victory or groans of defeat. Twinight double-headers cast an insomniac glow into our efficiency, and night after night my mother and I would lie sleepless, bathed in violet light, listening to megaphoned moans of "It's a homer! It's a homer!")

> —Laura Cunningham, *Sleeping Arrangements*
> (New York: Alfred A. Knopf, 1989).

In the still largely Jewish Bronx, the creation of the state of Israel engendered pride, and the nation's economic upturn led many Jews who were normally solidly aligned with the Democratic Party to desert and vote for Dwight D. Eisenhower in 1952. Gerald Rosen satirized both Cold War conformity and the new prosperity in the borough in his memoir, *Growing Up Bronx*.

> In the years 1945 through 1948 the world was generally good to people in our neighborhood. The boys were home, the peacetime economy began to be rebuilt, Western Europe began to be rebuilt, and the Yankees began to be rebuilt.
>
> 1948 was perhaps the best year of all. Of course, the Yankees finished

sadly out of the money, but this was compensated for by the founding of the
state of Israel. Everyone flew little blue and white flags with the Jewish star on
them and things appeared to be going our way.

Even my father seemed relatively content. He continued to work hard
after the war and then, in 1948, he bought a partnership in a liquor store....
In those days, for a person of our class, owning a liquor store was the equiv-
alent of a medical degree for people on a higher social stratum....

My Uncle Lenny bought them. The General Eisenhower ties. They were
maroon with three pictures of General Eisenhower on them and under each,
"I LIKE IKE." He gave me one and I wore it often.

Most of the people in our neighborhood were backing Ike as opposed to
Adlai Stevenson. Ike had "taken care of our boys" in World War Two and he
would take care of us now. He had stood up to Hitler and he would stand up
to Joe Stalin.

—Gerald Rosen, *Growing Up Bronx* (Berkeley,
Calif.: North Atlantic Books, 1984).

With the increasing prosperity of the time, middle-class Bronx families could
afford to purchase annual memberships in Shorehaven Beach Club located near
Long Island Sound on the upper East River. It had a cruciform salt-water pool, varied athletic facilities, a cafeteria, an outdoor stage for shows, and a river view. Poet
Gayl Teller was a member there for twenty-five years, and it played an important
role for three generations of her family. This is shown in her poem "Nets." Paul is the
author's son, and "my basketball star–accountant" became her husband. Moishe's
was a supermarket chain that sold ethnic Jewish foods.

> Summer was not official until the nets were raised,
> like Old Glory over our heads on the volleyball courts,
> stretched and spined across tennis greens,
> hitched to wave and droop from basketball hoops.
>
> draped across the ping-pong tables, colorfully
> restored like hope at the outset of each endeavor
> to grapple against the squash walls. We raised the nets
> so we could defy them without pulling them down.
>
> *Net ball! Do over. You touched the net! You're out!*
> *You were over the net! Under the net! Yanked the net!*
> *You're out! You're out! You're out!* Net tenets
> All knots sometimes, but sometimes all air,

where you found yourself moving through. For nets
cast shadows full of holes that caught the sun
of our striving. A laying of hands for a swift-
skimming slam just atop the volleyball net. . . .

We loved our nets, their magnanimous lets,
the erratic skips the ball like a heartbeat made
off the rim tipped into the granting a second chance.
Women wore them with sparkles in their hair
to wink as the stars of their striving at the dance

on Saturday nights, or they did themselves out
in fishnet stockings to catch transcendence,
often left with nettled legs. Outdoing herself
and Moishe's in a fishnet bag, mom packed

her homeground liver, her secret airiness—
a few Ritz crackers. We netted our lifelines out
on graph paper, studying for finals in June,
our scribbles what we caught in our looseleafs

from immense fleets of words with our clumsy nets
of understanding. Sprawled across the blanket
and each other in our shifting friendship network,
we read our fishy shadows of Plato, Melville, Bio.

Let there be A's in those boxes! Let there be
a white veil between us, me and my basketball star–
accountant, a switch hitter of net swishes
and net worth, and when we cast our mosquito nets

across Paul's carriage, *Let there be light*
but no stinger strong enough to tear that net
nor small enough to slip through, I prayed
to the sieve of the universe, under the sycamores,

their leafy nets so fine they could enmesh the sun
and keep their game going over our heads
all summerlong, as they did long ago, over the heads
of the Indian fishermen chanting *Let there be*

fish and favor by the spirits, as they cast out
their nets on the Sound, on this very ground
of our Shorehaven, where shared nets of knowing
caught us and knit us together to this place.

—Gayl Teller, "Nets," *Shorehaven* (Lewiston, N.Y.:
The Mellen Poetry Press, 1996).

The rising tide of prosperity engendered new desires. The American Dream no longer consisted of residing in a spacious apartment near parks and abundant public transportation. Now people could afford cars, and the new highway could lead them out of the city and The Bronx to the suburbs, where they could purchase their own homes through new federal programs. Gil Fagiani remembered growing up in the Bedford Park area of the northwestern Bronx and his family's later migration to the suburbs.

I lived the first five years of my life in a three-story apartment building on 204th Street, a block away from the Villa Avenue neighborhood. The heart of the neighborhood consisted of half a dozen city blocks filled with wood frame houses and tenements, interspersed with small shops that catered to the tastes of the mainly Southern Italian residents. A jeweler and shoe repair shop, along with a bread store, bars, restaurants, groceries, and butcher shop served the small community.

Around the corner on the Grand Concourse rose St. Philip Neri Catholic Church, a turn-of-the-century, gray stone structure, where until after World War II, masses were said in Italian. I remember my mother's words, "The church was built by Italian laborers but taken over by wealthy Irish parishioners." Much of the community's social life centered around activities sponsored by the church. Especially notable were the *festa* of Saint Anthony celebrated in June, and the *festa* of Saint Assunta celebrated in August, which were accompanied by colorful street parades, including marching bands, along the Concourse.

Villa Avenue had a brief moment of glory in the late 40's when a teenage boy claimed he saw the Madonna. My uncle Charlie remembers the Grand Concourse being jammed with thousands of people, forcing the police to close down a section of the city's second-widest boulevard. The people came seeking supernatural solace for their physical ailments and personal problems, or perhaps out of curiosity. Some claimed miraculous cures, while others reported seeing a halo in the sky. Today, next to a tall apartment building, can still be found a small shrine commemorating the vision.

Sweet and haunting memories remain of Villa Avenue. I remember entering St. Philip Neri with my grandmother being awed by the towering ceiling, the gleaming marble, and the smell of incense, or going with her to visit nearby family, friends, and amiable fruit and vegetable vendors. My biggest thrill was walking hand in hand with her under the colored lights of the summer street *feste* and eating tangy lemon ices.

In 1950, my father took advantage of a V.A. loan and bought a house in Springdale, Connecticut. . . .

I had mixed feelings about the move. I enjoyed the greater freedom that living in a house and frolicking in the countryside gave me, but I missed my mother's extended family, and their warm, friendly neighborhood.

—Gil Fagiani, "East Harlem and Vito Marcantonio: My Search for a Progressive Italian-American Identity," *Voices in Italian-America* (Fall 1994).

Beneath the facade of prosperity and good times, however, both personal and societal problems, previously kept secret, began to be revealed in the increasingly candid literature of the era. Pulitzer Prize–winning author Frank Gilroy, in his play about a Bronx Irish-American family, *The Subject Was Roses*, explored the problems of alcoholism and domestic abuse. In the play, later made into a motion picture, the Cleary family welcomes home their son, Timmy, from World War II. Timmy has developed a drinking problem in the service. His return exacerbates a conflict between John, his father, and Nettie, his mother. Trying to patch things up between his parents, Timmy buys Nettie roses, but tells her that they came from John. However, John lets it slip that he did not purchase them. After one cruel exchange on a Sunday morning, Nettie leaves. Later that Sunday night, she still has not returned. Timmy is drunk, and his self-pitying father is worried over Nettie's disappearance. They argue.

JOHN Do you have any idea how I looked forward to this morning? To Mass, and dropping in at Rafferty's afterwards with you in your uniform?

TIMMY Always the injured party.

JOHN You'll be the injured party in about two minutes.

TIMMY I already am.

JOHN Real rough you had it. Good food. Good clothes. Always a roof over your head.

TIMMY Heigh-ho, everybody, it's count-your-blessings time.

JOHN I'll tell you what rough is—being so hungry you begged. Being thrown out in the street with your few sticks of furniture for all the neighbors to enjoy. Never sleeping in bed with less than two other people. Always hiding from collectors. Having to leave school at the age of ten because your

father was crippled for life and it was your job to support the house . . .
had it rough, all right.

TIMMY   The subject was roses.

JOHN   Where I couldn't have gone with your advantages . . . What I couldn't
have been.

TIMMY   I still want to know why you told her about the roses.

JOHN   We were having words and it slipped out.

TIMMY   Words about what? . . . Well?

JOHN   Stop pushing or I'll tell you.

TIMMY   Go on! Go on!

JOHN   *The humping I'm getting is not worth the humping I'm getting.*

TIMMY   (*Rising*) You pig.

JOHN   I'm warning you!

TIMMY   *You pig.* (JOHN's *right hand shoots out, catches* TIMMY *hard across the
side of his face.*)

> —Frank D. Gilroy, *The Subject Was Roses*, in *About
> Those Roses or How Not to Do a Play and Succeed:
> and the Text of "The Subject Was Roses"* (New York:
> Random House, 1965).

Like Timmy, other Bronxites after the war had to cope with personal and family problems. Using the new medium of television, Paddy Chayefsky, in the teleplay *Marty*, later made into a film that won Ernest Borgnine the Oscar, explored the problems of a socially backward Bronx Italian butcher who still lived at home with his controlling mother. Marty, an ordinary man, struggled for his identity. He meets with his friends in a neighborhood Bronx bar, as usual, to decide what to do that night.

CRITIC: What's playing on Fordham Road? I think there's a good picture in
the Loew's Paradise.

ANGIE: Let's go down to Forty-second Street and walk around. We're sure to
wind up with something.

Slowly Marty begins to look up again. He looks from face to face as each speaks.

CRITIC: I'll never forgive La Guardia for cutting burlesque outta New York
City.

TWENTY-YEAR-OLD: There's burlesque over in Union City. Let's go to Union
City. . . .

ANGIE: Ah, they're always crowded on Sunday night.

CRITIC: So wadda you figure on doing tonight, Angie?

ANGIE: I don't know. [*Turns to the twenty-year-old.*] Wadda you figure on doing?

The twenty-year-old shrugs.

Suddenly Marty brings his fist down on the booth table with a crash. The others turn, startled, toward him. Marty rises in his seat.

MARTY: "What are you doing tonight?" "I don't know, what are you doing?" Burlesque! Loew's Paradise! Miserable and lonely! Miserable and lonely and stupid! What am I, crazy or something?! I got something good! What am I hanging around you guys for?!

He has said this in tones so loud that it attracts the attention of everyone in the bar. A little embarrassed, Marty turns and moves quickly to the phone booth, pausing outside the door to find his dime again.

Marty finally summons up the courage to repudiate his friends' opinions on the worth of women based on looks to pursue a plain woman he likes.

> —Paddy Chayefsky, "Marty," *Television Plays* (New York: Simon and Schuster, 1955).

Despite the general postwar prosperity of The Bronx, some struggled. These included members of the German-American family of poet Richard Foerster. Young Foerster grew up in the Norwood section in a superintendent's basement apartment, with its access to the back yard. He described his experiences there, and the hard and dirty job of stoking the coal-burning furnace, work shouldered by his mother, in his poem "The Superintendents of 3152 Hull Avenue."

> In that basement apartment of first memories
> I looked out of a skeletal whale,
> the ribbed cage of my bed, out through
> a deep-silled window, into midday
> caught as a brief slant of sunlight.
> There in the narrow sunken yard she'd send
> me out to play beside the rough
> foundation stones, which even now,
> just one of memory's ruins, seem colossal.
> The only colors were the blue straight up
> and the persistent sumacs' green that sprang
> from any crevice in those walls and hung

in midair, exotic as tropical palms
to a Bronx boy. My father hacked off all
that he could reach, as if grayness were
a virtue he could never quite perfect.
Instead, it was my mother who completed
those walls, gave them their lasting texture,
granular and oily, as soot will be:
Wandering back inside from play,
I found her, in a cavern heaped with coal,
stooped before open iron doors, feeding shovel
by shovel her secret uncontainable god.

> —Richard Foerster, "The Superintendents of 3152 Hull Avenue," *Sudden Harbor* (Alexandria, Va.: Ochises Press, 1992).

Like family dysfunction, poverty, and alcoholism, mental illness, formerly considered shameful and kept secret, became a controversial literary subject. Beat poet Allen Ginsberg, in "Kaddish," the Hebrew word for the prayer for the dead, boldly confronts how his mother's deteriorating mental state forced him, reluctantly and with great anguish, to commit her to an institution where she stayed for most of the remainder of her days.

At the time, his Aunt Elanor, his mother's sister, and her husband, Max, lived on Rochambeau Avenue in the Norwood section of The Bronx. The aging sisters had been ardent communists before the war and Naomi, Ginsberg's mother, felt comfortable in the borough's Leftist climate. After Naomi separated from Louis, her husband and Allen's father, she moved often. Eventually, she relocated to The Bronx to live with Edie, Max's sister, who agreed to take her in despite her own failing health. Edie lived in the same building as Elanor and Max. Eugene is Ginsberg's brother; "Dr. Isaac" was briefly Naomi's male companion.

Ginsberg uses some Hebrew words in the poem. *Shema Y'Israel* is the beginning of the basic Jewish declaration that God is One, while *Svul Avrum* is Ginsberg's Hebrew name. *Buba* is the Yiddish word for grandmother.

> . . . But then went half mad—Hitler in her room, she saw his moustache in the sink—afraid of Dr. Isaac now, suspected that he was in on the Newark plot—went up to Bronx to live near Elanor's Rheumatic Heart—. . . .
>
> Max's sister Edie works—17 years bookkeeper at Gimbels—lived downstairs in apartment house, divorced—so Edie took in Naomi on Rochambeau Ave—

Woodlawn Cemetery across the street, vast dales of graves where Poe once—Last stop on Bronx subway—lots of communists in that area.

Who enrolled for painting classes at night in Bronx Adult High School—walked alone under Van Cortlandt Elevated line to class—paints Naomi-isms—

Humans sitting on the grass in some Camp No-Worry summers yore—saints with droopy faces and long ill-fitting pants, from hospital—

Brides in front of Lower East Side with short grooms—lost El train running over the Babylonian apartment rooftops in the Bronx—

Sad paintings—but she expressed herself. Her mandolin gone, all strings broke in her head, she tried. Toward beauty? or some old life Message?

But started kicking Elanor, and Elanor had heart trouble—came upstairs and asked her about Spydom for hours,—Elanor frazzled. Max away at office, accounting for cigar stores till at night.

'I am a great woman—am truly a beautiful soul—and because of that they (Hitler, Grandma, Hearst, the Capitalists, Franco, Daily News, the '20s, Mussolini, the living dead) want to shut me up—Buba's the head of a spider network—'

Kicking the girls, Edie & Elanor—Woke Edie at midnite to tell her she was a spy and Elanor a rat. Edie worked all day and couldn't take it—She was organizing the union.—And Elanor began dying, upstairs in bed.

The relatives call me up, she's getting worse—I was the only one left—Went on the subway with Eugene to see her, ate stale fish—

'My sister whispers in the radio—Louis must be in the apartment—his mother tells him what to say—LIARS!—I cooked for my two children—I played the mandolin—'

Last night the nightingale woke me / Last night when all was still / it sang in the golden moonlight / from on the wintry hill. She did.

I pushed her against the door and shouted 'DON'T KICK ELANOR!'—she stared at me—Contempt—die—disbelief her sons are so naive, so dumb—'Elanor is the worst spy! She's taking orders!'

'— No wires in the room!'—I'm yelling at her—last ditch, Eugene listening on the bed—what can he do to escape that fatal Mama—'You've been away from Louis years already—Grandma's too old to walk—'. . . .

I've seen your grave! O strange Naomi! My own—cracked grave! Shema Y'Israel—I am Svul Avrum—you—in death?

Your last night in the darkness of the Bronx—I phonecalled—thru hospital to secret police

that came, when you and I were alone, shrieking at Elanor in my ear—
who breathed hard in her own bed, got thin—

Nor will forget, the doorknock, at your fright of spies,—I saw advancing,
on my honor—Eternity entering the room—you running to the bathroom
undressed, hiding in protest from the last heroic fate—

Staring at my eyes, betrayed—the final cops of madness rescuing me—
from your foot against the broken heart of Elanor,

your voice at Edie weary of Gimbels coming home to broken radio—and
Louis needing a poor divorce, he wants to get married soon—Eugene dreaming, hiding at 125 St., suing negroes for money on crud furniture, defending
black girls—

Protests from the bathroom—Said you were sane—dressing in a cotton
robe, your shoes, then new, your purse and newspaper clippings—no—your
honesty—

as you vainly made your lips more real with lipstick, looking in the mirror to see if the Insanity was Me or a carful of police.

Or Grandma spying at 78—Your vision—Her climbing over the walls of
the cemetery with political kidnapper's bag—or what you saw on the walls of
the Bronx, in pink nightgown at midnight, staring out the window on the
empty lot—

Ah Rochambeau Ave.—Playground of Phantoms—last apartment in the
Bronx for spies—last home for Elanor or Naomi, here these communist sisters lost their revolution—

'All right—put on your coat Mrs.—let's go—We have the wagon downstairs—you want to come with her to the station?'

The ride then—held Naomi's hand, and held her head to my breast, I'm
taller—kissed her and said I did it for the best—Elanor sick—and Max with
heart condition—Needs—

To me—'Why did you do this?'—'Yes Mrs., your son will have to leave
you in an hour'—The Ambulance

came in a few hours—drove off at 4 A.M. to some Bellevue in the night
downtown—gone to the hospital forever. I saw her led away—she waved,
tears in her eyes. . . .

—Allen Ginsberg, "Kaddish," *Collected Poems:*
1947–1980 (New York: Harper & Row, 1984).

Another troubled Bronx resident was the future assassin of John F. Kennedy,
Lee Harvey Oswald, who, as a teenager, moved from the South to the Tremont
neighborhood near the Bronx Zoo. Oswald's tormented Bronx sojourn was imagi-

natively re-created by Don DeLillo in his novel *Libra*. He began with the boy's mother's move to The Bronx and Lee's school truancy.

> She'd found three rooms on one hundred and something street, near the Bronx Zoo, which might be nice for a growing boy with an interest in animals. . . .
>
> It was a railroad flat in a brick-red tenement, five stories, in a street of grim exhibits. A retarded boy about Lee's age walked around in a hippy-hop limp, carrying a live crab he'd stolen from the Italian market and pushing it in the faces of smaller kids. This was a routine sight. Rock fights were routine. Guys with zip guns they'd made in shop class were becoming routine. From his window one night he watched two boys put the grocery store cat in a burlap sack and swing the sack against a lamppost. He tried to time his movements against the rhythm of the street. Stay off the street from noon to one, three to five. Learn the alleys, use the dark. He rode the subways. He spent serious time at the zoo. . . .
>
> . . . The zoo was three blocks away. There were traces of ice along the fringes of the wildfowl pond. He walked down to the lion house, hands deep in his jacket pockets. No one there. The smell hit him full-on, a warmth and a force, the great carnivore reek of raw beef and animal fur and smoky piss.
>
> When he heard the heavy doors open, the loud voices, he knew what to expect. Two kids from P.S. 44. A chunky kid named Scalzo in a pea coat and clacking shoes with a smaller, runny-nose comedian Lee knew only by his street name, which was Nicky Black. Here to pester the animals, create the routine disturbances that made up their days. He could feel their small joy as they spotted him, a little jump of muscle in the throat. Scalzo's voice banged through the high chamber.
>
> "They call your name every day in class. But what kind of name is Lee? That's a girl's name or what?"

> Later, Lee, who was seldom in school, was picked up by a truant officer and sent for psychiatric evaluation. He was found to be intelligent, but also remote and unreachable. His truancy increased. As a young adult the real Lee Harvey Oswald was attracted to the communist philosophy of the Soviet Union.
>
> —Don DeLillo, *Libra* (New York: Viking, 1988).

Many Bronxites had been dedicated to leftist causes for decades. The often unfounded charges of a communist conspiracy to overthrow the United States government begun by Senator Joseph McCarthy led to genuine fear among those who might have been suspected of liberal, socialist, or communist leanings. In E. L. Doctorow's novel (later made into a motion picture) *The Book of Daniel*, the national hysteria caused by McCarthyism burst upon a tranquil Bronx scene. The narrator, Daniel, the son of Paul and Rochelle Isaacson, often referred to himself in the third person. The fictional Isaacsons resemble Julius and Ethel Rosenberg of Manhattan who were executed for giving atomic secrets to the Soviet Union. Faye Emerson was a familiar television personality of the era. The fictional Mindish was a Jewish communist friend.

I went along the school fence to 174th Street, then down 174th Street still along the school fence, to Eastburn Avenue; across Eastburn; and another block past the shoemaker, the dairy, Irving's Fish Market, Spotless Cleaner, to Morris Avenue; across Morris; and in the middle of the block right between the candy store I didn't like, and Berger's Barber Shop, was Isaacson Radio, Sales and Repair.

A crowd had formed in front of his father's radio store.

There is no tension in the scene. It is a social occasion. It is the first television set to come to 174th Street, and it is sitting there in the window of Isaacson Radio, Sales and Repair, a great brown console, beaming its tiny moving pictures to the curious crowd.

I could have watched my mother's face at the moment she understood this. But I was pushing forward for a glimpse of Faye Emerson. I doubt if her face softened with relief. I doubt if she smiled at the foolishness of her foreboding.

My father came out of the store and worked his way through the group of people standing there, and ignoring him as he jostled through them. He did not have a coat on, only his shirt with the sleeves rolled up and his work apron with its pockets for tools. He took my mother's arm and together they walked a few feet away from the edge of the gathering, she still pushing the stroller.

"Where did you get that?" Rochelle said.

"It was on order. Listen—"

"Can we take it home?" I asked him.

"Just a minute, Danny. Let me talk to your mother. Mindish has been arrested."

"What!"

"Keep your voice down. Early this morning while he was eating breakfast. The FBI came and took him downtown."

"Oh, my God—"

"Don't say anything to anyone. Go about your business and let everything remain the same. I'll be home for supper, and then we'll talk."

Some days later, terror came to the Isaacson home. There was a knock on the door.

When Daniel opened the door, there stood the two FBI agents. Tom Davis and John Bradley. Behind them, across the street, frost in the crotches of the chain link fence of the schoolyard shone in the early morning sun like stars in Daniel's eyes.

"Hi, Danny. Is your Dad at home?"

"What is it, Daniel?" his mother called from the living room.

"It's those two men," Daniel replied.

Daniel and the FBI men listened to the sounds of his mother waking up his father. Daniel still held the doorknob. He was ready to close the door the second he was told to.

"What time is it?" said his father in a drugged voice.

"Oh my God it's six-thirty," his mother said.

She came into the hallway, pulling on her robe. Her long nightgown was thin cotton and Daniel panicked for a second because you could see the tips of her breasts through the material until she wrapped the robe around her and tied the belt. He glanced at the two men in the door to see if they saw, but there was nothing in their faces.

"Morning, Mrs. Isaacson. Can we come in?". . .

Either my mother nodded that they could come in, or they took her silence as permission. I know she would have been anxious to keep the cold out. They walked through the door and immediately there was an electric charge of life just outside, and right behind them came another man, then two more, then a few more, all warmly dressed and well tailored for the harsh autumn morning, a dozen FBI men, all told, bringing into our little splintery house all the chill of the outdoors on their bulky shoulders. They poured through the front door like an avalanche of snow.

"What is it now!" my mother shouted.

"Rochelle!" my father called.

I looked outside. Five or six sedans were double-parked along the street. Another car was pulling up. Two more of the G-men stood on the sidewalk. Another was going down the alley to come in through the basement. In my ears was the crackle of a turned-up police radio.

My father was shown the warrant for his arrest as he sat on his hide-a-bed with his bare feet on the floor. He groped around for his glasses. He told my mother he felt suddenly nauseous, and she had him bend over with his head between his knees till the feeling went away. She was furious.

"What are these men doing here?" she said to Bradley and Davis. "Do you think you've got John Dillinger? What are you doing?" Men were going through the bookshelves, the bedclothes, the mahogany wardrobe closet. Men were marching upstairs. . . .

"Murderers!" my mother cried. "Maniacs! Haven't you hounded us enough? Can't you leave us alone?"

She did not appear to realize that my father had been arrested.

> —E. L. Doctorow, *The Book of Daniel* (New York: Random House, 1971).

The arrogance of government power was also evident in the actions of Robert Moses, who combined in his person the leadership of several state and city agencies and independent authorities to create a network of superhighways. One of its elements, the Cross-Bronx Expressway, cut a wide swath through densely populated neighborhoods filled with apartment houses. The reaction in The Bronx was recounted by Marshall Berman in *All That Is Solid Melts into Air*.

In the spring and fall of 1953, Moses began to loom over my life in a new way: he proclaimed that he was about to ram an immense expressway, unprecedented in scale, expense and difficulty of construction, through our neighborhood's heart. At first, we couldn't believe it; it seemed to come from another world. First of all, hardly any of us owned cars: the neighborhood itself, and the subways leading downtown, defined the flow of our lives. Besides, even if the city needed the road—or was it the state that needed the road? (in Moses' operations, the location of power and authority was never clear, except for Moses himself)—they surely couldn't mean what the stories seemed to say: that the road would be blasted directly through a dozen solid, settled, densely populated neighborhoods like our own; that something like 60,000 working- and lower-middle-class people, mostly Jews, but with many Italians, Irish and Blacks thrown in, would be thrown out of their homes. The Jews of the Bronx were nonplussed: could a fellow-Jew really want to do this to us? (We had little idea of what kind of Jew he was, or of how much we were all an obstruction in his path.) And even if he did want to do it, we were sure it couldn't happen here, not in America. We were still basking in the afterglow of the New Deal: the government was *our* government, and it would

Construction of the Cross-Bronx Expressway in the 1950s. "The road would be blasted directly through a dozen solid, settled, densely populated neighborhoods like our own." —Marshall Berman. The Bronx County Historical Society Research Library.

come through to protect us in the end. And yet, before we knew it, steam shovels and bulldozers were there, and people were getting notice that they had better clear out fast. They looked numbly at the wreckers, at the disappearing streets, at each other, and they went. Moses was coming through, and no temporal or spiritual power could block his way.

For ten years, through the late 1950s and early 1960s, the center of the Bronx was pounded and blasted and smashed. My friends and I would stand on the parapet of the Grand Concourse, where 174th Street had been, and survey the work's progress—the immense steam shovels and bulldozers and timber and steel beams, the hundreds of workers in their variously colored hard hats, the giant cranes reaching far above the Bronx's tallest roofs, the dynamite blasts and tremors, the wild, jagged crags of rock newly torn, the vistas of devastation stretching for miles to the east and west as far as the eye could see—and marvel to see our ordinary nice neighborhood transformed into sublime, spectacular ruins.

—Marshall Berman, *All That Is Solid Melts into Air:*
The Experience of Modernity (New York: Simon and
Schuster, 1982).

Increasing numbers of Jews left The Bronx. Paralleling the decline in the borough's Jewish population was the waning use of Yiddish by younger, assimilated Jews who had grown up speaking English as their primary language. However, many of them never lost consciousness of their ethnic identity, and sprinkled their speech with Yiddish expressions. Irena Klepfisz's poem "*Der mames shabosim*/My Mother's Sabbath Days" illustrates this phenomenon. The poem was written in English with Yiddish and Polish words interspersed in it. *Erev shabes* is Hebrew and Yiddish for Friday evening; *fraytik* is Yiddish for Friday, while the day is called *pjontek* in Polish; and *treyf* is both Yiddish and Hebrew for unkosher food.

> So for us it was different. *Erev shabes* was plain *fraytik*
> or more precisely: *pjontek*.　I remember　summer evenings
> I'd wait for her　at the Mosholu stop of the Lexington line.
> Bright heat and light　at 6 o'clock.　She was full

Jerome Avenue between Mosholu Parkway and Gun Hill Road, 1973. "All the way up Jerome Avenue we'd walk past the Jewish deli / where we never ate." —Irena Klepfisz. The Bronx County Historical Society Research Library, Ralph Marx Collection.

of tales   of Miss Kant   the designer   a career woman
longing for home and family   in love with a handsome pilot
of Scottie   the model   who married smart   a wealthy buyer
and now sat brazenly chic   in a reform synagogue.
I listened   eager to understand   these widow tales   of romance
amid the rush of   each season's showing   and once   even
saw   on a page of the *Times*   a mannequin   dressed in
the very gown   Mamma Lo had made.

All the way up Jerome Avenue   we'd walk   past the Jewish deli
where we never ate   (what was the point if you could make it at home?)
past the pizza place   where occasionally   while shopping   she'd buy me
a slice   past the outdoor groceries   fruit stands   fabric   shoes
lingerie   and stationery stores—till Gun Hill Road   and Jade Garden.
Perhaps I knew it was *treyf*.   She certainly did
but was not concerned.   We'd order   the salty wonton soup
chow mein   or pepper steak   and though she mocked the food
she never resisted.
It was Friday.   The shop was closed.   We'd eat dinner and like the rich
lean leisurely back in our booth.   I didn't know it was *erev shabes*.
Still—she rested.

> —Irena Klepfisz, "*Der mames shabosim*/My
> Mother's Sabbath Days," *Gesher-Bridge: Feminist
> Newsletter of New Jewish Agenda* (July 1989).

Another postwar phenomenon was the emergence of a new media-driven teenage culture. Many houses of worship used their gathering halls to stage weekend dances for teenagers. Bill Fullham describes his experience of Friday night dances at St. Nicholas of Tolentine Church on Fordham Road and University Avenue.

The dress code was as strict as any nun's. Jackets and ties for the boys and skirts (no one ever wore a dress) for the girls. The fable of "black patent leather shoes" and the admonition regarding their reflective qualities was never raised. No sneakers. Definitely no jeans (see dungarees). Anyone who has undergone an inspection in the military will have some idea what entry to the dance was like. . . .

Each boy developed a style. Right hand high or low (not too low). Left hand holding hers, either wrapped around or intertwined. Most girls, accustomed to the awkward moves of these newfound partners, would, within reason, allow the gentlemen to make decisions in these areas.

However, if the style of dance was of such that children might result (the Arthur Fonzarelli-drape-yourself-all-over-the-lady style), one could always expect a visit from the chaperone. These volunteer parents were trained by the fiercest nuns and priests to assume that each male participant was a raging inferno of lust and the object of his interest was the chaperone's daughter.

Various clever phrases were employed to separate the offenders. "Let's leave room for the Holy Ghost" or "A little too close there." These admonitions were embarrassing for the girls but a point of pride for the guys. "Hey! Did you guys see that? Old Mr. McBride had to pry us apart with a crowbar."

—Bill Fullham, "Friday Night Dances," *Back in The Bronx* (vol. 7, issue 25, n.d.).

Whether dressed in bright, flashy colors, such as shocking pink or chartreuse, or in black leather jackets and blue jeans, the teenagers of the era readily embraced the new rock 'n' roll music to help set them apart from their elders. A new form of popular music took root in The Bronx. Small groups of teens gathered in hallways, schools, basements, and alleys to sing a cappella in mellow harmonies of such adolescent problems as young love. Morris High School became a center for young black singing groups who favored rhythm and blues music, while the Italian Americans of the Belmont neighborhood created the doo-wop style. As disk jockeys promoted the new music on radio and television, record companies scouted The Bronx for new talent. Janice Eidus, in her short story "Vito Loves Geraldine," tells of a fictional teenage girl's attraction to the lead singer in a Bronx-based doo-wop group.

Vito Venecio was after me. He'd wanted to get into my pants ever since the tenth grade. But even though we hung around with the same crowd back at Evander Childs High School, I never gave him the time of day. I, Geraldine Rizzoli, was the most popular girl in the crowd. I had my pick of the guys, you can ask anyone, Carmela or Pamela or Victoria, and they'll agree. And Vito was just a skinny little kid with a big greasy pompadour and a cowlick and acne and a big space between his front teeth. True, he could sing, and he and Vinny Feruge and Bobby Colucci and Richie DeSoto formed a doo-wop group and called themselves Vito and the Olinvilles, but lots of the boys formed doo-wop groups and stood around on street corners doo-wopping their hearts out. Besides, I wasn't letting any of them in my pants either.

Carmela and Pamela and Victoria and all the other girls in the crowd would say, "Geraldine Rizzoli, teach me how to tease my hair as high as yours and how to put my eyeliner on so straight and thick," but I never gave away my secrets. I just set my black hair on beer cans every night and in the morning I teased it and teased it with my comb until sometimes I imagined that if I kept going I could get it high enough to reach the stars, and then I would spray it with hairspray that smelled like red roses and then I'd stroke on my black eye liner until it went way past my eyes.

The kids in my crowd were the type who cut classes, smoked in the bathroom, and cursed. Yeah, even the girls cursed, and we weren't the type who went to church on Sundays, which drove our mothers crazy. Vito was one of the worst of us all. He just about never read a book or went to class, and I think his mother got him to set foot in the church maybe once the whole time he was growing up. I swear, it was some sort of a holy miracle that he actually got his diploma.

. . . But when Vito and the Olinvilles got themselves an agent and cut a record, *Teenage Heartbreak*, which Vito wrote, I started to see that Vito was different than I'd thought, different than the other boys. Because Vito had an artistic soul. Then, on graduation night, just a week after Vito and the Olinvilles recorded *Teenage Heartbreak*, I realized that, all these years, I'd been in love with him, too, and was just too proud to admit it because he was a couple of inches shorter than me, and he had that acne and the space between his teeth. There I was, ready for the prom, all dressed up in my bright red prom dress and my hair teased higher than ever, waiting for my date, but my date wasn't Vito, it was Sally-Boy Reticliano, and I wanted to jump out of my skin. About halfway through the prom, I couldn't take it any more and I said, "Sally-Boy, I'm sorry but I've just got to go over and talk to Vito.". . . I spotted him standing alone in a corner. He was wearing a tux and his hair was greased up into a pompadour that was almost as high as my hair. He watched me as I walked across the auditorium to him, and even in my spiked heels, I felt as though I was floating on air. He said, "Aay, Geraldine, how goes it?" and then he took me by the arm and we left the auditorium. It was like he knew all along that one day I would come to him. It was a gorgeous spring night, I could even see a few stars, and Vito put his arm around me, and he had to tiptoe a little bit to reach. We walked over to the Gun Hill Projects, and we found a deserted bench in the project's laundry room, and Vito said, "Aay, Geraldine Rizzoli, I've been crazy about you since tenth grade. I even wrote *Teenage Heartbreak* for you."

And I said, "Vito, I know, I guessed it, and I'm sorry I've been so dumb since tenth grade but your heart doesn't have to break any more. Tonight I'm yours."

And Vito and I made out on the bench for a while but it didn't feel like just making out. I realized that Vito and I weren't kids anymore. It was like we had grown up all at once. So I said, "Vito, take me," and he said, "Aay, Geraldine Rizzoli, all *right*!". . . Afterwards he walked me back to Olinville Ave. And he took out the car keys and carved "Vito Loves Geraldine" in a heart over the door of the elevator in my building, but he was careful to do it on another floor, not the floor I lived on, because we didn't want my parents to see. And then he said, "Aay, Geraldine Rizzoli, will you marry me?" and I said, "Yeah, Vito, I will." So then we went into the staircase of the building and he brushed off one of the steps for me and we sat down together and started talking seriously about our future and he said, "Aay, you know Vinny and Bobby and Richie and me, it's a gas being Vito and the Olinvilles and singing those doo-wop numbers, but I'm no fool, I know we'll never be rich or famous. So I'll keep singing for a couple more years, and then I'll get into some other line of work, and then we'll have kids, okay?" And I said sure, it was okay with me if he wanted to sing for a few years until we started our family. Then I told him that Mr. Pampino at the Evander Sweet Store had offered me a job behind the counter which meant that I could start saving money right away. "Aay, Geraldine, you're no fool," he said. He gave me the thumbs up sign and we kissed. . . . We agreed that we wouldn't announce our engagement until we each had a little savings account of our own. That way our parents couldn't say we were too young and irresponsible and try to stop the wedding, which my father, who was very hot-tempered, was likely to do.

The very next morning, Vito's agent called him and woke him up and said that *Teenage Heartbreak* was actually going to get played on the radio, on WMCA by the Good Guys, at eight o'clock that night. . . . Soon everyone on Olinville Ave. knew. . . .

Three days later *Teenage Heartbreak* made it to number one on the charts, which was unbelievable, like twenty thousand holy miracles combined, especially considering how the guidance counselor at Evander Childs used to predict that Vito would end up in prison. The disk jockeys kept saying things like, "these four boys from the streets of the Bronx are a phenomenon, ladies and gentlemen, a genuine phenomenon!"

> —Janice Eidus, "Vito Loves Geraldine," *Vito Loves Geraldine: A Collection of Stories* (San Francisco: City Lights Books, 1989).

While the fictional Vito Venecio lived in the northeastern section of The Bronx and his group, the Olinvilles, was named after that neighborhood, there was a real doo-wop star, Dion DiMucci, whose group, Dion and the Belmonts, took its name from their Italian neighborhood in the central Bronx. Dion, later inducted into the

Rock 'n' Roll Hall of Fame, explains how he was shaped by his Belmont surroundings in his memoir, *The Wanderer*.

> Keep going down Crotona Avenue to the main drag, 187th Street, and hang a left. You'll be heading right for Mount Carmel, the parish cathedral and the hub of my little kingdom. It was big and dark and kind of spooky inside that church; I can still smell the mustiness of old hymn books and incense. My dad brought me there every Sunday for the first eight years of my life, not because he was so pious, but because he liked to listen to the pipe organ. . . .
>
> . . . We liked to hang out the window of my grandmother's house during the religious festivals. The neighborhood would set up a stage, right below her apartment, painted with flowers and really ornate, and they'd get a band and an opera singer and they'd be music all night. From Maria's we had a box seat for it all and during the feast of Saint Anthony they'd wheel this statue down the middle of Crotona Avenue, with all the elderly ladies in black gowns and rosary beads following behind. The merchants in the neighborhood used to come out and pin money on the statue, and Ricky got to thinking. We could get our own statue, he said, and work Southern Boulevard. . . .
>
> The DiMuccis lived at 749 East 183rd Street on the top floor of a two story walk-up. . . .
>
> The rest of my family—aunts and uncles and second cousins and old ladies from the old country—were spread out all over the Bronx. During the holidays, or for a wedding or funeral, it seemed like they all came over to our place for dinner—two hundred and fifty Italians, all talking at once. . . .
>
> In a way, I'm constantly being reminded of what it was like to grow up in that neighborhood, at that time. Everywhere you look, you pick up the memories. Movies and TV celebrate the myth of the dago street kid, half Valentino, half Al Capone. From Fonzie to *The Lords of Flatbush*, I keep seeing the image of that little kingdom, hearing the music and the lingo that made it so special, so exclusive. . . . I'd stroll down the streets of the neighborhood shouting out to people I met. It was good to be alive on Crotona Avenue at the dawn of rock 'n' roll.

As a teenager, Dion felt at home in the Bronx streets and was attracted to the dangerous, but seemingly glamorous, gang life that formed around young men of his age.

> Ricky and I decided to join the Fordham Daggers, the gang that claimed our neighborhood as its turf. It's another one of those clichés that I actually

lived through. You know the image, from *West Side Story, Rebel Without a Cause,* and a dozen B-picture melodramas—the black leather jacket, Luckies in the T-shirt sleeve, and a tattoo that read "Live Fast, Die Young, and Leave a Good-Looking Corpse." I'm not sure Hollywood was copying us or the other way around, but I do know that myth was a reality, a reality that caught us up and sometimes carried us away. . . .

But it was no play acting. The trouble we caused ourselves and others was real. We didn't steal hubcaps or terrorize old ladies. It wasn't like that. We'd come together to protect the turf, a few blocks of tenements we called our own and staked out against the other gangs: the Imperial Hoods or the Italian Berrettas or the Golden Guineas. . . .

. . . A lot of guys went . . . to the grave. . . . By the time Ricky and I left the Daggers to join the Baldies, a bigger, tougher local gang that took its name from the American eagle, we'd been to more than our share of funerals. Zip gun fights, car crashes, knife wounds, a drunken stunt that went wrong: Friends of mine were checking out and nobody was asking why.

187th Street and Prospect Avenue in the late 1950s. "We'd come together to protect the turf, a few blocks of tenements we called our own and staked out against the other gangs." —Dion DiMucci. The Bronx County Historical Society Research Library, Max Levine Collection.

It was doo-wop music that rescued Dion.

Carlo Mastrangelo. Fred Milano. Angelo D'Aleo. They were the best in the neighborhood, maybe the best in the Bronx, and back then, in the middle of the Fifties, there was lots of competition for that crown. Seems like every street corner had its own harmonizing heroes back then; guys who would spend hours getting down their parts, riffing off the big doo-wop hits of the day, and dreaming, just maybe, that if they got good enough, if they could whip up that slick a cappella blend like topping on a sundae, it might just be their voices coming off the radio from a fire escape on a hot summer night.

Carlo, Freddie, and Angelo. I'd sung with them dozens of times on the front stoop or stopped on my way somewhere to take the lead on "Earth Angel," "I Love You So," or "Story Untold" underneath the streetlight. They were guys who'd drifted in and out of my scene for years, not close friends, not like Ricky, but guys you'd shout hello to from down the street. And who'd shout back.

The name they took was the Belmonts, after Belmont Avenue, and the music we made together was the pure sound of the neighborhood.

—Dion DiMucci with Davin Seay, *The Wanderer: Dion's Story* (New York: Beech Tree Books, William Morrow, 1988).

Bronx teenage gangs were usually organized along ethnic lines. There were confrontations between rival gangs "defending their turf." In "Summer Nights, Italian Bronx, 1959," poet Michael Gilmartin describes such a clash, based on a real event in the Italian Belmont neighborhood at the time of the feast of Our Lady of Mount Carmel.

On the evening the Monsignor visited,
We climbed to the rooftops
Overlooking the platform jutting from the street corner.
The moon bobbed in the city's summer breeze.
The girls' dresses blew.
Special lights spilled color into the stalls
Of sausage and cheese and chestnuts and bread.
For the feast of Our Lady of Mount Carmel,
Banners hung from the fire escapes.
There were cafes on the chalk-flecked street.

The night before, the big guys caught a Carlos Perez,
After some spics used belts
To slice open the eyes of one of ours.
The concrete sprouted blood flowers.
Perez was pushed into a sewer,
The manhole cover placed back over him
Neat as a thumbprint.
For hours they kept him there.
They let us peek through the gutter opening.
He was clinging to the iron rung steps.
Long before the cops came,
The whole block knew what was happening.

Now the Monsignor stood near there
Passing out blue and gold holy cards.
Pigeons whirred behind us.
Below us, booming up through the old, tile hallways,
The tenor, bass, falsetto, and lead,
Screwed out of their street corner for the second night running,
Still sang *a capella.*

> —Michael Gilmartin, "Summer Nights, Italian
> Bronx, 1959," *Esprit: A Humanities Magazine*
> (Spring 1984).

The rebellious teenage subculture and its accompanying delinquency marked by teenage gangs spilled over as violence in the schools. Soon, it began to affect teachers' attitudes toward their students and their jobs. Some descended into apathy, believing that nothing they could do would reach their pupils or encourage them to learn. In Evan Hunter's controversial novel—later made into a motion picture—*Blackboard Jungle*, Rick Dadier, a recently hired English teacher at the fictional North Manual Trades High School, is recovering from a stab wound inflicted by one of his students. As he enters the teachers' lounge, his fellow instructors are joking about the results of the examinations for hiring new teaching personnel just posted on the bulletin board and about their yearning to teach in an "easier" school, such as Julia Richmond High School.

Solly Klein stood near the bulletin board in the teachers' lunchroom and pointed a stubby forefinger at the school page of the *World-Telegram-Sun.*

"Another list of names," he said. "All the suckers who passed the elementary school exam this time." He shook his head, tapped the tacked page with his finger, and then walked back to the table. "They never learn," he said. "They get sucked in every year."

"The way you got sucked in," Lou Savoldi said, looking up from his tea.

"I got sucked in, all right," Solly answered. "Had I known what. . ."

"Had I but known," George Katz said, smiling. "Ah, had I but known."

"Read your history book," Solly said.

Rick Dadier enters the lunchroom.

"Look at all the happy faces," he said, smiling. . . .

"Who me?" Solly asked. "There's nothing funny about this dump, nothing. Except The Boss. He's a riot."

"He's not a bad fellow," Katz said.

"He's a prince," Solly said dryly.

"No, really. He's not bad at all."

"I said, didn't I? A prince. They all should send him someplace where royalty is appreciated."

"Well, I don't think he's doing a bad job here," Katz said staunchly.

"Nobody does a bad job here," Savoldi said sadly.

"Except you, Lou," Solly said.

Savoldi shrugged. "How can you do a bad job here?" he asked. "A bad job anyplace else is a good job here."

"He's finally catching on," Solly said. "He's been teaching here for eighty years, and he's just getting wise."

"I'm one of the Original Wise Men," Savoldi said.

"It is possible to do a good job here," Rick said softly.

"Here's Dadier again," Solly said. "Dadier, you'd better be careful or you'll wind up being a principal."

"He'd like that," Savoldi said sadly. "Wouldn't you, Dadier?"

"That's what I'm bucking for," Rick said, smiling.

"You can always tell the hot-rods," Solly said, wagging his head. "I spotted you for a hot-rod from go, Dadier. That's why your arm is in a bandage now."

"It's healing," Rick said, shrugging.

"Everything heals," Savoldi said.

"Time heals all wounds," Katz put in.

"Unless they use a zip gun on you someday. Try to heal a hole in your head," Solly said.

"They won't use a zip gun on me," Rick said confidently.

"Famous last words," Solly said. . . .

"How did your kids like the tie, Katz?" Manners asked.

"They thought it was very nice," Katz answered, still miffed.

"They don't know ties from garter snakes," Solly said.

"They're not that dumb," Rick contradicted.

"No, huh?"

"*I* don't think so."

"That's because you love them all, Dadier. There's nothing like a little knifing to generate love and devotion."

"Dadier is a professional hero," Savoldi said.

"He stops rapes and knifings," Manners said, "and is also available for Christmas shows, hayrides, and strawberry festivals."

"No *bar-mitzvahs*?" Solly asked.

"Those, too," Rick said, smiling. . . .

"I don't think it's proper to joke about Dadier's knifing," Katz said, really thinking it was not proper to joke about his gift tie.

"Who's joking?" Solly asked. "Dadier is a very brave man."

"A missionary," Manners said.

Solly turned, seemingly surprised. "Are you still around, Manners? I thought you'd be teaching at Julia Richmond by this time."

"I'm working on it," Manners said, smiling.

"It was," Katz said thoughtfully, "an act of bravery."

"What's that?" Solly asked.

"Dadier's knifing."

"Certainly. You have to be very brave to get all sliced up."

"You talk about it as if it were nothing at all," Katz said seriously. "As if it meant absolutely nothing."

"Knife wounds mean nothing to heroes," Manners said. He flicked an imaginary cut on his shoulder. "Just a scratch, man."

"That's Dadier's trouble," Savoldi said sadly. "He's a professional hero."

"No," Rick said, smiling. "I'm just a teacher."

—Evan Hunter, *Blackboard Jungle* (New York: Simon and Schuster, 1954).

The Bronx, which began the postwar years in the glow of prosperity, ended as a borough facing serious problems. Increasing youth unrest and a feeling of helplessness among those in a position to confront it proved a volatile mixture. In too many of the borough's once-stable neighborhoods, it created a pathological situation.

8

THE URBAN CRISIS

THE BRONX IN THE YEARS
OF CHANGE AND UNREST

1961–1980

IN THE SIXTIES AND SEVENTIES, THE ASSASSINATIONS OF NATIONAL leaders, along with the images of the Vietnam War and protests and demonstrations telecast into living rooms each night, brought violence and killing directly into the public consciousness. Confidence in the effectiveness of government was eroded by the fall of Saigon, the Watergate scandal, and the nuclear accident at Three Mile Island.

In accord with the mood of the times, writers focused on the negative changes then happening in The Bronx. Whatever positive note authors struck occurred in memoirs and other works in which they depicted an almost idealized past.

At that time, the drug epidemic led to increasing violence in the borough. Needing funds to pay for drugs to ease their cravings, addicts turned to crime, preying on the weak and elderly in particular. Some Vietnam veterans, introduced to drugs overseas, brought their habits back with them and swelled the ranks of the addicted. Popular culture sometimes glamorized drug use while downplaying the tragedy it caused.

Because of the drug epidemic and the allure of life in the suburbs, trends that had begun during the postwar years accelerated. Bronxites continued to leave the borough. Some moved from deteriorating neighborhoods to the new single-family homes, high-rise apartment houses, and gigantic cooperative developments erected on formerly empty lots in the northern and eastern Bronx.

At the same time, many people were attracted to The Bronx for the same reasons that had drawn previous groups. Unfortunately, their arrival coincided with a massive reduction in the need for low-skilled jobs, a mainstay for earlier immigrants. They also faced deteriorating housing, drugs, crime, and a system of schools and social services overwhelmed by the needs of the new, poorer residents. Many came to The Bronx because of the low rents in new public housing projects built for the poor, mostly in the South Bronx, and by the low rents for newly vacated apartments in existing privately owned apartment houses. But rents in private housing, still subject to wartime controls, did not provide enough funds for landlords to perform timely repairs on their aging buildings, and many deferred maintenance until it was long past due. Because the Federal Housing Administration refused to guarantee mortgages on multifamily dwellings inhabited by the unemployed and working poor, landlords, especially in the South Bronx, could not obtain bank loans to make substantial repairs. Unscrupulous landlords, abetted by corrupt building inspectors, collected rents without making repairs or paying property taxes. As conditions worsened, tenants left their buildings. In the end, vandals, looking for money to pay for more drugs, stripped those buildings of metal water pipes to sell for scrap, causing considerable water damage. Given this state of affairs, the unscrupulous landlords found it more profitable to destroy or abandon empty and ruined buildings.

By the end of the 1960s, some tenants used the law to stop their rent payments in response to landlord violations. Lacking funds, many decent landlords were unable to pay property taxes or make improvements. Further, the city preferred to give rehabilitation funds to landlords of already vacant buildings, rather than to those who still had tenants. Many old Bronx working-class neighborhoods fell into ruin. Almost anyone who could afford to move did so.

Other conditions contributed to the growing urban blight. The strong Democratic political machine erected by Edward J. Flynn in the 1920s and 1930s weakened. Although Charles Buckley, Flynn's successor, was strong enough to help elect John F. Kennedy in 1960, by the middle of the decade, his power waned. Professionally trained Jews and newly arrived blacks and Puerto Ricans demanded elected and appointed places in the government and party hierarchy consistent with their increased population in the borough. But Buckley insisted that the newcomers wait their turn as the Irish and working-class Jews who now controlled the party did in their time. This caused a split in the Bronx Democratic Party as a new reform movement challenged the regulars in primary elections. Unable to ensure votes for city, state, and national candidates as it once did, the divided Bronx party failed to address the growing crisis. In addition, during this era and later, several corrupt Bronx politicians were imprisoned for tax evasion, racketeering, extortion, and other charges. On top of that, New York City reached a financial crisis in the 1970s and was nearly bankrupt by 1976.

Poorer families from newer ethnic groups moving into an established neighborhood often faced resentment and hostility, which were frequently returned. Terence Winch's poem, "Six Families of Puerto Ricans," depicted the class conflict between Irish and Puerto Ricans on Daly Avenue. Winch noted that earlier Puerto Rican migrants, who had eventually been accepted, also moved away as the changes continued.

I guess it was the summer of nineteen
fifty five   I just got back from Rockaway
the first thing I heard when I got back
was the news that
six families of Puerto Ricans had moved
into nineteen fifteen Daly Avenue   the Mitchells'
building   as time went on
more and more pee ars moved into
the neighborhood   there was great hostility
on both sides   once on the fourth of July
Martin Conlon threw some cherry bombs
and ash cans through the windows of the Puerto
Ricans   they were just spics to us
I remember a Puerto Rican shooting
at me and some friends with a bee bee gun
from his roof   you could hear the bee bees
bouncing off the cars   bodegas opened
on Tremont Avenue   Spanish kids dropped
water balloons on Irish kids   there was
a Sunday mass in Spanish in the church basement
this was worse than a potato famine
and the Irish started moving out
Mr. Zayas moved in next door to us
where the Gormans had lived   Mr. Zayas
had a son named Efrain who married
a beautiful girl named Carmen   Puerto Rican men
played dominos on the sidewalk
when me and my father left the block
in the fall of nineteen sixty eight
we were among a handful of Irish still
in the neighborhood   things were so bad
by then that even the respectable Puerto Ricans
like Mr. Zayas were long gone. . . .

—Terence Winch, "Six Families of Puerto Ricans,"
Irish Musicians/American Friends (Minneapolis:
Coffee House Press, 1985).

In former Bronxite Richard Price's novel *The Wanderers*, later made into a motion picture, an alliance is formed among normally feuding Italian North Bronx gangs in order to confront a rival black alliance. They prepare for a "rumble" in which fists, bats, and other blunt instruments would be used as weapons. Lester Avenue is a thinly disguised Lester Street located near the low-income Parkside Houses projects where the author grew up. The Fordham Baldies got their name from the bald eagle on their jackets, not from shaved heads. The Wanderers is the narrator's gang.

> The only other gang worth being scared of was the Fordham Baldies, who were *so* fucking insane that they shaved their heads so their hair wouldn't get in their eyes in a fight. They were older too. About eighteen on the average. The toughest guy on the Baldies was Terror, a huge cross-eyed monster who even beat up on his own gang when they weren't fighting anyone else. But even *he* knew better than to fuck with the puniest guy on Lester Avenue. They'd come down like vigilantes and tear up the whole Fordham area, and they'd go down like that night after night until Terror gave himself up. Then a kangaroo court in some basement and even money Terror would be found in the trunk of a deserted car out in Hunt's Point the next week.

—Richard Price, *The Wanderers* (New York: Houghton Mifflin, 1974).

The increasing violence on the streets spilled into the schools. Poet w r rodriguez, in "logic," relates his experiences at the newly built Arturo Toscanini Junior High School on Teller Avenue and 164th Street.

> . . . me who learned in junior high school
> while the elders were not watching
> or saw only the past or pretended not to see
> when some gang walked into math class
> while the teacher was discussing how the hottentots
> could only count up to three and had no vision of infinity
> and beat up some girl who helped grade papers and left
> while the teacher did not move from his desk
> and no counselor came to counsel us
> and no principal stopped by to smile and say
> what an unfortunate incident this was and to lie
> that this would never happen again
> it was just business as usual at arturo toscanini junior high school
> where gangs chased intellectuals and jews

and anyone else who did not belong
and the social studies teacher taught
what a great melting pot this america was
when she wasn't at the police station filing assault reports. . . .

—w r rodriguez, "logic," *Dusty Dog* (January 1991).

The progression of gang violence from using fists, to knives, to guns is chronicled by black author Geoffrey Canada in his sociological memoir, *Fist Stick Knife Gun.*

When I was growing up in the South Bronx there were some natural checks on violent behavior. Most violence on the block was done with the fists in what we called a "fair one": two people fought until one was too hurt to continue or quit in defeat. There were people around to ensure the dispute was settled according to the rules. No "dirty" fighting was allowed, no kicking or biting, no weapons. If someone violated the rules he might be attacked or ostracized by the group. Violence against others who did not live on the block was not subject to the same rules—in these situations you could do anything you liked—but even so, because none of us had guns, knife fighting was usually the most extreme form these encounters took. Anyone who has ever fought with a weapon like a knife or a bottle knows there is no glamour in it. These fights are messy and dangerous, even deadly. The use of weapons usually occurred only in someone else's territory.

The first rules I learned on Union Avenue stayed with me for all of my youth. They were simple and straightforward: Don't cry. Don't be afraid. Don't tell your mother. Take it like a man. Don't let no one take your manhood. My teachers were the typical instructors on blocks like Union Avenue—the adolescents we all looked up to.

Cauldwell Avenue between Westchester Avenue and 156th Street about 1970. Note the children in the street. "My teachers were the typical instructors on blocks like Union Avenue—the adolescents we all looked up to." —Geoffrey Canada. The Bronx County Historical Society Research Library, Ralph Marx Collection.

. . . This was 1966, and America's inner cities had not turned into the killing fields that they are today. While it was clear that we ruled this block, that we were some of the toughest guys the Bronx had produced, none of us owned guns. Back then a man could pull a gun on a bunch of street toughs with a fair amount of certainty that he had the only gun on the block. . . .

The K55 knife was the weapon of choice among the older teenagers of the South Bronx.

One day, young Canada finds a K55 in the gutter. The knife gives him a feeling of security, especially in "enemy territory," where he walks in a distinctive manner to convey that he is street smart. Later, when conditions in The Bronx worsen, he feels he needs more protection.

In 1971, well before the explosion of handguns on the streets of New York City, I bought a handgun. I bought the gun legally in Maine, where I was in college. The clerk only wanted to see some proof of residency, and my Bowdoin College I.D. card was sufficient. For a hundred and twenty-five dollars I was the proud owner of a .25 caliber automatic with a seven-shot clip. The gun was exactly what I needed. It was so small I could slip it into my coat pocket or pants pocket.

I needed the gun because we had moved from Union Avenue to 183rd Street in the Bronx, but I still traveled back to Union Avenue during holidays when I was home from school. The trip involved walking through some increasingly dangerous territory. New York City was going through one of its gang phases and several new ones had sprung up in the Bronx. One of the gangs used to hang out right down the block from where we now lived on 183rd Street and Park Avenue. When I first went away to school I paid no mind to the large group of kids that I used to pass on my way to the store or the bus stop back in the Bronx. The kids were young, fourteen or fifteen years old. At nineteen I was hardly worried about a bunch of street kids who thought they were tough. But over the course of the next year the kids got bolder and more vicious. On several occasions I watched with alarm as swarms of teenagers pummeled adults who had crossed them in one way or another. Everyone knew they were a force to be reckoned with, and many a man or woman crossed the street or walked around the block to keep from having to walk past them.

And I crossed the street also. And there were times that I went out of my way to go to another store rather than walk past the rowdy group of boys who seemed to own the block. On more than one occasion I rounded a corner only to come face to face with the gang. I could feel their eyes on me as I looked straight ahead, hoping none of them would pick a fight. That September in 1971, when I got to the serenity of Bowdoin College I was more tense than usual. I realized that those kids had me scared. After having survived growing up in the Bronx, here I was scared to go home and walk down my own block. The solution was simple, and as I held the small gun in my hand I knew I found the answer to my fears.

> —Geoffrey Canada, *Fist Stick Knife Gun: A Personal History of Violence in America* (Boston: Beacon Press, 1995).

Along with the increasing ownership of deadly arms among the young, drug abuse became more prevalent in The Bronx. In his essay "The Battle of Bean Hill," Gil Fagiani recounts how two brazen barbituate addicts, Tommy O'Toole and Two-Fingers Frank Galuzzo, confront each other, frightening the clientele at a local coffee shop on Fordham Road, the main shopping district.

Fordham Road at its junction with Kingsbridge Road, about 1960. "Over the years the area near Fordham Road in the Bronx . . . came to be referred to by locals as Bean Hill." —Gil Fagiani. The Bronx County Historical Society Research Library, Max Levine Collection.

Strung out on barbituates, the bean heads were considered the lowest of the low by other junkies. Over the years the area near Fordham Road in the Bronx where they hung out came to be referred to by locals as Bean Hill. . . .

One day shortly before Christmas, a group of holiday shoppers was crowded into a coffee shop on Bean Hill when Tommy and Two-Fingers began to argue outside. They were both "beaned" to the gills and as they cursed at each other they wobbled like their joints were made of rubber. Then they began to throw punches, their arms moving slowly as if they were underwater. After Tommy took a left hook to the nose that drew blood, he staggered backwards and pulled off his thick brass-buckled belt. He began to lash Two-Fingers with the belt, and although he couldn't swing with much force, the buckle end of the belt soon left a meshwork of bloody streaks across Two-Fingers's face. The blood dripping down his face didn't seem to faze Two-Fingers at all, and he continued to throw slow-motion punches Tommy's way. Finally, Tommy dropped his belt and pulled out of a holster strapped to his right ankle a linoleum knife with a long, curved blade. Everybody in the coffee shop cringed in anticipation of Two-Fingers being hacked into hamburger meat. But no sooner had Tommy unsheathed his knife than it fell out of his hand, and when he bent down to pick it up, Two-Fingers kneed him in the face sending him sprawling across the sidewalk. "Look at da muddafucka now," he beamed, resting one of his feet on Tommy's bean-kiestered butt and waving his two-fingered hand in the air like he was flashing the peace sign.

—Gil Fagiani, "The Battle of Bean Hill," unpublished short story.

The poverty and the dehumanizing living conditions among the mostly black and Puerto Rican population that now inhabited the South Bronx also led to the widespread use of narcotic drugs and to crime. Desperate junkies often preyed on family, neighbors, and local residents to get the money to buy expensive heroin to feed their insatiable urge. With grim humor, former South Bronx resident and poet w r rodriguez captures the pain caused by drug addiction in a South Bronx neighborhood in "blinky."

blinky

had a glass eye that didn't fit well
but he was too poor to get another
so folks called him blinky   the one eyed junkie

because he was a junkie   & twitched a lot
trying to keep his eye from falling out

he wasn't like the other junkies who weren't like him
& who hung around   wasted   waiting to score
watching who to rob   & mugging people
angel's father's head bloodied   stabbed in the chest too
not because he fought back   but because they wouldn't take chances

or waste time asking   & in a rush they pushed maria
who lived next door & was seventy six years old
down the stairs   took her pocketbook   the social security money
just enough to pay the rent   & buy thirty dollars food each month
she spent ten weeks in the hospital   with fractured ribs
& a broken hip   so they could get their fix
but blinky wasn't like them

maybe he didn't have much of a habit to support
or maybe he dealt on the side
but he'd just hang around the supermarket
carry packages home for a quarter or half-a-buck
take odd jobs   paint apartments
sweep sidewalks   bring down the garbage for the super
in bad times he'd beg by the subway

one night blinky overdosed in some basement
folks said he didn't move an eyelid
when the cops carried him to the ambulance

word got around he was dead
someone painted a cross on the sidewalk
put a bouquet of plastic flowers next to a hat
read the bible & took a collection   *for blinky's funeral*
he said   & the old women walking home from the stores
dropped in dimes & quarters
some stopped to listen to the prayers

two weeks later blinky returned
he woke up in lincoln hospital   stole some clothes & walked out
right past the cops & nurses   back to 138th street hoping for a fix

when he saw the cross still painted on the sidewalk
& found out about our donations
he had some fine ideas on spending the money
so he & a few friends went looking for the man who took the collection

but no one could ever find him

—w r rodriguez, "blinky," *the shoe shine parlor et al.*
(Madison, Wisc.: Ghost Pony Press, 1984).

The increasing plague of addiction led to escalating crime rates and to the destruction of families and neighborhoods. The process is described by Jill Jonnes in her study *We're Still Here.*

As the junkies multiplied, longtime merchants closed their doors for good, including Jake the Pickle Man. He retired after forty-five years as a premier pickle maker, but continued to live on Jennings Street. He who had once been the terror of the housewives was now scared of addict-muggers. One neighbor remembered him calling up his stairs to make sure no one was lurking. On June 10, 1963, Jacob Shertzer was found murdered in his apartment, his hands tied behind him, the gas on, his mouth stuffed with a rag. Jake's brutal murder sent waves of fear through the nearby street and shops. What kind of animal would kill an old, helpless man like that? In a neighborhood that had never seen a mugging from one year to the next, it now seemed there were vicious killings every two or three weeks. More of the old stores closed on Jennings Street—Rosenblatt's dry goods, Stern's bakery, Weintraub's ladies wear, and Ralph's grocery.

By 1967 when Patrolman Sam Strassfield of the Forty-first Precinct (soon to attain widespread infamy as "Fort Apache") was assigned to the Jennings Street–Charlotte Street foot patrol, the addicts were as bad as a plague of locusts—they swarmed everywhere and were just as destructive. "So many people OD'ed," remembers Strassfield, "we used to get them all the time in the hallways and vacant lots. Who had time to deal with the drugs? Our job was to protect lives and property. The junkies went to the roofs and cellars to transact their business."

—Jill Jonnes, *We're Still Here: The Rise, Fall, and Resurrection of the South Bronx* (Boston: The Atlantic Monthly Press, 1986).

The social upheaval of the sixties also affected girls and young women. In the still largely Irish working-class neighborhood of Highbridge, an early introduction to sexual relations, smoking, drinking, and performing daredevil high jinx was aided by the rocky topography overlooking the Harlem River that hid such activities from view. The resulting dangers are described by Joan Murray in her poem with separately numbered sections, "Coming of Age on the Harlem." The Circle Line operates boats taking tourists around Manhattan Island, including the portion on the Harlem River that borders The Bronx.

> . . . Just before ten, just before your father's curfew,
> you can station yourself on the highway bridge, where
> it joins the ramp from the river park
> to see the couples rise up on the evening tide:
> the sooty venuses with dirty hand marks
> on white and fondled blouses, and
> their boyfriends swaggering in teenage jeans.
> You laugh, and send your first awakening lust
> to follow them back to the neighborhood
> where someday all will notice that you've grown.
> And small children will stand on bridges
> to flank your path
> as you make your debut entry
> to the nightly river-park cotillion, on the arm
> of some lanky boy with a dangling black curl,
> and the cleanest, oh the cleanest hands.
>
> . . . It's the boys with sprouts of pubic hair
> who have the manliness to strip and jump
> while tourists on the Circle Line around
> Manhattan watch with Brownie cameras.
> Bright-faced fathers and mothers, pointing out
> the river life to their children.
> They look for street kids in straw hats,
> the Tom Sawyers and Huck Finns of the Harlem,
> but only get an upraised finger.
> Behind the nude boys who perch on the river rocks
> and invite the sun to their members,
> a dozen girls, in tight black shorts and
> ponytails, keep a coy but glancing distance. . . .
>
> . . . In Undercliff Park, below Washington Bridge,
> I play stretch and toe-knee-chest-nut with

my father's pocketed army knife.
A dangerous age. Threats are cutting through the air:
the flailing depantsings, the groping bra quests for
a wad of cotton or a nylon stocking.
A dangerous age, with the deadly fear
of being found a child.
To relieve it one day, we hang a tire in a tree and
swing in packs out over the cliff edge,
until the boy beside me loses his grip, and lies
below, as quiet as an infant in a lullaby.
Weeks later, we visit him at home, sign his casts
and giggle at his immature pajamas.
He lifts his mattress to show
an arsenal of thirty knives and ice picks,
and lets each girl pick a pocket lighter
shoplifted from Woolworth's.

. . . Hung by my hands above water,
I am dangled by boys from the ledge
of the Washington Bridge abutment.
Twelve years old, twelve feet from the surface,
I do not trust boys, but love their giddy danger
like a windflaw teasing with a sail.
And while we dangle, the boys hurl rocks
at the river, waiting for the splash that will leap
up to our blouses and clutch the outlines
of our forming breasts.
Soaked through, we climb the naked limbs
of a shore tree and sprawl in the afternoon sun.
Above, a boy hovers in the branches,
reaches for my hand a moment and is gone,
leaving something growing in me
that holds me separate from my friends
as we walk together to our father's houses,
wearing our secret scent of the river. . . .

—Joan Murray, "Coming of Age on the Harlem,"
The Same Water: Poems (Hanover, N.H.: Wesleyan
University Press, 1990).

From the distance of later years, when buildings of the area were burned down and bulldozed, Joan Murray recalls the sexual assault, rape, and murder of several little girls in the Highbridge neighborhood in her poem "The Unmolested Child." She also reimagines the killing of six-year-old Kathy Hagman, bribed by candy or money to a rooftop and then dropped to her death, probably by another child. From Kathy's viewpoint, she could see the Polo Grounds, the Manhattan ballfield once used by the New York Giants and New York Mets; the Wilson Tower, the home of the H. W. Wilson Company that publishes *The Readers' Guide to Periodical Literature* in Highbridge; the low-income Highbridge Gardens housing projects; the Washington, Third Avenue, and Macombs Dam bridges, which all still cross the Harlem River connecting The Bronx with Manhattan; and the IRT shuttle bridge, which carried subway trains across the river from the Polo Grounds to the Jerome Avenue elevated subway line and was abandoned after the New York Giants left for San Francisco. The highway footbridge spanned the Major Deegan Expressway, which still parallels the river, while "the older river one" referred to the High Bridge itself, where Edgar Allan Poe once walked when he resided in his cottage where he wrote the poem "Ulalume."

> . . . An unprecedented vantage. From here a child could scan all
> the architectonics of the Harlem: the disjunct perspective
> of buildings not yet burned, and down to her left,
> Yankee Stadium. And the Polo Grounds
> still standing to her right, and, closer,
> the Wilson Tower, where neighbor wives
> bring to light *The Readers' Guide to Periodical Literature*
> and still are home by five. And the meat
> *loafs* in its pan. And each thing finds its place. . . .
>
> But held aloft now, over the ledge, Kathy Hagman
> can see at once all the bridges of our Harlem, the lengths
> we all have crossed: the Washington, Third Avenue and
> Macombs Dam. The IRT shuttle bridge, soon left open,
> the highway footbridge, and the older river one
> with its aqueduct and arches that will one day appear so
> famously in our high-school Latin books, on whose
> span the widowed Poe once walked, waving to demons in
> the tide, and thought to make that walk his last.
> But he turned instead through farmers' fields, across
> the Bronx to the straw-stuffed bed we looked at once,
> and wrote a consolation, an explanation for

all these things: the garbled lamentation, "Ulalume."
So let's be off to rave and run our circles, to clean and
put away the pans, to welcome to our burned-out shelters,
the pending, black ball that makes room for others,
to be gone before she lands.

> —Joan Murray, "The Unmolested Child," *The Same Water: Poems* (Hanover, N.H.: Wesleyan University Press, 1990).

Many girls grew up too quickly on the streets of The Bronx. Teenage pregnancy increased. Young mothers, often unable to shoulder the responsibilities of parenting, sometimes endangered the welfare of their children. Neglect, abandonment and infant mortality were all too frequent. In his short story "Elba," South Bronx resident Abraham Rodriguez, Jr., whose book was a *New York Times Book Review* Notable Book of the Year in 1992, explored what happened to two fictional eighth graders, Elba and Danny.

> They caressed each other in darkened movie theaters and deserted beaches.
> "If only we had a car," Danny lamented as they sat on the stoop of her building on Tinton Avenue.
> Two days later after entering the eighth grade, after a few tokes on an old roach, Danny took her to an empty lot on Fox Street. Their sneakers struggled over jutting bricks and crackling wooden beams while a red sun splattered the sky and spilled through gaping windows.
> "I picked the place out yesterday," he said like a newlywed. He lifted her up and carried her through the dark hallways as he had seen men do in old movies on TV. He carried her down steps and over decaying planks of wood, nails sticking out of them like teeth. . . .
> They came to their little hideaway three or four times a week, loving furiously, until one strange morning when Elba felt sick. She threw up twice and felt dizzy. She began missing school, her body a stranger that throbbed and ached. Her mother seemed to know what was up.

Pregnant and afraid, Elba refuses to abort the baby. Months later, Danny, the baby's father, agrees to marry her.

> Her mother was ecstatic, helping her pick out a pretty dress. The ceremony was quick and brief. There were no relatives. Rows of near-empty pews greeted them in the desolate Pentecostal church her mother attended. There

A lot filled with rubble and abandoned buildings between 146th and 147th Streets west of St. Ann's Avenue, June 27, 1972. "He carried her down steps and over decaying planks of wood, nails sticking out of them like teeth." —Abraham Rodriguez, Jr. The Bronx County Historical Society Research Library.

was no honeymoon. Danny rented a two-room apartment in a private house on Kelly Street. He worked as a mechanic's assistant at Meineke on Bruckner Boulevard. Elba wasn't too impressed with any of it. The empty rooms depressed her.

Danny begins abusing Elba and staying out late alone, returning drunk. Elba misses the freedom of her single life. *Chica* is Spanish for girl, while a *puta* is a whore.

She'd stare out the window at the groups of kids hanging out, smoking and gyrating to music. They'd say, "Come on, *chica*, join us," but she'd shake her head sadly. Their laughter would drift up to her while she slept or washed dishes or changed little Danny's diapers. She felt old and lonely and abandoned, a lifer in a prison cell waiting for the chair.

The day she turned sixteen, Danny didn't even come home. He stumbled in at about six in the morning, outraged that she complained, storming off to work without so much as a kiss. The talk on the street was he was spending his nights drinking at Los Chicos, staring at the flabby go-go girls. She complained. She was tired of getting fucked violently by him, so one night she screamed and pushed him off her. She told him she wasn't his fucking *puta* to just get fucked whenever he felt like it, that it was time he cut the shit and tried to grow up like she was trying to do, to accept his responsibilities and start spending more time with his wife and kid and less time at Los Chicos. It was a good speech, but she only got so far before he swung at her like a cornered animal, his blow throwing her off the bed.

The blow still stung, the sound of it reverberating in her head. She leaned on the crib and stared down at the baby without seeing him. She stormed away from the crib, pulse throbbing in her temples wildly, a terrible defiance taking hold of her. She peeled off her panties and turned on the shower, the room filling up with vaporous steam. The baby began to cry.

"Fuck you!" she screamed. "Fuck you! Getcha father to take care a you!"

The teenage mother turns her rage and resentment on her wailing infant.

The baby was shrieking, its red face visible over the rim of the crib, creased like a battered peach. "If you shit yaself, tough!" she yelled. "Get ya father to take care a you!" The baby wailed louder, as if it understood. She locked the windows and left the stereo on. . . .

Two steps from the door she paused to listen, satisfied that she couldn't really hear the baby anymore as she made her way down the creaking stairs in her high heels.

—Abraham Rodriguez, Jr., "Elba," *The Boy without a Flag: Tales of the South Bronx* (Minneapolis: Milkweed Editions, 1992).

Some white ethnic Bronxites who never succeeded in life often had to cope with violence and emptiness. John Patrick Shanley's play *Danny and the Deep Blue Sea* brought together two social outcasts in a seedy Bronx bar near the Parkchester neighborhood where the playwright was raised. Danny, a troubled James Monroe High School dropout, has spent time in a juvenile facility. Roberta, a drug-abusing single mother, lives with her parents. They discuss the history of Zerega Avenue, a street paralleling Westchester Creek in the Castle Hill section of the eastern Bronx where Danny lives. The area had been heavily industrialized in the 1960s with the creation of the Zerega Industrial Park. Earlier, it had been a countrified, marshy habitat.

Zerega Avenue at the corner of Lafayette Avenue about 1975. "Ain't no frogs 'round Zerega." —John Patrick Shanley. The Bronx County Historical Society Research Library, Ralph Marx Collection.

ROBERTA. Where you from?

DANNY. Zerega.

ROBERTA. Yeah? I used to catch frogs 'round Zerega.

DANNY. Ain't no frogs 'round Zerega.

ROBERTA. Not now. When I was a kid.

DANNY. Ain't never been no frogs 'round Zerega.

ROBERTA. Yes, there was. There used to be a little like marsh over on Zerega, and it had frogs in it.

DANNY. When?

ROBERTA. A long time ago. . . . You from Zerega whaddaya doing here?

DANNY. There's nothing goin on over Zerega.

ROBERTA. Nothing going on here.

DANNY. Yeah, well maybe I like that. Peaceful.

ROBERTA. You don't look peaceful to me.

DANNY. I'm peaceful. But people fuck with me.

Roberta brings Danny back to her Bronx apartment. They discover that they have both grappled with feelings of low self-esteem. She tells him that she had once stumbled into sex with her father when she was a teenager, and that she blames herself for the incident. After hearing a distant ship's horn, Roberta shares a strange opium-induced dream with Danny, which exaggerates her neighborhood's proximity to the ocean.

Westchester Square is the modern starting point for Westchester Creek. While small barges and boats navigating the waterway encouraged industrialization along its banks, no ocean-going vessel could navigate it. The creek flows into the upper East River, which is often confused with Long Island Sound.

> ROBERTA. . . . (*A distant boat horn sounds.*) Listen! (*It sounds again, and then once more.*) There. You hear it?
>
> DANNY. What is it?
>
> ROBERTA. Big boats.
>
> DANNY. Ain't no boats around here. There's no water.
>
> ROBERTA. Yeah, there is. It's not a block over or like that, but the ocean's right out there. (*The horn sounds again.*) See? That's a big boat goin down like some river to the ocean.
>
> DANNY. Whatever you say.
>
> ROBERTA. That's what it is. There's boats right up by Westchester Square. What's that, twenty blocks? Look sometime, you'll see 'em. Not the real big ones, but big. Sea boats. . . . I dreamed about the ocean. It was real blue. And there was the sun, and it was real yellow. And I was out there, right in the middle of the ocean, and I heard this noise. I turned around, and whaddaya think I saw? Just about right next to me. A whale! A whale came shootin straight outta the water! Yeah! And people on the boat said, Look! The whales are jumpin! And no shit, these whales start jumpin outta the water all over the place. . . . And then, after a while, they all stopped jumpin. It got quiet. Everybody went away. The water smoothed out. But I kept lookin at the ocean. So deep and blue. And different. It was different then. 'Cause I knew it all had them whales in it.

Touched by Roberta's dream of symbolic rebirth, Danny proposes to her. Roberta accepts, even though they have known each other for only a few hours.

—John Patrick Shanley, *Danny and the Deep Blue Sea: An Apache Dance* (New York: Dramatists Play Service, 1984).

The increasing disintegration of families and the prevalence of muggings and more violent crimes even began to affect the elegant Grand Concourse, once the pride of the borough. One of the victims of crime was Cynthia Ozick's fictional Ruth Puttermesser in *The Puttermesser Papers*. A scholarly civil servant who grew up in a Grand Concourse apartment, Puttermesser remains there as an adult. But her still elegant and beloved Bronx apartment is subject to the depredation affecting the borough; it is ransacked by thieves and charred by a fire they set.

> Her majestic apartment on the Grand Concourse in the Bronx, with its Alhambra spaciousness, had been ravaged by arsonists. Even before that, the old tenants had been dying off or moving away, one by one; junkies stole in, filling empty corridors with bloodstained newspapers, smashed bottles, dead matches in random rows like beetle tracks. On a summer evening Puttermesser arrived home from her office without possessions: her shoes were ash, her piano was ash, her piano teacher's penciled "Excellent," written in fine large letters at the top of "Humoresque" and right across the opening phrase of "Für Elise," had vanished among the cinders. Puttermesser's childhood, burned away. How prescient her mother had been to take all of Puttermesser's school compositions with her to Florida! Otherwise every evidence of Puttermesser's early mental growth might have gone under in that criminal conflagration.
>
> —Cynthia Ozick, *The Puttermesser Papers* (New York: Alfred A. Knopf, 1997).

Many deteriorating Bronx apartment houses became hazardous to their inhabitants. Some corrupt inspectors were bribed to look the other way, but in "The Building Inspector," poet Joan Murray chronicles the discoveries of one who cannot ignore the cost in human suffering.

> This is a poem of stairs,
> a poem by my father,
> a poem of tunnelling
> the East Bronx
> step by step
> to shine the light
> on a life
> in a coal room;
> then across a rooftop,
> stop in the electrocution of an old mind
> torn in tennis shoes;
> go down the landing
> in tenement dark

a nude woman waits
for anyone;
then through wild dog streets
of freezing rain
sharp like the knives behind any door
where you'll find
rats, lice, bedbugs, waterbugs,
a woman dying for a month
with no water,
a man sleeping in his feces
for a year;
now up a flight,
"no heat in my prayer room"
no place on the city form
for prayers
no time:
rush upstairs
two cluttered rooms,
young mother, four babies,
their window crashed
to the yard,
glass flying,
plaster falling,
wailing sad eyes
that send you home
in jagged dreams. . . .

—Joan Murray, "The Building Inspector," *Egg Tooth* (Bronx, N.Y.: Sunbury Press, 1975).

Living conditions of many tenants in South Bronx apartment houses were squalid. Garbage was often strewn in hallways and alleys. Many of the newcomers were poorer and less educated than former residents, and the newly arrived Puerto Ricans often spoke little or no English. Journalist Herb Goro recorded the frustration and helplessness of the new residents and the teachers, block workers, landlords, and children in the area of 180th Street and Third Avenue, a poor neighborhood. One young female resident reports stoically on the difficulty of ridding her apartment of vermin.

Well, we were sleeping and it was two or three o'clock in the morning when I heard a rat scratching on my bed, so I woke up my mother. Then the rat runned away over my sister's arm and my sister woke up and started screaming. Then two or three days passed and my mother was sleeping in the little bed, and a bigger rat than the other climbed up on the bed and tried to get between my mother's legs. My mother shook her leg, and he run away. Yesterday I was watching the TV and I seen a rat—a big, big rat standing next to the refrigerator looking at us.

You couldn't sleep at night. I let my baby sleep with me, 'cause we were afraid to let her sleep in the crib. And it got so that like sometimes you would come through here at night and they would run out from under the chairs and you're screaming all over the place and waking up everybody.

Rats, big rats. I see them. I told Mr. Gonzalez, the landlord. He put poison. But I didn't put it because then the rat dies and smells no good. I can't eat and long time smells no good in my apartment. It smells, smells. I open all the windows.

—Herb Goro, *The Block* (New York: Random House, 1970).

Housing deterioration was often accompanied by the destruction of family life. Bronx Latina author Sandra María Esteves recalls the building where she grew up, which was stripped, abandoned, and finally bulldozed to the ground by the city. The apartment house where her father had lived also became an empty shell, as shown in her poem "Father's Day on Longwood Avenue."

Returning to that abandoned past of youth,
Bronx neighborhood of her father's house.
A five story structure, still, but standing.
Where once his tall husky frame sat
in a top floor window, drinking beer.
As she watched from below,
in awe of this person, she barely knew.

Three blocks south from him
the Beck Street tenement she first claimed home,
last year, torn to the ground.
Nineteen years tumbled into shadows,
dust traces of rubble remain,
names of neighbors, best friends, disappeared.

And in the place where her room once held her,
where she became alive, cried,

and learned to love her mother,
studying world through windows facing sun,
chanting incantations to the Moon
of top forty hit parades
in fourth floor ghetto repertoire.
Space of broken concrete, limping paint,
so dear, the only water she knew,
now a lane through a park where lovers walk
over new matted rugs of prefabricated astroturf.
While memories of building linger in trees,
Titi Julia's apartment one, where life began,
now air and space where birds fly in symbolic liberation
of land reclaimed by wind,
spirit of her home set free,
an unraveled karma.

While the shell of her father's house endures,
a monument braced against the elements.
Roof leaking to basement, only rats take notice.
Winds howling lonely sonatas, no one hears.
A single pigeon flies west, silhouetting sunset.
She remembers a young woman of thirteen
looking for the last time
at this stranger not seen for twenty-six years,
wondering
who he was.

> —Sandra María Esteves, "Father's Day on Long-
> wood Avenue," *Bluestown Mockingbird Mambo*
> (Houston: Arte Público Press, 1990).

Some highway construction shattered whole neighborhoods. When Robert Moses built new highways, such as the Cross-Bronx Expressway, most Bronxites accepted the resulting neighborhood deterioration with resignation. A few balked. One of these, Marshall Berman, notes the effect on the once-stable Tremont neighborhood after the construction of the Cross-Bronx Expressway was completed.

> Indeed, when the construction was done, the real ruin of the Bronx had just begun. Miles of streets alongside the road were choked with dust and fumes and deafening noise—most strikingly, the roar of trucks of a size and power that the Bronx had never seen, hauling heavy cargoes through the city,

bound for Long Island or New England, for New Jersey and all points south, all through the day and night. Apartment houses that had been settled and stable for twenty years emptied out, often virtually overnight; large and impoverished black and Hispanic families, fleeing even worse slums, were moved in wholesale, often under the auspices of the Welfare Department, which even paid inflated rents, spreading panic and accelerating flight. At the same time, the construction had destroyed many commercial blocks, cut others off from most of their customers and left the storekeepers not only close to bankruptcy but, in their enforced isolation, increasingly vulnerable to crime. The borough's great open market, along Bathgate Avenue, still flourishing in the late 1950s, was decimated; a year after the road came through, what was left up went up in smoke. Thus depopulated, economically depleted, emotionally shattered—as bad as the physical damage had been the inner wounds were worse—the Bronx was ripe for the dreaded spirals of urban blight.

—Marshall Berman, *All That Is Solid Melts into Air: The Experience of Modernity* (New York: Simon and Schuster, 1982).

The unstoppable Robert Moses also built the Bruckner Expressway, which became the New England Thruway farther north, through Hunts Point. The narrator of Herman Wouk's novel *Inside, Outside* recalls his old neighborhood and mourns the loss of the building that housed his father's Fairy Laundry.

All at once the recollection comes upon me in an overpowering wave—I smell the steamy soap-and-chlorine air of the laundry, and hear the machines clattering and rumbling, and see the sweaty women in white smocks out on the main floor, working the presses and feeding the mangles. Gone, all gone! The New England Thruway obliterated that Bronx neighborhood. The Fairy Laundry is as lost as Atlantis. And to think that that building was my father's life; that was all he ever did with his mind and his gifts!

—Herman Wouk, *Inside, Outside* (Boston: Little, Brown & Company, 1985).

The same highway also affected Pelham Bay Park in the northeastern Bronx neighborhood of Cynthia Ozick. In her allegorical short story "The Pagan Rabbi," she tells of the effect on the park caused by highway construction. The fictional narrator of the story is drawn to a tree in the park upon which a brilliant and pious young rabbi had hung himself after being seduced by a sprite sent by the pagan god Pan. In an attempt to understand why he chose to kill himself, and why on that spot, the narrator pauses to absorb the scene, including the new highway.

> On the day I came to see the tree the air was bleary with fog. The weather was well into autumn and, though it was Sunday, the walks were empty. There was something historical about the park just then, with its rusting grasses and deserted monuments. In front of a soldiers' cenotaph a plastic wreath left behind months before by some civic parade stood propped against a stone frieze of identical marchers in the costume of an old war. A banner across the wreath's belly explained that the purpose of war is peace. At the margins of the park they were building a gigantic highway. I felt I was making my way across a battlefield silenced by the victory of the peace machines. The bulldozers had bitten far into the park, and the rolled carcasses of the sacrificed trees were already cut up into logs. There were dozens of felled maples, elms, and oaks. Their moist inner wheels breathed out a fragrance of barns, countryside, decay.
>
> —Cynthia Ozick, "The Pagan Rabbi," *The Hudson Review* (Autumn 1966).

The World War I Memorial in Pelham Bay Park, summer 1988. "In front of a soldiers' cenotaph a plastic wreath left behind months before by some civic parade stood propped against a stone frieze of identical marchers in the costume of an old war." — Cynthia Ozick. The Bronx County Historical Society Research Library, gift of Raanan Geberer.

As people fled from heavily populated Jewish neighborhoods, Yiddish literary culture all but disappeared from its old Bronx strongholds. I. J. Schwartz, one of the original group of Bronx Yiddish writers, outlived most of his compatriots and died in neglect and poverty in his old Bronx neighborhood. In "The Boarder," poet Frederick Feirstein recounts a visit to see Schwartz. Feirstein calls him by his Yiddish nickname, "Yud." Sholem Asch was an author who had written best-selling novels in English on Jewish themes.

> Stubborn Spring pushed through the cold twigs
> In the small park across the street
> From where Yud Schwartz, the poet, lived
> With a deaf butcher and the butcher's wife
> In one room cluttered as his grief:
> Pictures of his dead wife on his desk
> And of Schwartz, Sholem Aleichem and Sholem Asch—
> Three cypresses on a Bronx street,
> Two of them dead, Yud Schwartz
> Cut down as well. His bookcase was

A crypt; his Yiddish tongue was dust;
And she dead a week—
Ruts for the skidding wheels of a Ford.

"How do I feel? I woke at dawn
In a yellow sweat, my sheets wet,
My guts wood, my head stuffed with grass,
With bluebird bones, fragments of poems.
I dressed. Buttoning my shirt was hard,
Believe me. 'There's one choice,' I said.
'Make up your mind!' and I half-walked
Down to the park. Forty-six steps—
I counted every one of them.
The clouds were rinsed of simile,
The sky bluer than Galilee.
The buds were out. I touched them: frail
As a wren's tongue, pale. The earth felt
Like bear's fur. Good, damn it, it's good.

How do I feel?" He read a poem:
About wind, papers wrapped tight on his calves
As he walked Sholem Aleichem's streets, the old shops
Gone, slush soaking his shoes—gone poor.
Spanish in the tenement rooms
Where he spent his Sabbath afternoons
With his young wife, his poet-friends,
Peeled yellow apples and munched nuts,
Munched figs, and vowed to eat the world.

In Fall I telephoned. "Who?" said the butcher's wife.
"The poet." "Who?" "The boarder!" "Dead.
Last Spring. He left no money and no clothes."

—Frederick Feirstein, "The Boarder," *New and Selected
Poems* (Brownsville, Ore.: Story Line Press, 1998).

One of the last remaining Yiddish poets in The Bronx, the award-winning
Gabriel Preil, lived on the Grand Concourse. In his poem bearing the title of that
great boulevard, written especially for this book, he recounted the waning Jewish
presence there.

Frozen skies above buildings
Enveloped in wool-white haze.
A Sabbath evening, northern, unJewish
Extends along the avenue budding with signal lights
An endless, unknowing now.

Five Jews live here
From cage to cage
Five stalks of corn, marginal
And the lonely Sabbath locks herself in
Like a dying queen.

> —Gabriel Preil, "Grand Concourse," trans. Estelle
> Gilson, unpublished poem.

The cause of the rapid changes in The Bronx led to provocative speculation. Noted black author James Baldwin, observing the rapidity of neighborhood transformation, detects racism as the cause.

The life of the city, watching it—I watched—well, I grew up in Harlem, and when we were able, when we made a little money, enough to put something aside—and do not underestimate that effort; it is hard for everybody, but, baby, try it if you're black—we began to move across the river to the Bronx, all those people who had lately become white fled in terror, and one of the results of that is the present disaster called the South Bronx where nobody can live. The motion of the white people of this country has been—and it is a terrifying thing to say this, but it is time to face it—a furious attempt to get away from the niggers.

> —James Baldwin, "The Language of the Streets," in
> *Literature and the Urban Experience*, ed. Michael C.
> Jaye and Ann Chalmers Watts (New Brunswick, N.J.:
> Rutgers University Press, 1981).

However, Marshall Berman, former Bronx resident, sees the exodus from the borough as a continuation of the process of fulfilling the American Dream.

The Bronx of my youth was possessed, inspired, by the great modern dream of mobility. To live well meant to move up socially, and this in turn meant to move out physically; to live one's life close to home was not to be alive at all. Our parents, who had moved up and out from the Lower East Side, believed this just as devoutly as we did—even though their hearts might break when we went. Not even the radicals of my youth disputed this dream—and the Bronx of my childhood was full of radicals—their only complaint was that the dream wasn't being fulfilled, that people weren't able to move fast or freely or equally enough. But when you see life this way, no neighborhood or environment can be anything more than a stage along life's way, a launching pad for higher flights and wider orbits than your own. . . . Thus we had no way to resist the wheels that drove the American dream, because it was driving us ourselves—even though we knew the wheels might break us. All through the decades of the postwar boom, the desperate energy of this vision, the frenzied economic and psychic pressure to move up and out, was breaking down hundreds of neighborhoods like the Bronx, even where there was no Moses to lead the exodus and no Expressway to make it fast.

Thus there was no way a Bronx boy or girl could avoid the drive to move on: it was planted within us as well as outside. Moses entered our soul early. But it was at least possible to think about what directions to move in, and at what speed, and with what human toll. One night in 1967, at an academic reception, I was introduced to an older child of the Bronx who had grown up to be a famous futurologist and creator of scenarios for nuclear war. He had just come back from Vietnam, and I was active in the anti-war movement, but I didn't want trouble just then, so I asked about his years in the Bronx instead. We talked pleasantly enough, till I told him that Moses' road was going to blow every trace of both our childhoods away. Fine, he said, the sooner the better; didn't I understand that the destruction of the Bronx would fulfill the Bronx's own basic moral imperative? What moral imperative? I asked. He laughed as he bellowed in my face: "You want to know the morality of the Bronx? 'Get out, schmuck, get out!'" For once in my life, I was stunned into silence. It was the brutal truth: I had left the Bronx, just as he had, and just as we were all brought up to, and now the Bronx was collapsing not just because of Robert Moses but also because of all of us. It was true, but did he have to laugh?

—Marshall Berman, *All That Is Solid Melts into Air:
The Experience of Modernity* (New York: Simon and
Schuster, 1982).

Clearly, there was no consensus on what caused the collapse of the South Bronx, but the result of the urban crisis was dramatic. The changes that overcame The Bronx were also typical of other American cities. The Bronx was generally not the center of well-publicized protests, organized marches, or demonstrations that called attention to the plight of the poor. Media attention at the time concentrated on Harlem, Bedford-Stuyvesant, and Brownsville in New York City, and on Newark, Chicago, Detroit, and the Watts section of Los Angeles in the rest of the nation. Indeed, journalists, ignoring the restive poor of the borough, referred to the South Bronx of the 1960s and the first half of the 1970s as the Silent Ghetto. For many who fled New York City for its northern suburbs, The Bronx became merely a place to pass through at high speed to and from home and work.

9

DEVASTATION

THE BRONX IS BURNING

1965–1991

THE WORLD WAS SHOCKED IN 1977 WHEN PRESIDENT JIMMY CARTER was photographed walking on Charlotte Street, formerly a densely populated, middle-class Jewish area filled with apartment houses. The landscape was now a vacant ruin of blocks upon blocks of rubble. Those apartment houses had been burned and razed to the ground. The horror was compounded during the World Series when a camera from a blimp overlooking Yankee Stadium focused upon a building ablaze in the inky night. The combination of these two events fixed The Bronx as an international symbol of the nation's urban crisis upon the minds of millions of people. Many observers compared the devastation to that of the bombed-out cities of Europe during World War II. Why did this happen?

Mario Merola, who was a city councilman from The Bronx and became Bronx County district attorney in 1973, compares the borough of his youth to the devastation of the time in his memoirs.

> Soon after I became district attorney in 1973, we realized the extent of the problem. From my office on the sixth floor of the Bronx County Courthouse, I was hearing so many fire engines racing up and down the Grand Concourse that I finally asked, hey, what's going on? It got to be a regular event. I'd look out the window and spot the black smoke rising over the rooftops. Or Eddie McCarthy would come in, point out the window, and we'd stand and watch still another building disappear. You could see it all along the horizon, the black smoke and flames, the torched buildings left behind. When you got out of your car in the morning, you could smell smoke hanging in the air from the night before.
>
> … First, we allowed the problem to fester by ignoring the conditions that led to it. We weren't building enough housing for low- and middle-class families to replace and supplement the affordable housing stock we did have—

which all too often consisted of run-down tenements, ripe for arson. We never came up with creative ideas to cope with the educational, health, social, political, and economic problems that were strangling communities and keeping neighborhoods in turmoil. We believed that the way to stabilize families and neighborhoods was simply to hand out a monthly check, with no responsibility attached. And when the fires occurred, we had a system of rewards, both for tenants and landlords. Looking back on it, we might as well have lit the match for some of those people, who were looking to make a little insurance money, or get out of an unprofitable business, or were angry at a lover and wanted revenge, or just liked to set fires for kicks. It was that bad. Our laws and politicians were providing incentives for people to destroy neighborhoods.

There were a lot of ways the arson game was played. Soon after we zeroed in on the problem, we were able to piece together some of the scenarios. The landlords who burned their property for profit often followed a pattern. First, they got the tenants on the upper floors, especially in the top rear apartments, to move out of the building. Then they would hire someone for a few bucks, maybe a kid in the neighborhood, and have him pour gasoline or some other accelerant through holes drilled in the roof and light the fire. Once the roof went, the building was considered uninhabitable. Then came the profit: insurance money, sometimes a lot more than the building was worth; government funding to purchase the site from the landlord or help him rebuild; a virtual tax pardon—no law said that property taxes had to be paid out of the proceeds. Is it any wonder that most of the torched buildings were in tax arrears? And is it any wonder that we had burned-out buildings and empty lots all over the place? The insurance companies never even investigated those fires and never forced the landlords to rebuild. They just paid out the claims and passed the expense on to everyone else in the form of higher premiums. Talk about take the money and run.

Vandalized, abandoned apartment house at the corner of Third Avenue and Cyrus Place, May 1978. "There were scavengers who wanted to clear out buildings so they could strip them of their valuable plumbing and construction materials. There were people who set fires on the lower floors of buildings so they could burglarize top-floor apartments while the buildings were being evacuated. There were youths who simply liked to vandalize other people's property." —Mario Merola. The Bronx County Historical Society Research Library.

Entrance of 546 East 145 Street near St. Ann's Avenue, a building destroyed by fire, December 13, 1972. "There were kids who set fires because they enjoyed seeing the fire engines roll by and were caught up in the media excitement of the arson wave. There were pyromaniacs who did it for sexual thrill. And, of course, there were the common criminals who set fires to spite, to frighten, to extort, to kill." —Mario Merola. The Bronx County Historical Society Research Library.

Then there were those tenants who burned their own buildings so they could collect welfare money. Just as we had no central repository of insurance records to allow us to check up on some of the arsonist landlords, the city had none for tenants who submitted claims for relocation money. We found people who'd burned themselves out seven, eight times. They'd put all of their furniture out on the sidewalk, tell everyone in the building to get out, and then set their apartment on fire. They would go to the Department of Social Services, claim that they'd been burned out, and collect the $2,000 stipend to replace furniture and pay for moving expenses. Virtually no questions asked.

There were also tenants who burned themselves out because they wanted to leave their privately owned tenements and move into better-maintained public housing. Fire victims always went to the top of the waiting lists for apartments in city projects.

There were scavengers who wanted to clear out buildings so they could strip them of their valuable plumbing and construction materials. There were people who set fires on the lower floors of buildings so they could burglarize top-floor apartments while the buildings were being evacuated. There were youths who simply liked to vandalize other people's property. There were social activists who believed that burning out a neighborhood would force the government to pay attention to their group's needs. There were kids who set fires because they enjoyed seeing the fire engines roll by and were caught up in the media excitement of the arson wave. There were pyromaniacs who did it for sexual thrill. And, of course, there were the common criminals who set fires to spite, to frighten, to extort, to kill. Because so few arsonists are actually caught, no one knows which kind of criminal sets the most fires.

—Mario Merola, *Big City D.A.* (New York: Random House, 1988).

Fear struck people in every Bronx neighborhood in the wake of the maelstrom in the South Bronx. As Jill Jonnes recorded:

Year by year as the arson epidemic raged, Melrose, Mott Haven, Hunt's Point, Morrisania, West Farms, Tremont, Concourse, Highbridge and Morris Heights were overwhelmed, immobilized, destroyed or subsumed by the "South Bronx." No one who observed this South Bronx cancer could believe the rapidity with which it struck. . . .

The South Bronx made a terrific stage for passing politicians, a Pope, radicals, journalists, assorted do-gooders, and hustlers of every hue. . . .

President Jimmy Carter walks on the rubble of a once-vibrant Charlotte Street, October 5, 1977. "The South Bronx made a terrific stage for passing politicians, a Pope, radicals, journalists, assorted do-gooders, and hustlers of every hue. . . . Charlotte Street became a must for political aspirants." —Jill Jonnes. The Bronx County Historical Society Research Library.

Charlotte Street became a must for political aspirants. Teddy Kennedy made an appearance there in March, 1980, just before the New York presidential primary, in the company of Herman Badillo, who squired Kennedy around in the rain, taking him to the very spot where Carter stood. With this most dramatic of backdrops—dead buildings, the famous mountain range of rubble—Badillo extended his arm and indicted the landscape and the president. "Take a look around you, Senator, and see for yourself what the Carter promises have done." Ronald Reagan came for his turn. . . . Reagan emerged from his limousine into the blazing sunlight and stood on Charlotte Street in his cream-colored suit. . . . Across the street, a hostile crowd of sixty or seventy chanted, "You ain't gonna do nothing," and "Go back to California."

—Jill Jonnes, *We're Still Here: The Rise, Fall, and Resurrection of the South Bronx* (Boston: The Atlantic Monthly Press, 1986).

Watching the fires burn, and even setting them, became a neighborhood sport for some South Bronx teenagers, as described by Abraham Rodriguez, Jr., in his novel *Spidertown*. Firebug, the fictional neighborhood arsonist, is the crash-pad roommate of Miguel, a drug runner trying to get out of the business. "A wienie roast" is the term used for a set fire. Amelia is Miguel's friend.

"There's a wienie roast tonight," Firebug whispered, eyes luminous. "You inta' comin'? I wanna know if you can pick Amelia up f' me like always."

Miguel leaned against the cold wall. "You got another one?"

"Yup. I'm a real busy man."

Miguel thought for a moment about the big fire he had seen two nights ago, the big tenement on Jackson Avenue. Rolling clouds of black smoke blotted out the sky while brilliant sheaths of flame slithered out of every window. Rows of engines clogged the streets, red lights pulsing like strobes in a disco. Miguel and Amelia sat on the hood of his Impala, his '68 four-door cherry leather Impala. They had been two blocks away, across an empty lot, and they could still feel the heat on their faces.

"He's gettin' better," Amelia had said, munching loudly. She passed him the bag of popcorn and he handed her the bottle of beer, while small clusters of grieving tenants clutched blankets and stood out in the cold, some barefoot, some in ragged slippers and tattered robes, some crying, screaming, yelling anxiously for their children, a fat mother with steel-wool hair frantically counting heads. Amelia had pointed out a man who stood by a lamp-post, clad only in underwear, his thin legs trembling. She laughed and laughed. There was a time when Miguel used to laugh too, enjoying the show from his front-row seat. Now he felt disgusted.

A fire in an apartment house at Fox and 163rd Streets. "Rolling clouds of black smoke blotted out the sky while brilliant sheaths of flame slithered out of every window." —Abraham Rodriguez, Jr. The Bronx County Historical Society Research Library, Dennis P. O'Connell, photographer.

Miguel lives in an area that has been devastated by the arson fires.

The private house where he used to live was still there across from the church, empty windows gaping, an ugly burnt-out hulk. Like an old garish hooker wearing too much eyeliner, it called to him. "Come back." His old window was shattered and blackened. No matter where he turned there was an old empty building waiting for him, an ugly fragment of past, an old dead life. Seventeen almost, but he felt like he was already fifty, looking back on a long, cluttered road. How would he ever be a kid? He was trying to make big decisions about life and about love, whatever the fuck THAT was.

Although Miguel attends the South Bronx "wienie roasts," he no longer has the stomach for the devastation they cause or for the pain they inflict on innocent tenants. Domino is a member of the arsonists' pack.

Miguel didn't even know why he was going to the roast. He approached the burning building, fire trucks scattered across his path like children's toys, when he noticed that the building was the same one he had stopped in to chat with Domino.

Firebug's groupies were across the street by one of the engines. He leaned against his car and lit a cigarette. The small building stood with one side of its face in flames, tongues of fire flicking up defiantly through the rolling black smoke and the stabbing beams of water. Miguel recognized a fat woman across from him in a tattered housedress and thong sandals, one of which had ripped and dangled and dragged as she marched up and down the street screaming and crying. Her words were not words but howls, her fists beating her chest. Miguel focused on Domino, his green beret over his head of stiff frizz, laughing and getting poked by a girl named Stephanie, who was trying to get him to stop. Miguel looked back at the woman. "That one," Domino had said to him that day she passed them on the stairs, glaring. "She's one a' them. Fucken tenant organizers." It made Miguel think of what the Nazis used to do. . . .

—Abraham Rodriguez, Jr., *Spidertown* (New York: Hyperion, 1993).

Dennis Smith was a fireman in Engine Company 82 on Intervale Avenue near 167th Street in the South Bronx. In the early 1970s, it was the busiest firehouse in the world, averaging 700 calls a month. He relates one incident caused by the chaos engulfing the South Bronx. Mike is a fellow firefighter.

Anything that had the smallest benefit for firemen would interest Mike, and he worked untiringly for the men in the firehouse.

Then a nine-year-old boy reached up and pulled the alarm-box handle. Kids do this a lot in the South Bronx. His friends giggled, and they all ran up the street to watch the fire engines come. The box came in on the bells—2787—Southern Boulevard and 172nd Street. Mike pulled himself up on the side step of the apparatus. The heavy wheels turned up Intervale Avenue, the officer's foot pressing hard on the siren. At Freeman Street the apparatus turned right, and Mike lost his grip. He spun from the side step like a top. Marty Hannon and Juan Moran jumped off the apparatus even before it came to a screeching stop. There was blood all over. They could see that Mike had stopped breathing. Marty cleared some of the blood away with a handkerchief, and began mouth-to-mouth resuscitation. He told me all he remembers of those agonizing minutes was the Battalion Chief's voice blaring over the Department radio: *"Transmit signal ten ninety-two for Box 2787. Malicious false alarm."*

The following day the city's newspapers ran the story stating that the Uniformed Firefighters Association was offering a thousand dollars' reward for information leading to the arrest of the person who pulled the box. That afternoon a nine-year-old boy was led through the heavy iron doors of the Forty-first Precinct House. News spreads quickly in the South Bronx, and the boy's friends told their parents, who called the cops.

While the boy was being questioned at the police station, people from the Hoe Avenue Association, a neighborhood action group, painted alarm box number 2787 black, and hung a sign around it. The sign was in two parts, the top half in Spanish, and the bottom in English. It read: A FIREMAN WAS KILLED WHILE COMING HERE TO A FALSE ALARM. Before the paint was dry another false alarm was pulled at the same box, and the men of Engine 82 took the sign down.

Mike had two sons, one seven, the other nine—two brave and frightened boys now walking on either side of their mother, walking slowly behind a shining red fire engine that moves between endless rows of their school chums, and hundreds of firemen. They look up at the flag-draped casket on top of the fire engine and feel proud that their daddy is the cause of all this ceremony, but they are also frightened because they are old enough to realize that there is a tomorrow, and it is going to be different without him.

The young boy at the police station is frightened, too, but in a different way. He is confused and wonders why everyone is so upset. All the kids pull false alarms. At least the kids he pals around with do. He came to this

An unidentified block in the South Bronx in the late 1970s. "You can play in the abandoned buildings, they told him, or on the towering trash heaps in the backyards, or in the musty, rat-infested cellars. There used to be a boys' club in the neighborhood, but it burned down and never reopened." —Dennis Smith. The Bronx County Historical Society Research Library, Sy Rubin, photographer.

country from Puerto Rico five years ago, and the kids on the block taught him that you have to make your own fun in the South Bronx. You can play in the abandoned buildings, they told him, or on the towering trash heaps in the backyards, or in the musty, rat-infested cellars. There used to be a boys' club in the neighborhood, but it burned down and never reopened. He learned, too, that pulling the handle of a fire-alarm box causes excitement, and a certain pleasure that comes with being responsible for all the noise, the sirens, the air horns. Why is everyone so upset?

I know why I am upset. My company alone, Engine 82, responded to over two thousand false alarms last year. Many of them were caused by kids like this. Kids with no place to go, nothing to do.

—Dennis Smith, *Report from Engine Company 82*
(New York: Saturday Review Press, 1972).

With block after block of burned-out shells of apartment buildings on their hands, city agencies tried to camouflage the emptiness of entire neighborhoods by slapping decals over their boarded-up windows. The decals showed partly opened louvered shutters and window-sill flower pots to fool passing motorists on the highways into briefly believing the houses were still inhabited. Poet Katherine Soniat captured the scene in "Skirting It: The Bronx."

Decals in the windows of buildings off the Cross-Bronx Expressway near Crotona Park, 1987. *"The City Planning Commission / spreading hope with picture decals / on abandoned buildings' walls: / . . . Such a picture, / Such a Main Street of the seasonal / when the weather's coming down hard / on this by-pass to the next state."* —Katherine Soniat. The Bronx County Historical Society Research Library, Ted Tobar, photographer.

Like memories of a voice
that called you in at dark,
the proper image is struck—
The City Planning Commission
spreading hope with picture decals
on abandoned buildings' walls:
one offers green shutters, a window box
of geraniums, another holds a boy
smiling astride a cherry-ribboned
Christmas bike. Such a picture,

Such a Main Street of the seasonal
when the weather's coming down hard
on this by-pass to the next state,
spilling into broken windows
that will not refill with glass
and give the world back shiny,
slightly muted by rain.

      —Katherine Soniat, "Skirting It: The Bronx,"
Cracking Eggs (Gainesville: University Presses of Florida, 1990).

To the aging Jewish immigrants who still resided in the South Bronx, as well as to the black and Hispanic elders who had moved there during the past three decades, the ever-advancing fires evoked painful memories of conditions from which they had fled. The Bronx was certainly no longer the idealized working-class haven it had once been for them. Marc Kaminsky, writer and psychotherapist, recounts the effect in 1978 of the conflagration on the minds of the elderly members of a senior center on Tremont Avenue gathered in a workshop on living history.

For nearly forty years, my grandmother Esther had lived two blocks away, in the grandly styled Marjorie Hall. This apartment complex, built just before the First World War, consisted of five connected buildings that enclosed a formal garden with a fountain at the center. It combined the imagery of the medieval walled city, the Jewish ghetto, and the aristocratic pleasure garden that itself reproduced the traditional image of paradise. "The green and pleasant parks of the Bronx"—so read the handbill my grandfather Alter picked up on Delancey Street one day in 1913—became the middle-class idea of the heavenly city that my immigrant grandparents pursued after abandoning, without apparent difficulty, the Messianic hopes of their Orthodox fathers and, a few years later, again without much soul-

Abandoned buildings on Clay Avenue south of the intersection with Webster Avenue and Claremont Parkway, March 1981. Note the recently revealed early twentieth-century billboards advertising an elegant Harlem department store. "The social history of every old one in the group included the narrative of a journey that had this place as its terminus: a common migration that had taken them, at some period in their lives, through Harlem. . . . And all of them had moved 'up from the ghetto' to this 'good neighborhood' in the Bronx, where they now watched the flames climb up from the valley below Third Avenue, gutting abandoned and tenanted buildings in a steady advance westward." —Marc Kaminsky. The Bronx County Historical Society Research Library, Robert Apuzzo, photographer.

wrenching, the socialist dream of a redeemed life in a just society. Now, sixty-five years later, less than a mile away, the fires that were razing the refuge they had once found here could be seen, past midnight, from the bedroom and living room windows of the ten old people in the workshop.

With members of the workshop, Kaminsky draws an analogy between the burning of Troy in the *Iliad* and the fires in the South Bronx.

> Our Troy was the South Bronx. Here was our common ground, the final and major connection among us. The social history of every old one in the group included the narrative of a journey that had this place as its terminus: a common migration that had taken them, at some period in their lives, through Harlem. And it was the last in a series of remarkable commonalities that we discovered among them. With one exception, every person in the workshop had lived in Harlem: the Jews more than half a century ago, when its boundaries included a "Little Russia" as well as a large population of German-Jewish merchants; the Blacks and Puerto Ricans had lived there in the Forties and Fifties. And all of them had moved "up from the ghetto" to this "good neighborhood" in the Bronx, where they now watched the flames climb up from the valley below Third Avenue, gutting abandoned and tenanted buildings in a steady advance westward.
>
> —Marc Kaminsky, "All That Our Eyes Have Witnessed: Memories of a Living History Workshop in the South Bronx," *Twenty-five Years of the Life Review: Theoretical and Practical Considerations,* ed. Robert Disch (New York and London: The Haworth Press, 1988).

It seemed unthinkable to long-time Bronx residents that once-proud middle-class neighborhoods would turn into crime- and drug-infested ruins. Such conditions, prevalent at the same time buildings were burning, were captured by the poet Florence Holzman in "The Death of the Bronx."

> Snow storms of the forties
> forts and snowball fights
> drying mittens on the hallway radiator
> of the brick apartment building
> drinking hot chocolate
> curtains pinned on a stretcher to dry

> Mom ironing heavily starched shirts,
> socks, even our shoe laces.
> our waterfall
> a board against the pavement catching rain
> mothers chattering from windows
> watching out for each other's children
> refusing to accept what was happening
> it all seemed to suddenly change
> crime and drugs
> buildings burning
> people I knew all moving away
> syringes in the hallways.
>
> —Florence Holzman, "The Death of the Bronx,"
> *Impulse* (May 1995).

A long-time resident, poet Virginia Scott, was also forced to come to terms with the fires after the building next door burned. In "Limoges," she celebrates her hard-working Canadian ancestors who passed down to her their strength and endurance. The Limoges china represents the beauty and continuity of her family tradition. It is kept in her apartment on Sedgwick Avenue in the hilly western Bronx.

> . . . When my mother, Janie, died,
> she left me her most exquisite
> possession, her *Limoges.*
>
> Plates, cups, bowls
> are in The Bronx now.
> The building next door,
> six story brick,
> has burned
> and is gutted.
>
> The Bronx is hilly
> and crowded with people
> *living under the delicate blue bowl*
> *of the arching sky.*
>
> . . . From one generation
> to the next,

plates, cups, bowls
pass.

There is in people,
There is in women

an exquisite possession:
golden, flowered, delicate,
enduring, transmittable.

My mother left me her *Limoges*,
which her mother gave her,

and in The Bronx,
I am buoyed
by that elegance,

rose-petalled.

> —Virginia Scott, "Limoges," *The Witness Box*
> (Pittsburgh: Motheroot Publications, 1984).

During and after the period of arson fires, crack cocaine replaced heroin as the drug of choice for many users. The demand for this highly addictive substance devastated a large segment of Bronx residents as its use spread in the 1980s. Its effect is implied by black poet, playwright, and former Bronx resident Ed Bullins in his poem "Whiteness in the '80s (Short Ode to a Lost Generation)."

A black boy
On a black corner
after dark
Wears black
black pants
black shirt
black sox and shoes
Black all over
With small white rocks
in his black hands.

> —Ed Bullins, "Whiteness in the '80s (Short Ode to
> a Lost Generation)," unpublished poem.

Crime and violence affected even those residing in the most stable areas untouched by fires. Ninth-grader Latoya Hunter, a fourteen-year-old black girl from a Jamaican family living in a northern Bronx neighborhood near Gun Hill Road, recorded in her diary the emotional trauma she experiences after a local shooting.

January 9, 1991

Dear Janice,

Today gunshots echo in my head. They are the same gunshots that killed an innocent human being right across from my house last night. They are the same gunshots that have scarred me, I think, forever.

Late last night, I was in bed when I heard a man screaming for a police officer. I told myself, I didn't hear the four gunshots that followed his cry for help. I lay there in bed and it was like I was frozen. I didn't want to move an inch. I then heard hysterical crying. I ran to the window when I couldn't keep myself back any longer. What I saw outside were cops arriving. I ran into my parent's room and woke them up. By that time, tears were pouring unstoppingly from my eyes. I couldn't stop shaking. My parents looked through the window and got dressed. They rushed outside and I followed them. It turned out that I knew the person who got shot. He worked at the store at the corner. He was always so nice to me, he was always smiling. He didn't know much English but we still managed a friendship.

I can't believe this happened. Things like this happen everyday in N.Y., but not in my neighborhood, not to people I know.

January 15, 1991

Dear Janice,

Since the murder I haven't been particularly interested in going outside. Today I was thinking about everything. My friends have been doing things and I haven't been there. They'll tell me what's happened the previous day, and I'll feel left out. I was thinking I shouldn't spend so much time in the house anymore. I think tomorrow I'll go outside for a while. This is going to sound funny but for every car that passes me by while I'm walking down the street, a thought comes to me. It says, "I'm going to die now, the person in the car is going to pull out a gun and shoot." The funny thing is when that thought occurs, I don't feel scared that much. I feel calm and ready to face my death. I've discovered about myself that when the day of my death comes, I'll be ready and I'll have a calm soul.

—Latoya Hunter, *The Diary of Latoya Hunter: My First Year in Junior High* (New York: Crown Publishers, 1992).

The constant reports of fires, the widespread use of drugs, and the rampant crime that made headlines in the nation's newspapers and nightly features on television news shows also had an effect on the image of the borough held by non-Bronx residents. Tom Wolfe catered to this image when he pinpointed The Bronx as the setting of *Bonfire of the Vanities*, a satirical novel skewering the pretensions of the greedy and grasping 1980s yuppies.

This fear is first felt by a wealthy and married Manhattan stockbroker, Sherman McCoy, driving with his mistress, Maria, from the airport back to Manhattan over the Triborough Bridge. Unable to move his Mercedes into the lane that leads to the

Bruckner Boulevard at 138th Street in the 1980s. "EAST 138TH . . . a ramp. . . . All at once there was no ramp, no more clean cordoned expressway. He was at ground level. . . . He seemed to be underneath the expressway." —Tom Wolfe. The Bronx County Historical Society Research Library.

Manhattan off-ramp because of the press of traffic, he is forced to get off at the exit leading to The Bronx.

A vague smoky abysmal uneasiness was seeping into Sherman's skull. The Bronx . . . He had been born and raised in New York and took a manly pride in knowing the city. *I know the city.* But in fact his familiarity with the Bronx, over the course of his thirty-eight years, was derived from five or six trips to the Bronx Zoo, two to the Botanical Gardens, and perhaps a dozen trips to Yankee Stadium, the last one in 1977 for a World Series game. He did know that the Bronx had numbered streets which were a continuation of Manhattan's. . . . How bad could it be?

The tide of red taillights flowed on ahead of them, and now they bothered him. In the darkness, amid this red swarm, he couldn't get his bearings. His sense of direction was slipping away. He must be heading north still. The down side of the bridge hadn't curved a great deal. But now there were only signs to go by. His entire stock of landmarks was gone, left behind. At the end of the bridge the expressway split into a "Y". MAJOR DEEGAN GEO. WASHINGTON BRIDGE . . . BRUCKNER NEW ENGLAND . . . Major Deegan went upstate . . . NO! . . . Veer right . . . Suddenly another "Y" . . . EAST BRONX NEW ENGLAND . . . EAST 138TH BRUCKNER BOULEVARD . . . Choose one, you ninny! . . . Acey-deucey . . . One finger, two fingers . . . He veered right again . . . EAST 138TH . . . a ramp. . . . All at once there was no more ramp, no more clean cordoned expressway. He was at ground level. It was as if he had fallen into a junkyard. He seemed to be underneath the expressway. . . .

Sherman McCoy gets out to remove a tire in the roadway that blocked the car.

Two figures! . . . two young men—black—on the ramp, coming up behind him. . . .

"Yo!" said the big one. "Need some help?"

It was a neighborly voice. *Setting me up! One hand inside his jacket pocket!* But he sounds sincere. *It's a set-up, you idiot!* But suppose he merely wants to help?: *What are they doing on this ramp?* Haven't done anything—haven't threatened! But they *will.* Just be nice. Are you *insane?* Do something! Act! A sound filled his skull, the sound of rushing steam. He held the tire up in front of his chest. *Now!* Bango—he charged the big one. . . . the brute fell over the tire. . . .

"Sherman!"

Maria was behind the wheel of the car. The engine was roaring. The door on the passenger side was open.

"Get in!"

The other one, the skinny one, was between him and the car . . . a terrified look on his mug . . . eyes wide open. . . . Sherman was pure frenzy . . . Had to get to the car! . . . He ran for it. He lowered his head. He crashed into him. The boy was spinning back and hit the rear fender of the car but didn't fall down.

"Henry!"

The big one was getting up. Sherman got into the car.

At the wheel, the frenzied Maria throws the car into reverse.

The skinny one standing right there. . . . The rear end fishtailed . . . *thok!* . . . The skinny boy was no longer standing. . . . Maria fought the steering wheel. . . . She floored it. . . . A furious squeal . . . The Mercedes shot up the ramp. . . .

On the way back to Manhattan, Sherman ruminates on the possibility that one of the young men has been killed or injured.

. . . *thok!* . . . the sound of the rear fender hitting something and the skinny boy disappearing from view. . . .

. . . he could hear it again. The little *thok!* And the skinny boy was gone.

"Maria, I think you—I think we hit one of them."

In Wolfe's burlesque, the national paranoia about blacks and Hispanics and the streets and neighborhoods of The Bronx also grips the white ethnic elite who run the borough. The huge cube-shaped Bronx County Building on the Grand Concourse and 161st Street is likened to a citadel like the Rock of Gibraltar where they barricade themselves. Larry Kramer, a new assistant district attorney, describes the terror felt by the staff.

It was not just young assistant D.A.'s like him and Andriutti and Jimmy Caughey. All over Gibraltar, at this moment, from the lowest to the highest, the representatives of the Power in the Bronx were holed up in their offices, shell-backed, hunched over deli sandwiches, ordered in. . . . You could ascend to the very top of the criminal justice system in the Bronx and eat deli sandwiches for lunch until the day you retired or died.

The Bronx County Building on the Grand Concourse between 158th and 161st Streets, October 1984. "All over Gibraltar, at this moment, from the lowest to the highest, the representatives of the Power in the Bronx were holed up in their offices, shell-backed, hunched over deli sandwiches, ordered in. . . . There were holdups on the crest of the Grand Concourse, this great ornament of the Bronx, at 11:00 a.m. on nice sunny days. . . . There were assistant D.A.'s who had worked in Gibraltar for ten years who couldn't tell you, on a bet, what was on 162nd Street or 163rd Street, a block off the Grand Concourse." —Tom Wolfe. The Bronx County Historical Society Research Library.

And why? Because they, the Power, the Power that ran the Bronx, were terrified! They were terrified to go into the heart of the Bronx at high noon and have lunch at a restaurant! Terrified! And they ran the place, the Bronx, a borough of 1.1 million souls! The heart of the Bronx was now such a slum that there was no longer anything even resembling a businessman's sit-down restaurant. But even if there were, what judge or D.A. or assistant D.A., what court officer, even packing a .38, would leave Gibraltar at lunchtime to get to it? First, there was plain fear. You walked from the Bronx County Building across the Grand Concourse and down the slope of 161st Street to the Criminal Courts Building, a distance of a block and a half, when you had to, but the prudent bearer of the Power kept his wits about him. There were holdups on the crest of the Grand Concourse, this great ornament of the Bronx, at 11:00 a.m. on nice sunny days. And why not? More wallets and handbags were out on foot in the middle of nice sunny days. You didn't go beyond the Criminal Courts Building at all. There were assistant D.A.'s who had worked in Gibraltar for ten years who couldn't tell you, on a bet, what was on 162nd Street or 163rd Street, a block off the Grand Concourse. They had never been to the Bronx Museum of Art on 164th. But suppose you were fearless in that sense. There remained another subtler fear. You were an alien on the streets of the 44th Precinct, and you knew at once, every time Fate led you into *their* territory. The looks! The looks! The deadly mistrust! You were not wanted. You were not welcome. Gibraltar and the Power belonged to the Bronx Democratic Party, to the Jews and Italians, specifically, but the streets belonged to the Lockwoods and the Arthur Riveras and the Jimmy Dollards and Otis Blakemores and the Herbert 92X's.

> —Tom Wolfe, *The Bonfire of the Vanities* (New York: Farrar, Straus and Giroux, 1987).

Because of the national, and even international, attention focused upon The Bronx in the wake of the fires that beset large portions of the borough, the reputation of the area plummeted. It was depicted in films, video games, and in other areas of popular culture as a crime-ridden wasteland where decent people ventured at their own peril. Visitors to New York City satisfied their need to see such extraordinary ruins only by taking escorted bus tours through the area. One such tour and its effect on the people in the area is revealed in Don DeLillo's novel *Underworld*. Sister Grace, referred to as Gracie, is a fictional Catholic nun helping the poor in a devastated Bronx neighborhood.

> Gracie dropped the crew at their building just as a bus pulled up. What's this, do you believe it? A tour bus in carnival colors with a sign in the slot reading *South Bronx Surreal*. Gracie's breathing grew intense. About thirty Europeans with slung cameras stepped shyly onto the sidewalk in front of the boarded shops and closed factories and they gazed across the street to the derelict tenement in the middle distance.
>
> Gracie went half berserk, sticking her head out the van and calling, "It's not surreal. It's real, it's real. Your bus is surreal. You're surreal.". . .
>
> Gracie shouting, "Brussels is surreal. Milan is surreal. This is real. The Bronx is real."

> —Don DeLillo, *Underworld* (New York: Scribner, 1997).

10

COPING

THE BRONX ENDURES

1961–1988

I N THE 1960S, BEFORE THE ARSON FIRES BEGAN, DESPITE THE PROBLEMS that faced The Bronx or, perhaps, because of them, Bronxites began to celebrate their borough. In 1964, a Golden Jubilee celebration was staged to mark the fiftieth anniversary of the creation of Bronx County. By that time, Ogden Nash's 1930 humorous quip about the borough's name began to sting. Abraham Tauber, dean of faculty at Bronx Community College, asked the poet to write a new work for the occasion. Nash made amends.

> I wrote those lines, "The Bronx? No thonx!"
> I shudder to confess them.
> Now I'm an older, wiser man
> I cry, "The Bronx? God bless them!"
>
> —Ogden Nash, untitled poem, *The Bronx County Historical Society Journal* (July 1964).

Soon afterward, Ruth Lisa Schechter, then arts coordinator for the newly founded Bronx Council on the Arts, wrote the poem "Bronx," in which she celebrates the landmarks of the borough, past and present.

She refers to the orange, white, and blue striped flag of The Bronx with a shield in the center bearing a sun surmounted by an eagle on a hemisphere and a ribbon below it bearing the Latin motto, *Ne Cede Malis*, Yield Not to Evil, all enclosed in a laurel wreath. Herman Melville, Joseph Pulitzer, and Fiorello La Guardia are all buried in Woodlawn Cemetery. In 1797, President John Adams resided in his daughter's house in Eastchester, now part of The Bronx, while yellow fever raged in Philadelphia. In the 1850s, American Shakespearean actor Edwin Forrest built a castle for his home, which is now on the Bronx campus of the College of Mount Saint Vincent. Schechter refers to Maritime and Einstein, other institutions of higher education in The Bronx, and to a branch of N.Y.U., where the Goldman Band used to perform. The Jerome Park Race Track was on the site of the current Jerome

Park Reservoir. "Rochdale principles" refers to the governing rules of the Amalgamated Houses, first used in 1844 for a cooperative grocery in Rochdale, England. The rotary printing press was invented by Richard M. Hoe, who resided in The Bronx in the mid-nineteenth century. Starlight Park was an amusement park that flourished in the center of The Bronx between the wars.

Bronx Borough President Joseph Periconi affixes a sign to a lightpole announcing the Golden Jubilee in 1964 when The Bronx celebrated its fiftieth anniversary as a county of New York State. "I cry, 'The Bronx? God bless them!'" —Ogden Nash. The Bronx County Historical Society Research Library, Max Levine Collection.

> Ghosts trail like wedding veils, north, south
> to Yankee Stadium. As in a parable stopping, going
> on trains to Mosholu where a moment known is—
> Herman Melville rests at Woodlawn, safe
>
> from winning, losing the big, white whale. HAIL
> the beginning of the Bronx on 42 square miles
> holding Moby Dick in "why" and "how," climbing
> hill by hill as on a monorail, right or wrong
>
> divided by the Harlem River to Spuyten Duyvil
> myth year by year or any day on wings to Pelham
> Bay, east, west, pushing back Starlight Park towards
> Yonkers, New Rochelle. In clear or muddled lines
>
> maps design the Communities of 1914, catching
> the careless day under orange, white, blue
> summer sky like Bronx flag waving *Ne Cede Malis*
> waving promised birds in Van Cortlandt Park
>
> to the Botanicals, past our homes, past Giles Place
> in spite of hurricanes where the Penman
> of the Constitution signs another time and puts
> his pen aside. HAIL Morris of Morrisania flying
>
> yellow fever, near the residence of President
> Adams. Eastchester, Bronx. As we go down together
> bumping into history where we look: indentured
> servants, old land grants, Washington, Rochambeau
>
> and Indian tribes round campfires lit before—
> Edgar Allan Poe musing stanzas on Highbridge, moving

The monorail, to the left, at the mainland side of the City Island Bridge in Pelham Bay Park in 1909. A postcard photograph. Passengers from the horsecar that just arrived from City Island to the right are transferring. ". . . climbing / hill by hill . . . on a monorail." —Ruth Lisa Schechter. Barbara Unger Collection.

The entrance to Starlight Amusement Park at 177th Street and Devoe Avenue, 1923. A postcard photograph. "HAIL / . . . Starlight Park." —Ruth Lisa Schechter. Barbara Unger Collection.

to Fordham house, house of green shutters, moving
with Annabel Lee; dying 19th century, moving

to La Guardia, Pulitzer in Woodlawn trailing ghosts
and names off Gun Hill Road to Bronx Zoo. Near our homes,
Mark Twain of Riverdale, near our homes
freedom fighter, Anne Hutchinson and Siwanoy

Indians fall. Far from Boston, Blue Hill Avenue
new to my eyes as a child, distinguishing forms
on the other foot, observing Bronx flag starts
in sun seal, eagle hemisphere, alert to peace

and liberty, courthouse, smallpox, the Lindy
Hop near Franz Sigel Park. While Shakespearean
drama sets up its castle on Mount St. Vincent
lawn. HAIL the Borough of Universities lights up

students at Fordham campus in peace processions
near our homes, Jerome race track round the reservoir
and Loew's Paradise, Merchant Marine, Maritime
and Einstein. HAIL the first Rotary Press like

three-striped flag, *Yield Not to Evil* in laurel wreath
and bronze integrity. Up in air
the Hall of Fame, N.Y.U. and Goldman's Brass Band
booms; near Poe Cottage, Jimmy Baldwin on the way

to DeWitt Clinton school, dreaming metaphors
    of fire
next time, near garment workers building Rochdale
principles, Sholem Aleichem, Trotsky, Tolstoy
and old Dutch Bronck family waving HELLO

Puerto Rico HELLO Italy HELLO Ireland HELLO
refugee from Warsaw Ghetto HELLO churches, syn-
    agogues
from Grand Concourse to Throgs Neck dreaming
    Bronx
dreaming white to purity, blue to orange to City

The Bronx flag. "Under orange, white, blue / summer sky like Bronx flag waving Ne Cede Malis */ . . . three-striped flag,* Yield Not Evil *in laurel wreath."—Ruth Lisa Schechter. The Bronx County Historical Society Reserach Library.*

Island, Orchard Beach like Sargasso Sea
black, brown. And what is color but a pigment
of the imagination? Near our homes, north, south
in noise of The Penman of the Constitution scratching

his fine pen again like a found poem, singing across
Van Cortlandt Park, singing what is not corruptible.

> —Ruth Lisa Schechter, "Bronx," *The Bronx County
> Historical Society Journal* (July 1971).

In addition to its distinguished history, one point of Bronx pride was the continued success of the New York Yankees at Yankee Stadium, at least until the team went into a decade and a half slump after 1964. One famous fan was poet Marianne Moore, a Brooklyn resident who followed the games on radio, and even listened to the postgame broadcasts. She celebrated the team in "Baseball and Writing," mentioning the names of many Yankee players of the first half of the 1960s.

. . . It is a pitcher's battle all the way—a duel—
a catcher's, as, with cruel
    puma paw, Elston Howard lumbers lightly
        back to plate. (His spring
        de-winged a bat swing.)
    They have that killer instinct;
    yet Elston—whose catching
    arm has hurt them all with the bat —
            when questioned, says unenviously,
    "I'm very satisfied. We won."
            shorn of the batting crown, says, "We";
            robbed by a technicality.

When three players on a side play three positions
and modify conditions,
    the massive run need not be everything.
        "Going, going . . ." Is
        it Roger Maris
    has it, running fast. You will
    never see a finer catch. Well . . .
    "Mickey, leaping like the devil"—why
        gild it, although deer sounds better

Yankee Stadium in the 1950s. A postcard photograph. "In that galaxy of nine, say which / won the pennant? Each." —Marianne Moore. The Bronx County Historical Society Research Library.

snares what was speeding towards its treetop nest,
　　　　　one-handing the souvenir-to-be
　　　　　meant to be caught by you or me.

Assign Yogi Berra to Cape Canaveral;
he could handle any missile,
　　He is no feather. "Strike! . . . Strike *two!*"
　　　Fouled back. A blur.
　　　It's gone. You would infer
　　that the bat had eyes.
　　He put the wood to that one.
Praised, Skowron says, "Thanks Mel.
　　I think I helped a *little* bit."
　　　　　All business, each, and modesty.
　　　　Blanchard, Richardson, Kubek, Boyer.
　　　　In that galaxy of nine, say which
　　　　won the pennant? *Each.* It was he.

Those two magnificent saves from the knee—throws
by Boyer, fitness in twos—
    like Whitey's three kinds of pitch and pre-
      diagnosis
      with pick-off psychosis.
    Pitching is a large subject.
    Your arm, too true at first, can learn to
    catch the corners—even trouble
      Mickey Mantle. ("Grazed a Yankee!
My baby pitcher, Montejo!"
      with some pedagogy
      you'll be tough, premature prodigy.)

. . . victory

sped by Luis Arroyo, Hector Lopez
deadly in a pinch. And "Yes,
    it's work; I want you to bear down,
      but enjoy it
      while you're doing it."
    Mr. Houk and Mr. Sain,
    if you have a rummage sale,
    don't sell Roland Sheldon or Tom Tresh.
      Studded with stars in belt and crown,
the Stadium is an adastrium.
      O flashing Orion,
      Your stars are muscled like the lion.

> —Marianne Moore, "Baseball and Writing," *The Complete Poems of Marianne Moore* (New York: The Macmillan Company/The Viking Press, 1967).

The devastation caused by the arson fires affected much of The Bronx. Reactions were diverse. While many people continued to move out of the borough, not all residents wanted to leave. In several areas, they organized to preserve their neighborhoods. This often became a point of pride and borough loyalty. Some people beautified their neighborhoods; others tried to stablize their areas.

In the South Bronx area just south of Longwood Avenue, filled with brownstone-like townhouses, the resident-owners organized to save their neighborhood. Their efforts are recognized by Diane Winston in her essay "Beyond Landmark Status."

The two-and-one-half story buildings of pink, brown or maroon display elegant architectural flourishes: bay windows with ornamental columns, sloping slate roofs, curved cornices and amethyst doorknobs.

This small oasis has been painstakingly safeguarded from destruction by local homeowners. Working together as the Longwood Community Historic District Association, they have achieved a remarkable record of success in a very short time. . . .

"You can now say, 'I live in the South Bronx' with a lot of pride," says Marilyn Smith, co-chairperson of the association. Smith, an attractive woman with a hearty laugh who works as a probation officer for the Bronx Family Court, moved to Longwood in 1960 as a young bride. Today she lives on East 156th Street with her husband, three daughters, grandmother and aunt. "I have absolutely no desire to move," she says. "Where else could I live so inexpensively and so well?" Her street, 156th, like others in the district, has a turn-of-the-century quality. . . .

The architectural integrity of the area, as well as the beauty of the buildings, moved New York City's Landmark Preservation Committee in July 1980

Alexander Avenue south of 139th Street, part of the Mott Haven Historic District, January 3, 1991. "The architectural integrity of the area, as well as the beauty of the buildings, moved New York City's Landmarks Preservation Committee in July 1980 to designate it a historic district, the second such designation in the South Bronx—Mott Haven was the first—and the 39th in New York City." —Diane Winston. The Bronx County Historical Society Research Library.

to designate it a historic district, the second such designation in the South Bronx—Mott Haven was the first—and the 39th in New York City. . . .

The association's other co-chairperson, Tom Bess, is a second-generation Longwood resident. Born in Harlem, Bess' family moved to his present home at 947 E. 156th St. in 1944, the fourth black family to buy a home in the area. The neighborhood then was mostly Jewish, Irish and Italian; today it is equally divided between blacks and Hispanics.

"I've seen the neighborhood go from comfortable middle-class to low-moderate," says Bess, 46, who supervises court reporters for the criminal court of the city of New York. "The fact that neighbors and friends have stayed here made us begin to work on our homes. When the area began to burn, we dug in. I could have moved, but where else would I find such a gorgeous brownstone?". . .

It was in the mid-'70s that Bess and Smith decided it was time to organize. Each block already had its own block association, vestiges of the 1940s and '50s, but they wanted to pull the entire neighborhood together.

"We called a community meeting," recalls Bess, an engaging, articulate man with an easy laugh. "Our first venture was a community sweep. It worked. People saw us and, as sophomoric as it sounds, they got involved." After that they walked through the neighborhood, knocked on the 128 doors, and told residents they had two options: They could either get together in a unified body and storm every city agency to save their houses or they could sit by and let the neighborhood burn—it was 1977 and the community was still burning. . . .

. . . The group named block captains who supervised their areas and monitored ancillary services such as the police, sanitation, the fire department and the community board. Next, they looked into programs for rehabilitation loans and grants. But the combination of governmental red tape and their own inexperience stymied these efforts.

Finally, in 1980, the turning point came when Longwood was given landmark status. After receiving the designation, individual homeowners became eligible for city grants for facade improvement. In addition, the association could apply for state and federal grants and loans, which assist inner-city historic districts. . . .

. . . Although residents are gratified, at last, to have grant funds and landmark status, they feel it was only deserved, for they knew way back that their community was special. Agnes Holloway and her husband bought their home at 568 Dawson Street for $13,000 in 1950. They were the fourth black family on the street and Mrs. Holloway recalls that when she saw the red-

and-white limestone building with its interior amber-colored murals of pastoral scenes, she went straight to the real estate agent and bought it.

"In the whole of New York City, I don't think you can find any better buildings than you see on this block," she says, adding, "every landlord who purchased a home years ago saw something in these buildings. The landmark designation put an asterisk on that. It's something that will make us fight a little more."

—Diane Winston, "Beyond Landmark Status,"
¡Mira! (Spring 1982).

In 1970, local clergymen started the Northwest Bronx Clergy Conference, consisting of sixteen Catholic parishes, to organize the people of the area to prevent blight. They obtained financial assistance from large corporations and from government agencies for housing renovation, and received cooperation from local banks and insurers that enabled local landlords to repair their buildings. Mary McLoughlin is a layperson who became involved with the Coalition in an attempt to reverse the deterioration that had beset the apartment house on Sedgwick Avenue in Kingsbridge Heights in which she has lived since 1948. Her story is told by Jill Jonnes in her study of the borough.

Throughout the 1970s the situation deteriorated. The landlord accepted new tenants who stayed up all night playing loud music and defaced the halls with graffiti. He rented part of the basement to a social club. "I was told they were looking for a go-go girl," Mrs. McLoughlin says wryly.

A core of fed-up tenants organized. Then, in August of 1979, the landlord removed the boiler and never bothered to replace it. The new tenants' association went to housing court, and the landlord agreed to reinstall the boiler. The building's back retaining wall collapsed, threatening to undermine the whole structure. The desperate tenants sought a City housing administrator. The case dragged on for more than a year. Worn down and discouraged, the tenants still persevered, attending more than one hundred meetings with City agencies and court hearings, many of which were canceled or postponed. A mysterious fire broke out above Mrs. McLoughlin's apartment.

Only a rare and faithful citizen could hang on through these seemingly fruitless dealings with the housing bureaucracy. Yet the coalition's secret was to persist doggedly in apparently hopeless causes. "The coalition helped us right down the line," says Mrs. McLoughlin, who some called an "unsung saint." "They gave us technical assistance and drove us to court and provided backup." Mrs. McLoughlin wears a neat navy dress with a leaf pattern and has her shoulder-length brown hair pulled back with bobby pins. "I said to myself, 'This is a good building. I am not going to move. I am not going to allow a lousy landlord to deprive me of a place to live.'" And so she continued the struggle. She had what people in the South Bronx had lacked—a larger organization to guide them and give them heart, and, just as important, new City programs that would enable an administrator to restore their buildings.

—Jill Jonnes, *We're Still Here: The Rise, Fall, and Resurrection of the South Bronx* (Boston: The Atlantic Monthly Press, 1986).

Although most people moved from the ravaged areas of the South Bronx to other parts of the borough or elsewhere, some occupied their abandoned buildings, rehabilitated them, and ended up owning them cooperatively.

Banana Kelly . . . began to fight housing abandonment in the Longwood section of the South Bronx in the mid-1970's. The group took its name from the sweeping banana-shaped block of Kelly Street, where it began organizing "sweat equity" projects, in which residents rebuild abandoned shells basically by themselves.

—Alan Finder, "Nonprofit Community Groups Rebuild Housing in the Bronx," *New York Times* (March 11, 1990).

While no one could remain oblivious to the staggering social problems facing The Bronx, many people residing in the borough for years were determined to survive and endure. Like the members of the Longwood Community Historic District Association and Mary McLoughlin's tenants' group, the fictional Salvatore and Angelina in Nancy Charvat-Nagle's poem "The Fig Trees of Arnow Avenue" exemplify the desire to conserve what was good in an established way of life. Arnow Avenue is in the northeastern part of The Bronx between Pelham Parkway and Gun Hill Road, an area that remained mostly free of severe housing deterioration, abandonment, and arson.

If you are not from the
  Bronx,
If you have never seen them
  with your own eyes,
You would never believe it!
Those trees!

In front of two story
  brick houses
And just as tall.
The linoleum trees,
  we used to call them
In the days when

it was linoleum,
and not vinyl.

At the corner house,
The old gentleman
Carries the ladder
    from the garage
Places it carefully
    against the tree
And the old woman,
Frowning face peering
    between curtains
    at the window,
    worries.
His sons should be here,
    they have a duty.
The vertical lines
    between her dark brows
    deepen,
    remembering
    the phone calls.

Tony said he had to go
    to a wedding,
His wife's cousin, he said.
"Next week, Pop,
    I can help next week."
Sal said,
    "Not this weekend, Pop,
    I got things to do;
You know how it is, Pop,
    with kids."
Pop knew,
    Pop said nothing.
"The week after,
I gotta go to Joanne's family
    on Saturday.
A week from Sunday,
I'll come, Pop,

promise."
Frankie said "Aw, Pop,
Whaddaya fool with
    that thing for?
This weekend,
    I got plans.
You oughtta sell that place
    in the Bronx, Pop.
Come to the Island with me
    and Marlene.
We'll fix a nice apartment
    downstairs.
The Bronx is no place
    anymore, Pop."

Salvatore di Giuseppi
    hung up the phone.
His wife stood silently
    drying her hands
    on her apron.
Salvatore's lower lip
    pushed up against
    his upper lip
Chin lifted,
    jaw muscles tightened.
"My sons are too busy
    to help their father.
They say 'wait one week,'
    'wait two weeks.'
Frankie, when he's a boy
Want everything yesterday.
Now he say wait!
An old man don't wait!
Death don't wait!
Winter don't wait!
I do the tree today,
    myself,
Like in the old days."
Angelina's thoughts

Filled the silence
Between them.
But the tree
    was much smaller
In the old days,
And you were
    much stronger.
She watched him
    open the basement door,
Heard his footsteps
    irregular on the stairs.
His hip is bothering him
    again, she thought,
Smoothing out her apron.
She watched her husband
Slowly climb the rungs
    of the ladder,
Pruning shears in one
    hand.
Angelina let the curtains
    fall closed.

The boys, they want us to
    move with them,
    to Long Island.
Sometimes, I think,
    it's not such a bad idea.
Frankie has the room
    for us.
Her lips tightened
    into a line.
But this is where
I raised my boys.
This is my home!
She looked out the window
    again.
And he would never
    leave The Tree. . . .
. . . Salvatore brought that
    tree to America

A leafless twig
    wrapped in cloth.
They wouldn't care
That the figs in summer
Were as sweet
As the memory
    of home.
They wouldn't wrap it
Against the New York
    winter
Like my Salvatore.

She heard the snapping
    of branches
Being cut close.
Soon she would hear
The old living room carpets
    being dragged
    out of the garage.
Heavy work
For an old man.
Angelina sighed,
Went down the stairs,
Opened a closet and
    removed a garbage can
    with no cover.
She dusted it, carefully,
    Heard her husband
Struggling with the rug.
Angelina put the can down,
    gently
Reached into the closet
For the plastic clothesline.
Slowly she walked outside,
Stood out of the way
As Salvatore wrapped
    The Tree. . . .

The linoleum would be
    easier,

If the wind stayed away.
She looked at the sky.
The still air was cool.
Blue sky, no clouds,
The sun as hot on her face
  as home.
She walked back
  to the closet
  for more line.
Salvatore climbed down
  again
Limping a little,
He dragged the long roll of
  yellow and red linoleum.
The sound,
Like coarse sandpaper
  on wood,
Filled the garage.
She followed him
  to the front yard,
The brown trash can
  and an old bathmat
  in one hand,
Another coil of clothesline
  in the other.
Her arms swung
  as she walked,
A rolling gait that comes
With sixty years
Of walking on
  bowed legs.

She watched her Salvatore
In silence
Wrapping the huge hub

  of the tree
In worn linoleum
Tying the knots
That would not
Pull loose
In the wind.
Throwing the faded
  pink bathmat
Over the crown.
Angelina reached up
With the can.
Salvatore slipped it over
  the bathmat,
Taped it down.
Tied it to the lines
Binding the linoleum.

The sun was low
When Salvatore di Giuseppi
Stood beside Angelina
Their faces solemnly raised
looking at The Tree,
The last fig tree
On Arnow Avenue.
It was turning cold
In the setting sun,
Angelina shivered,
Golden light
Fell upon them and
Their shadows cast
Long and grey-blue
Beside the longer shadow
Of the fig tree
  from home.

—N. R. Charvat-Nagle, "The Fig Trees of Arnow Avenue," unpublished poem.

Angelo Mazza, a character in Pulitzer Prize–winning novelist Anna Quindlen's book *Object Lessons,* is a cemetery caretaker who dedicates his life to maintaining and beautifying his little corner of the northern Bronx. Calvary Cemetery appears to be modeled on St. Raymond's Cemetery in the Throggs Neck section, a tightly knit neighborhood of mostly Irish, Italian, and German residents that has changed very little over the decades.

> Outside, over the low stone wall just behind the rose garden, was the neighborhood—blocks of clapboard row houses shining clean and quiet in the sun, like so many others in the North Bronx, the backyards filled with tomato plants and the ornamental urns filled with hydrangeas. . . . When Angelo Mazza had taken over the place it had seemed half empty, tombstones only on one side, although a good many of the other plots had been purchased by families moving into the area around it. It had looked a little like a golf course, satisfyingly green and yet a bit austere, with its great metal gates crowned with one enormous cross flanked by two smaller ones. Angelo had gone to work.
>
> On either side of the gates he had planted pink azaleas, and along the

East Tremont Avenue at Waterbury Avenue just outside the gates of St. Raymond's Cemetery, November 1982. "On either side of the gates he had planted pink azaleas, and along the fence . . . he had put a wisteria." —Anna Quindlen. The Bronx County Historical Society Research Library.

Arthur Avenue at 186th Street in the 1980s. "About a mile from the housing project where I grew up is the small insular Italian neighborhood of Belmont, whose main artery is Arthur Avenue. . . . Arthur Avenue is lined with Italian bakeries, fruit and vegetable markets, Italian restaurants and cafes. The neighborhood thrives, especially on the weekends when a lot of the Italians, Irish, and Jews who grew up in the Bronx but have since moved north to Westchester come back to shop and dine." —Michael Covino. The Bronx County Historical Society Research Library, Ken Fisher Collection.

fence that separated the cemetery from a back alley and a block of backyards he had put a wisteria, a stick of a thing with three skinny tendrils. Along the fieldstone wall he had planted orange lilies he had found beside a creek one day in Westchester County, growing wild in mats of green foliage. He put violets around his own front door, which duplicated themselves as fast as field mice, and around back he put the rose garden and vegetable garden and herb patch.

—Anna Quindlen, *Object Lessons* (New York: Random House, 1991).

Other Bronx neighborhoods, such as Belmont in the central Bronx, remained relatively untouched. In many ways, the pattern of life there remained similar to that of the days before The Bronx became a by-word for the urban crisis. Michael Covino, who grew up in a housing project on Gun Hill Road and White Plains Avenue and later departed to the San Francisco Bay area, discovered that fact on a trip back to The Bronx in 1989.

About a mile from the housing project where I grew up is the small insular Italian neighborhood of Belmont, whose main artery is Arthur Avenue. It is one of those Italian neighborhoods that still persist in New York and that are so puzzling to outsiders, a neighborhood that, despite being in the heart of the wrecked Bronx, has one of the lowest crime rates in the five boroughs. Old people sit on the stoops late at night. People walk their dogs after midnight. Young people sit at outdoor cafe tables sipping espressos. The handball wall in the playground, painted with the tri-colors of the Italian flag, might be the only handball wall in all New York not defaced with graffiti.

Arthur Avenue is lined with Italian bakeries, fruit and vegetable markets, Italian restaurants and cafes. The neighborhood thrives, especially on the weekends when a lot of the Italians, Irish, and Jews who grew up in the Bronx but have since moved north to Westchester come back to shop and dine.

—Michael Covino, "The Neighborhood," *Express: The East Bay's Free Weekly* (January 12, 1990).

In many Irish-American Bronx neighborhoods, family life went on as it had before. Irish pubs and restaurants continued to be centers of social life, and such rituals as a family meal after a burial still were honored. This is all revealed in National Book Award winner Alice McDermott's novel *Charming Billy*.

Somewhere in The Bronx, only twenty minutes or so from the cemetery, Maeve found a small bar-and-grill in a wooded alcove set well off the street that was willing to serve the funeral party of forty-seven medium-rare roast beef and boiled potatoes and green beans almondine, with fruit salad to begin and vanilla ice cream to go with the coffee. Pitchers of beer and of iced tea would be placed along the table at intervals and the bar left open—it being a regular business day—for anyone who wanted a drink.

The place was at the end of a sloping driveway that started out as macadam but quickly diminished to dirt and gravel. There was an apron of dirt and gravel in front of the building, potholed, and on the day of the funeral filled with puddles, and the first ten cars parked here, including the black limousine Maeve had ridden in. The others parked up along the drive, first along one side, then the other, the members of the funeral party walking in their fourth procession of the day (the first had been out of the church, the second and third in and out of the graveyard), down the wet and rutted path to the little restaurant that, lacking only draught Guinness and peat fire, might have been a pub in rural Ireland. Or, lacking dialogue by John Millington Synge, the set of a rural Irish play.

How in the world she ever found this place was a mystery, despite the question of being asked again and again as Billy's friends and family filed in—the women, in high heels, walking on tiptoe down the sloping path, the men holding their wives' arms and umbrellas that had already been well soaked at the side of the grave. All of them, in their church clothes, gave a formal air to the gray day and the ragged border of city trees and wet weeds.

—Alice McDermott, *Charming Billy* (Rockland, Me.: Wheeler Publishing, Inc., 1998).

Some people who had left The Bronx earlier were drawn back. One was a fictional successful advertising executive and father of two from Great Neck, Steve Robbins, the hero of Avery Corman's novel *The Old Neighborhood*. Unhappily caught in a mid-life crisis, Robbins is drawn back to the Bronx neighborhood where his youthful dreams had been hatched, hoping for a new direction. In the 1970s, he takes the subway to the borough's busiest retail commercial center at the Grand Concourse and Fordham Road.

When I stepped out onto the street I became dizzy with the flood of memories. The physical landscape was essentially as it had been twenty years before. The overall look was shabbier, somewhat dirtier, but nothing had been torn down, nor had any new buildings been constructed. Alexander's Department Store was there on Fordham Road, and the Dollar Savings Bank Building, and the Wagner Building to which my father had reported for civilian defense duty during World War II. Where stores had been located, stores existed. On 188th Street and the Grand Concourse, the place I now stood, Bickford's cafeteria, the seltzer stop for the local horseplayers, was out of business. With appropriateness the location had been taken over by an off-track betting parlor.

I saw a sign on the other side of the street for Krum's but when I entered I found it was no longer a soda parlor, it was a candy and card shop....

I walked north along the Grand Concourse and crossed Fordham Road, which was busy with shoppers. The people were mostly Hispanics and blacks. Looking east and west along Fordham Road I could see it was still thriving with retail stores. Just north of Fordham Road, Sutter's Bakery was in its old location on the Grand Concourse. I had been dispatched there for a coffee ring on many a weekend morning, my parents were lucky if the cake arrived home with the pecans. I bought half of a coffee ring on this day and began to devour it outside the bakery....

I continued along the Grand Concourse, walking slowly, trying to absorb the sensations, worried that I was about to come upon a row of condemned buildings, burnt mattresses in the street, cars abandoned and stripped—my childhood neighborhood desecrated. But this section of the Bronx, north of Fordham Road near Kingsbridge Road, was not blighted. I reached Poe Park, it seemed the neighborhood was still predominantly Irish Catholic and Jewish. In the park, young mothers sat on benches as their children played, some of the old people were involved in shuffleboard games or were playing cards and checkers. I searched for a familiar face. I recognized no one. At the end of the park, still standing, was Poe Cottage, a farmhouse where Edgar Allan Poe had lived. I had first visited it with class 1–1 of P.S. 86, nearly forty years before.

I took a deep breath anticipating what I was to do next. I crossed to the west side of the street and walked down the hill of Kingsbridge Road and entered my old neighborhood. On both sides of the street the stores were fully rented. The Fishers were gone from the candy store, and the Rosens were gone, but it was still a functioning neighborhood, drug store, fish store, kosher butcher, coffee shop, pizza store, shoppers were on the streets, cars and buses were moving along. Kingsbridge Road was virtually as it had been when I left. I looked at the side streets, the red brick buildings had become murky with age, the white brick buildings had yellowed, but these apartment houses were occupied, sheet metal did not cover the windows, garbage was not scattered through the streets as in the photos I had seen of the South Bronx. I stopped in front of Beatrice Arms and I shuddered from the impact of seeing the building again. I looked up at the window where my mother had tossed down shopping money wrapped in a handkerchief. . . .

I walked back to Kingsbridge Road, the neighborhood was busy with street life, teenagers were gathered in front of the pizza store, people were walking dogs, the stores were busy with shoppers. Even on a warm summer day the pulse was more active than anything I had known in the suburbs. I took the subway and returned to Great Neck by train.

I was back the next day. And the next. And the next. I kept coming back. . . . I haunted my old neighborhood like a restless ghost.

Soon Robbins moves into an apartment in his old neighborhood and finds a job making malteds in a Bronx candy store.

—Avery Corman, *The Old Neighborhood* (New York: The Linden Press/Simon and Schuster, 1980).

In 1969, writer Gil Fagiani actually returned to live in his old neighborhood on the Grand Concourse near Kingsbridge Road and, writing in the mid-1980s, he found the area still vital, although the ethnic mix had changed.

Kingsbridge Armory at Kingsbridge Road and Jerome Avenue in the summer of 1978. "Although the Bronx has become a media metaphor for urban blight, I love my neighborhood. It has a unhewn, heroic quality to it that both the suburban outlands and the bloodless, gentrified tracts of Manhattan lack. . . . A few blocks away is the Kingsbridge Armory—the largest in the world." —Gil Fagiani. The Bronx County Historical Society Research Library.

The building I have been living in for eight years was almost solidly Jewish in the 1950s. The mezuzah, like a cocked, all-protective eye in the frame of my front door, is a testament to that long bygone period. Now I would estimate that 70% of the tenants are Puerto Rican, 20% white and 10% are black. The surrounding neighborhood was traditionally Irish and Jewish, a mixture of middle, professional and working class families. Today, the neighborhood is predominantly third world and poor. Some people call it a neighborhood in transition and decline. I call it a victim of class and racial warfare. Last week my insurance agent reminded me that since I live one block south of Kingsbridge Road, I am considered a resident of the South Bronx. But this is a kind of racial geography because physically I live in the Northwest Bronx. This distinction translates into higher insurance rates, fewer mortgages, poorer services and all the other mean and petty consequences of racial discrimination.

Although the Bronx has become a media metaphor for urban blight, I love my neighborhood. It has an unhewn, heroic quality to it that both the suburban outlands and the bloodless, gentrified tracts of Manhattan lack. Across the street from my home is the cottage-residence of the demoniac genius Edgar Allan Poe. A few blocks away is the Kingsbridge Armory—the largest in the world. Down Fordham Road are the Botanical Gardens and the Bronx Zoo. The descendants of the laborers who built these cultural gems live in the adjacent Italian community of Arthur Avenue. My great grandfather owned a tavern on 187th Street. No matter how much the Bronx has changed in ethnic composition, on a hot summer night the sidewalks of the Arthur Avenue neighborhood are still cluttered with elderly Italian men and women, sitting and communing with the fresh air and each other on their block. Their neighborhood remains strong and they stick out a collective tongue at the politics of neglect and fear.

New immigrants from Korea, the Dominican Republic, Thailand, Yugoslavia, Albania, Italy and the West Indies have poured into the Kingsbridge neighborhood in recent years. It bristles with the hues of many skin colors and the musicality of many tongues. They dream in common, though, of a better place to live and raise their children.

—Gil Fagiani, "Stirrings in the Bronx," *Forward Motion* (October-November 1985).

Many of the Jews who chose to remain in The Bronx relocated to the Riverdale, Pelham Parkway, and Co-op City neighborhoods in the northern part of the borough. Co-op City is a huge, government-subsidized, high-rise middle-class housing development in the northeastern corner of The Bronx. Thus, these formerly countrified areas developed as their population increased. The springing up of new dwellings and neighborhood businesses is recalled by Cindy Beer-Fouhy in her poem "Bronx Childhood."

> Vacant lots were meadows.
> Between the milkweed,
> queen anne's lace and
> tiger lilies set a
> centerpiece on tables made of slate.
>
> Black-eyed Susans webbed
> through tree house windows,
> sumac branches, shades;
> white wall tires hung from
> boughs, swinging shadows
> over vines of morning glory,
> ivy in the afternoon.

Cement and iron seal their graves
below a diner parking lot;

But seed is strong as memory.

Across the street,
in concrete dwellings,
grass sprouts through
a sidewalk crack.

> —Cindy Beer-Fouhy, "Bronx Childhood," unpublished poem.

As in the 1920s, moving from one neighborhood to what was looked upon as a better one was still considered taking a step up the socioeconomic ladder, as described by Milton Kessler in his poem "Mover."

During the night a mover came
and lifted
      lightly lightly
our whole apartment building
and all our broken glass-wings
and carried us
      lightly lightly
up to the Grand Concourse.

> —Milton Kessler, "Mover," *The Grand Concourse* (Binghamton, N.Y.: MSS-SUNY Binghamton, 1990).

Many elderly residents coped uneasily with change, hoping improvement would come. Leonard Kriegel depicts a young family visiting grandparents in the northern Bronx neighborhood of Norwood. The narrator suggests that perhaps America has robbed the people of The Bronx. He employs the Yiddish phrase *Amerika goniff!* (America, the thief), a term which had been used by the Jewish social activists and unionists in the 1930s, who also hoped life in America would improve. He thinly disguises the real names of Steuben Avenue, Rochambeau Avenue, Gun Hill Road, the Montefiore Medical Center, and the Valentine-Varian House, now the Museum of Bronx History. The Oval refers to Williamsbridge Oval Park, a former reservoir.

The Valentine-Varian House/Museum of Bronx History at Bainbridge Avenue and 208th Street, November 1969. "My sons and I stand in front of the old stone house. It has been moved across the street from where it used to stand. The old stone house is a museum now and it squats in front of the Oval. . . . It was our avenue to history, its importance somehow confirmed by the names of the surrounding streets." —Leonard Kriegel. The Bronx County Historical Society Research Library, gift of Ronald Schliessman.

My sons and I stand in front of the old stone house. It has been moved across the street from where it used to stand. The old stone house is a museum now and it squats in front of the Oval. To its left, an incongruous statue of a Civil War soldier holding a rifle. The statue puzzles me, for the house dates from before the Revolutionary War. Or so we believed. It was our avenue to history, its importance somehow confirmed by the names of the surrounding streets—Jones, Lafayette, Russell, Stoval, Coldfield, Coleman Place, Hodges Place, Partridge Avenue. An American litany. The statue insists on a different America. Village greens in small Indiana towns. On the other side, the flag snaps in the breeze-spit sun. A blue sign with yellow lettering marshals the gate.

CARLETON MUSEUM OF BRONX HISTORY
Open Sundays 1–5 P.M.
Admission: Adults 25¢
Children Under 16 Free (only in the company of adults)
PARKS, RECREATION, AND CULTURAL AFFAIRS ADMINISTRATION
CITY OF NEW YORK
BRONX COUNTY HISTORICAL SOCIETY

"Can we go inside?" Bruce asks. He does not know the house is history. But he wants to go inside.

"Not today. It's not open today."

They do not protest. They remember the promise of the track. We drift toward the tunnel entrance to the Oval. A brass tablet informs me that the flagpole has been donated by the Jewish War Veterans of America.

FOR ALL BRONX HEROES

WHO MADE THE SUPREME SACRIFICE
TO KEEP AMERICA FREE

The landscaped arc that embraces the Oval is spotted with ugly bare patches. The walls of the tunnel are graffitied—sullen, fading protest. Red paint spread everywhere. The tunnel was always filled with protests. Always open season for private revenge or public accusation. Each dutifully recorded on its walls. Like an early warning system of a brittle time to come. The boys run back and forth through the tunnel. Bruce whoops gleefully, trying to catch the echo. Mark spots his grandparents, shouts, and runs on ahead.

Later, the boys' grandfather expresses his frustration with the perception that the overwhelmed South Bronx includes everything south of Fordham Road. He considers the stabilizing presence of the nearby Montefiore Medical Center, a massive complex that has been in the neighborhood since 1912. The cemetery is Woodlawn Cemetery, a site of over four hundred acres that contains the magnificent mausoleums and simple graves of many of old New York's commercial and cultural elite.

"They say it saves the neighborhood, the Hospital," my father muses. "So it won't be like on the Concourse. On account the Hospital is here, they won't let this neighborhood go down." He does not explain who *they* are. He assumes that I know. And I do. *They* are the mysterious forces now ruling the Bronx. Like god, *they* create their own rules. My father now conceives his function as that of a survivor trying to do what has been expected of him. The Concourse has been doomed, at least below Fordham Road, simply because *they* had given it to *them*. The fate of the neighborhood has not yet been decided....

... My children kiss their grandparents good-by. I make sure my sons have strapped their safety belts in the back seat. We drive up the avenue to Coldfield Road. We pass the old stone house and the Oval, with its emptiness, with my past, with the October sun and the cancer tower and the senior citizens in their center. Unburied ghosts. Fleshed out in the very loss. Instead of turning left at Coldfield Road, I drive straight on. Past the Shrine Church of St. Rose and the Daughters of Israel Home for the Aged. I turn right at the corner. I drive into the cemetery. I want to look for Melville's tomb. I drive slowly past the markers and tombs and all the heaped-up remnants of nineteenth-century New York, squinting in the sun as I search the bookkeeping

Woodlawn Cemetery. "I turn right at the corner. I drive into the cemetery. I want to look for Melville's tomb. I drive slowly past the markers and tombs and all the heaped-up remnants of nineteenth-century New York, squinting in the sun as I search the bookkeeping of an alien time. We park the car and get out." —Leonard Kriegel. The Bronx County Historical Society Research Library.

of an alien time. We park the car and get out. What are we doing in a cemetery? Mark wants to know. Bruce examines a gravestone. I cannot find Melville's tomb. I feel very foolish. Once I walked here with a girl, I was a college sophomore then. Such memories are inane. Time reduced to words, language to memory. *Amerika goniff!* the union people laughed. Senior citizens is what they are now. *Amerika goniff!* For them and for Melville. But for me?

> —Leonard Kriegel, *Notes for the Two-Dollar Window: Portraits from an American Neighborhood* (New York: Saturday Review Press/E. P. Dutton & Co., 1976).

Despite the massive shift of Jews to the northern Bronx and elsewhere, a handful of elderly Jewish people remaining in the South Bronx took steps to preserve a way of life that was fast disappearing. Despite their dwindling numbers that changed so much in their lives, they still manage to go to their synagogue and socialize. Jack Kugelmass, a cultural anthropologist, believes that their very existence in the midst of such conditions is virtually a miracle.

Intervale Jewish Center at Intervale Avenue and 165th Street, 1997. "The shul—the Intervale Jewish Center—stands in the heart of the South Bronx. . . . Like all local institutions, the shul is subjected to repeated vandalism from marauding groups of youths." —Jack M. Kugelmass. Lloyd Ultan Collection, Joan Abbey, photographer.

The shul—the Intervale Jewish Center—stands in the heart of the South Bronx, a part of New York City inhabited predominantly by Puerto Ricans, interspersed with pockets of black residents. Crime, arson, and urban decay have been so widespread in this area that the 41st Precinct, in which the shul is located, was nicknamed "Fort Apache" by the police. Like all local institutions, the shul is subjected to repeated vandalism from marauding groups of youths, although it is so denuded of artifacts that there is scarcely anything left to steal. The silver ornaments that decorated the Torah scrolls disappeared years ago, and a large, discolored patch indicates the space on the wall from which vandals removed the bronze memorial plaque listing the names of deceased members of the congregation. The roof, too, has suffered from numerous attempts to penetrate the building. Periodic downpours have left the building with a musty odor, rotting wood floors, peeling paint, and falling plaster. The Torahs, hidden from view inside the Holy Ark, are covered with plastic garbage bags to protect them from the rain.

Some of the decay is a result of the shul's declining membership and the diminishing finances of the few remaining congregants. Built in 1923, when the south and central Bronx contained more than a quarter-million Jews, the shul could then barely house the hundreds of White Russian–Jewish immigrants who competed for seats. Nearby, rows of stores catered to the culinary needs of observant Jews. Today, the once plain but solid rows of middle-class houses and apartment buildings are pockmarked by vacant rubble-strewn lots. Dug into the ground like an exposed bunker, the shul seems to shrink from its neighbors: an abandoned six-story apartment building on one side; a garbage strewn lot on the other.

Inside, a half dozen stairs lead down from the entrance to a main hall large enough to seat five hundred people. The dozen or so congregants who still attend services are scattered throughout this room. Some sit alone, others in small groups. A few roam about the hall, checking for needed repairs, while others busy themselves at the rear of the shul, preparing the food and wine for the kiddush. . . .

What is most striking about these people is their ability to lead active lives in an area where few New Yorkers care to venture, let alone live. Their determination is all the more remarkable considering their advanced age and physical vulnerability. The neighborhood, like their age, sets the framework within which they live, but it does not determine, in a deeper sense, the quality of their lives. For most of them, the decay of the South Bronx is an adversary much like death. It is inevitable. One cannot flee from it, yet some form of resistance is necessary.

—Jack M. Kugelmass, "The Miracle of Intervale Avenue," *Natural History* (December 1980).

In the South Bronx, one of the few aspects of stability was the local playground. For children living on the increasingly mean streets of the Mott Haven section, St. Mary's Park offered a respite and a refuge, as shown in w r rodriguez's poem "st. mary's park."

> this is the first playground
> of the bronx its asphalt skin
> is cracked and gray
> children are busy
> with childhood
> there is nothing but this moment
> of fun
> here the poor forget hunger
> here the meek are not afraid

here the sad are lost in laughter
the innocent time before gangs
graffiti the rocks
before the sun is malignant
and the moon a mere golf course
there is nothing but
the exhilaration of life
gravity cannot hold us
we are seeds on the wind
sent forth from timeless trees
the falling from youth
seems eternal
the flight of maple wings
the plunge of acorn and pod
we land in the green world of infinite summer
the trees will not grow old
the trees will keep us forever safe
in the shade of knowledge and life
saint mary's park is heaven on earth
hell is the streets where we suffer and die

—w r rodriguez, "saint mary's park," unpublished
poem.

For teenagers, music has always been a means of coping with their lives. Popular music also became a route to success for some young blacks. An expression of the reality of their Bronx lives came in a new sound, hip-hop. Hip-hop's origins in The Bronx were recounted in a *Time* magazine feature story.

The hip-hop world began in The Bronx in 1971. Cindy Campbell needed a little back-to-school money, so she asked her brother Clive to throw a party. Back in Kingston, Jamaica, his hometown, Clive used to watch dance-hall revelers. He loved reggae, Bob Marley and Don Drummond and the Skatalites. He loved the big sound systems the deejays had, the way they'd "toast" in a singsong voice before each song. When he moved to the U.S. at age 13, he used to tear the speakers out of abandoned cars and hook them onto a stereo in his room.

The after-school party, held in a rec room of a Bronx high-rise, was a success: Clive and Cindy charged 25¢ for girls and 50¢ for boys, and it went till 4 a.m. Pretty soon Clive was getting requests to do more parties, and in

1973 he gave his first block party. He was Kool Herc now—that was the graffito tag he used to write on subway cars—and he got respect. At 18 he was the first break-beat deejay, reciting rhymes over the "break," or instrumental, part of the records he was spinning. He had two turntables going and two copies of each record, so he could play the break over and over, on one turntable and then the next. Americans didn't get reggae, he thought, so he tried to capture that feel with U.S. funk songs—James Brown and Mandrill. He had dancers who did their thing in the break—break dancers, or, as he called them b-boys. As they danced, Herc rapped, "Rocking and jamming / That's all we play / When push comes to shove / The Herculoids won't budge / So rock on, my brother. . . ."

Joseph Saddler loved music, too. He thought Kool Herc was a god—but he thought he could do better. Saddler figured most songs had only about 10 seconds that were good, that really got the party going, so he wanted to stretch those 10 seconds out, create long nights of mixing and dancing. Holed up in his Bronx bedroom, he figured out a way to listen to one turntable on headphones while the other turntable was revving up a crowd. That way a deejay could keep two records spinning seamlessly, over and over again. Herc was doing it by feel. Saddler wanted the show to be perfect.

So he became Grandmaster Flash. He played his turntables as if he were Jimi Hendrix, cuing records with his elbow, his feet, behind his back. He invented "scratching"—spinning a record back and forth to create a scratchy sound. He tried rapping, but he couldn't do it, so he gathered a crew around him—the Furious Five, rap's first supergroup.

Things happened fast. This is the remix. There were start-up labels like Sugar Hill and Tommy Boy. Then in 1979 came *Rapper's Delight*—the first rap song most people remember. Grandmaster Flash warned, "Don't touch me 'cause I'm close to the edge."

—Melissa August et al., "Hip-Hop Nation," *Time* (February 8, 1999).

Former Bronxite Marshall Berman exhorts Bronx youth to continue the success achieved by residents in the past. He imagines a project that would help inspire future generations and counteract some of the destructive effects of the Cross-Bronx Expressway. He proposes that a mural be painted along the highway's length that would depict the proud history of the borough and celebrate some of the famous people who came from The Bronx.

The Bronx Mural, as I imagine it, would be painted onto the brick and concrete retaining walls that run alongside most of the eight miles of the

Cross-Bronx Expressway, so that every automobile trip through and out of the Bronx would become a trip into its buried depths. In the places where the road runs close to or above ground level and the walls recede, the driver's view of the Bronx's past life would alternate with sweeping vistas of its present ruin. The mural might depict cross-sections of streets, of houses, even of rooms full of people just as they were before the Expressway cut through them all.

But it would go back before this, to our century's early years, at the height of the Jewish and Italian immigration, with the Bronx growing along the rapidly expanding subway lines, and (in the words of the *Communist Manifesto*) whole populations conjured out of the ground: to tens of thousands of garment workers, printers, butchers, house painters, furriers, union militants, socialists, anarchists, communists. Here is D. W. Griffith, whose old Biograph Studio building still stands, solid but battered and neglected, at the Expressway's edge; here is Sholem Aleichem, seeing the New World and saying that it was good, and dying on Kelly Street (the block where Bella Abzug was born); and there is Trotsky on East 164th Street, waiting for his revolution (did he ever really play a Russian in obscure silent films? we will never know). Now we see a modest but energetic and confident bourgeoisie, springing up in the 1920s near the new Yankee Stadium, promenading on the Grand Concourse for a brief moment in the sun, finding romance in the swan boats in Crotona Park; and not far away, 'the coops,' a great network of workers' housing settlements, cooperatively building a new world beside Bronx and Van Cortlandt parks. We move on to the bleak adversity of the 1930s, unemployment lines, home relief, the WPA (whose splendid monument, the Bronx County Courthouse, stands just above Yankee Stadium), radical passions and energies exploding, street-corner fights between Trotskyites and Stalinists, candy stores and cafeterias ablaze with talk through the night; then to the excitement and anxiety of the postwar years, new affluence, neighborhoods more vibrant than ever, even as new worlds beyond the neighborhoods begin to open up, people buy cars, start to move; to the Bronx's new immigrants from Puerto Rico, South Carolina, Trinidad, new shades of skin and clothes on the street, new music and rhythms, new tensions and intensities; and finally to Robert Moses and his dread road, smashing through the Bronx's inner life, transforming evolution into devolution, entropy into catastrophe, and creating the ruin upon which the work of art is built.

The mural would have to be executed in a number of radically different styles, so as to express the amazing variety of imaginative visions that sprang from these apparently uniform streets, apartment houses, schoolyards, kosher butcher shops, appetizing and candy stores. Barnett Newman,

Stanley Kubrick, Clifford Odets, Larry Rivers, George Segal, Jerome Weidman, Rosalyn Drexler, E. L. Doctorow, Grace Paley, Irving Howe, would all be there; along with George Meany, Herman Badillo, Bella Abzug and Stokely Carmichael; John Garfield, Tony Curtis' Sidney Falco, Gertrude Berg's Molly Goldberg, Bess Myerson (an iconic monument to assimilation, the Bronx's Miss America, 1945), and Anne Bancroft; Hank Greenberg, Jake La Motta, Jack Molinas (was he the Bronx's greatest athlete, its most vicious crook, or both?); Nate Archibald; A. M. Rosenthal of the *New York Times* and his sister, the communist leader Ruth Witt; Phil Spector, Bill Graham, Dion and the Belmonts, the Rascals, Laura Nyro, Larry Harlow, the brothers Palmieri; Jules Feiffer and Lou Myers; Paddy Chayefsky and Neil Simon; Ralph Lauren and Calvin Klein, Garry Winogrand, George and Mike Kuchar; Jonas Salk, George Wald, Seymour Melman, Herman Kahn—all of these, and so many more.

Children of the Bronx would be encouraged to return and put themselves in the picture: the Expressway wall is big enough to hold them all; as it got increasingly crowded, it would approach the density of the Bronx at its peak.

> —Marshall Berman, *All That Is Solid Melts into Air: The Experience of Modernity* (New York: Simon and Schuster, 1982).

Indeed, there certainly is a reservoir of good will among the Bronxites who had deserted the borough. In 1988, Avery Corman, the author of *The Old Neighborhood*, went back to The Bronx to report on his reactions for a *New York Times* article.

> Something about the Bronx . . . has a powerful emotional hold on people. Part of it has to do, I think, with a sense of loss. The culture in which we grew up there has vanished. In the 1960s and 1970s urban blight swept across the Bronx with such ferocity that its burned, abandoned housing looked like pictures we'd seen of London during the Blitz. . . . Another reason for people's connection to the place, and my own, I suspect, is the way we romanticize our childhood. For people now middle-aged, the years in the 1940s and 1950s were clearly simpler, more innocent times. But there is something undeniably special about those old Bronx neighborhoods . . . which many of us miss today. . . . You can take the boy out of the Bronx, but you can't take the Bronx out of the boy, and I am still rooting for the place.

> —Avery Corman, "Grand Concourse: A Writer's Return," *New York Times Magazine* (November 20, 1988).

11

THE PHOENIX

THE BRONX RISES FROM THE ASHES

1975–2000

A S THE THE 1970S WANED, THE ARSON FIRES THAT HAD PLAGUED THE South Bronx abated. Even as The Bronx was burning, however, the seeds of restoration were being planted. Increasingly, government funds rebuilt the burned-out areas of the South Bronx. Plans went forward with strong initiative from neighborhood residents working in cooperation with local government agencies. Often this process was facilitated by the active participation of the clergy and church organizations. The Bronx Democratic party revived under the leadership of George Friedman and Roberto Ramirez, the first Puerto Rican to lead a county political party. Under the aegis of Borough President Fernando Ferrer, The Bronx experienced a renaissance so swift and startling that, in 1997, the National Civic League named Bronx County an All-America City, the first borough of New York ever to win that prestigious award.

This did not seem a likely outcome at the end of the 1970s. At that time, the devastation in the South Bronx was widespread. Because the city, plagued by a serious fiscal crisis, could not address the situation, all it could do was to allow neighborhood residents to plant temporary community gardens on vacant lots. The church as a major force was illustrated by Don DeLillo in his novel *Underworld*. Two fictional nuns, Sister Grace and Sister Edgar, take a van to deliver food to the unfortunate homeless and squatters who live a semi-feral existence in the ruins.

The two women look across a landscape of vacant lots filled with years of stratified deposits—the age of house garbage, the age of construction debris and vandalized car bodies, the age of moldering mobster parts. Weeds and trees grew amid the dumped objects. There were dog packs, sightings of hawks and owls. City workers came periodically to excavate the site and they stood warily by the great earth machines, the pumpkin-mudded backhoes and dozers, like infantrymen huddled near advancing tanks. But soon they left, they always left with holes half dug, pieces of equipment discarded, styrofoam cups, pepperoni pizzas. The nuns looked across all this. There were

Kelly Street and Westchester Avenue, 1982. "A landscape of vacant lots filled with years of stratified deposits . . . house garbage . . . construction debris and vandalized car bodies . . . moldering mobster parts." —Don DeLillo. The Bronx County Historical Society Research Library.

networks of vermin, craters chocked with plumbing fixtures and sheetrock. There were hillocks of slashed tires laced with thriving vine. Gunfire sang at sunset off the low walls of demolished buildings. The nuns sat in the van and looked. At the far end was a lone standing structure, a derelict tenement with an exposed wall where another building once abutted. This wall was where Ismael Muñoz and his crew of graffiti writers spray-painted a memorial angel every time a child died in the neighborhood. Angels in blue and pink covered roughly half the high slab. The child's name and age were printed under each angel, sometimes with cause of death or personal comments by the family, and as the van drew closer Edgar could see entries for TB, AIDS, beatings, drive-by shootings, measles, asthma, abandonment at birth—left in dumpster, forgot in car, left in Glad Bag stormy night.

The area was called the Wall, partly for the graffiti facade and partly the general sense of exclusion—it was a tuck of land adrift from the social order.

"I wish they'd stop with the angels," Gracie said. "It's in totally bad taste. A fourteenth-century church, that's where you go for angels. This wall publicizes all the things we're working to change. Ismael should look for positive things to emphasize. The townhouses, the community gardens that people plant. Walk around the corner you see ordinary people going to work, going to school. Stores and churches.". . .

Edgar laughed inside her skull. It was the drama of the angels that made her feel she belonged here. It was the terrible death these angels represented. It was the danger the writers faced to produce their graffiti. There were no fire escapes or windows on the memorial wall and the writers had to rappel from the roof with belayed ropes or sway on makeshift scaffolds when they did an angel in the lower ranks. Ismael spoke of a companion wall for dead graffitists, flashing his wasted smile. . . .

They stopped at the friary to pick up groceries they would distribute for the needy. The friary was an old brick building wedged between boarded tenements. Three monks in gray cloaks and rope belts worked in an anteroom, getting the day's shipment ready. . . .

Edgar liked seeing the monks in the street. They visited the homebound, ran a shelter for the homeless, they collected food for the hungry. And they were men in a place where few men remained. Teenage boys in clusters, armed drug dealers—these were the men of the immediate streets. She didn't know where the others had gone, the fathers, living with second or third families, hidden in rooming houses or sleeping under highways in refrigerator boxes, buried in the potter's field on Hart Island.

Brother Mike requests the sisters to inquire about a twelve-year-old girl who lives in the ruins and who constantly runs away whenever he tries to speak to her. After loading the food into their van, the nuns visit Ismael Muñoz, who raises money by salvaging automobiles dumped into the Bronx River and donates some of the proceeds to the nuns. The nuns climb the needle-strewn stairs of the building inhabited by squatters living without heat, light, and water to Ismael's third-floor headquarters. Muñoz tells them that no money is available this time because he plans to use it to provide the building with the services it thus far lacks.

Edgar looked out a window and saw someone moving among the poplars and ailanthus trees in the most overgrown part of the rubbled lots. A girl in a too-big jersey and striped pants grubbing in the underbrush, maybe for something to eat or wear. Edgar watched her, a lanky kid who had a sort of feral intelligence, a sureness of gesture and step—she looked sleepless but alert, she looked unwashed but completely clean somehow, earth-clean and hungry and quick. There was something about her that mesmerized the nun, a charmed quality, a sense of something favored and sustaining.

She gestured to Gracie. Just then the girl slipped through a maze of wrecked cars and by the time Gracie reached the window she was barely a flick of the eye, lost in the low ruins of an old firehouse.

"Who is this girl," Gracie said, "who's out there in the lots hiding from people?"

Ismael looked at his crew and one of them piped up, an undersized boy in spray-painted jeans, dark-skinned and shirtless.

"Esmeralda. Nobody knows where her mother's at."

Gracie said, "Can you find the girl and then tell Brother Mike?"

"This girl she be real quick."

A murmur of assent.

"She be a running fool this girl."

Heads bobbing above the comic books.

"Why did her mother go away?"

"She be a addict. They un, you know, predictable."

All street these kids. No home or school. Edgar wanted to get them in a room with a blackboard and then buzz their heads with Spelling and Punctuation. She wanted to drill them in the lessons of the Baltimore Catechism. True or false, yes or no, fill in the blanks.

Ismael said, "Maybe the mother returns. She feels the worm of remorse. But the truth of the matter there's kids that are better off without their mothers or fathers. Because their mothers or fathers are dangering their safety."

"Catch her and hold her," Gracie told the crew. "She's too young to be on her own. Brother Mike says she's twelve."

"Twelve is not so young," Ismael said. "One of my best writers, he goes wildstyle, age eleven or twelve. Juano. I send him down in a rope to do the complicated letters."

In subsequent weeks, the two nuns try to make contact with Esmeralda, and Ismael succeeds in wiring his building with electricity. Sister Grace then finds out from the local precinct that poor Esmeralda has been raped and thrown off a roof. The two distraught nuns ask Ismael to find the killer, which he indicates would be impossible. Then, over an old flickering television set, CNN shows the Wall and the scene of the crime. Sister Edgar cannot watch. One of Ismael's children sprayed Esmeralda's angel onto the Wall, depicting her in running clothes and a pair of white Nike Air Jordan sneakers.

Then the stories begin, word passing block to block, moving through churches and superettes, maybe even garbled slightly, mistranslated here and there, but not deeply distorted—it is clear enough that people are talking about the same uncanny occurrence. And some of them go and look and tell others, stirring the hope that grows when things surpass their limits.

They gather at dusk at a windy place between bridge approaches, seven or eight people drawn by the word of one or two, then thirty people drawn by the seven, then a tight silent crowd that grows bigger but no less respectful, two hundred people wedged onto a traffic island in the bottommost Bronx where the expressway arches down from the terminal market and the train yards stretch toward the narrows, all that old industrial muscle with its fretful desolation—the ramps that shoot tall weeds and the waste burner coughing toxic fumes and the old railroad bridge spanning the Harlem River, an openwork tower at either end, maybe swaying slightly in the persistent wind.

They come and park their cars if they have cars, six or seven to a car, parking tilted on a high shoulder or in the factory side streets, and they wedge themselves onto a concrete island between the expressway and the pocked boulevard, feeling the wind come chilling in and gazing above the wash of standard rip-roar traffic to a billboard floating in the gloom—an advertising sign scaffolded high above the riverbank and meant to attract the doped-over glances of commuters on the trains that run incessantly down from the northern suburbs into the thick of Manhattan money and glut.

Over the objections of Sister Grace, Sister Edgar insists upon viewing the vision that has drawn so many people. They both go down one night and stand among a large throng in the moonlight.

They follow the crowd's stoked gaze. They stand and look. The billboard is unevenly lighted, dim in spots, several bulbs blown and unreplaced, but the central elements are clear, a vast cascade of orange juice pouring diagonally from top right into a goblet that is handheld at lower left—the perfectly formed hand of a female caucasian of the middle suburbs. . . .

Edgar doesn't know how long they're supposed to wait or exactly what is supposed to happen. Produce trucks pass in the rumbling dusk. . . . After twenty minutes there is a rustle, a sort of perceptual wind, and people look north, children point north, and Edgar strains to catch what they are seeing.

The train.

She feels the words before she sees the object. She feels the words although no one has spoken them. This is how a crowd brings things to single consciousness. Then she sees it, an ordinary commuter train, silver and blue, ungraffit'd, moving smoothly toward the drawbridge. The headlights sweep the billboard and she hears a sound from the crowd, a gasp that shoots into sobs and moans and the cry of some unnamable painful elation. A blurted sort of whoop, the holler of unstoppered belief. Because when the train lights hit the dimmest part of the billboard a face appears above the misty lake and it belongs to the murdered girl. A dozen women clutch their heads, they whoop and sob, a spirit, a godsbreath passing through the crowd.

Esmeralda.

Esmeralda.

Sister is in body shock. She has seen it but so fleetingly, too fast to absorb—she wants the girl to reappear. Women holding babies up to the sign, to the glowing juice, let it bathe them in baptismal balsam and oil. And Gracie talking into Edgar's face, into the jangle of voices and noise.

"Did it look like her?"

"Yes."

The crowd believes they have witnessed a miracle, concluding that they have seen a vision of Esmeralda. To be certain of what they saw, the nuns wait for the next train. Sister Edgar moves closer for a better view. The train lights again hit the billboard.

> She sees Esmeralda's face take shape under the rainbows of bounteous juice and above the little suburban lake and there is a sense of someone living in the image, an animating spirit—less than a tender second of life, less than half a second and the spot is dark again.
>
> She feels something break upon her. An angelus of clearest joy.
>
> —Don DeLillo, *Underworld* (New York: Scribner, 1997).

Although Esmeralda's mystical resurrection suggested divine intervention, her rebirth seemed to parallel actual events. Just as the raped and murdered street urchin scavenger emerged as an angel and an object of awe, so, too, did the devastated South Bronx rebuild and become a subject of amazement.

The effective rebuilding of The Bronx began when Mayor Edward I. Koch placed Edward J. Logue in charge of the South Bronx Development Organization. Beginning with the Charlotte Street made notorious by President Jimmy Carter's visit, his purview extended over a much wider area. In 1984, he surveyed his handiwork with Jill Jonnes, as recounted in her study *We're Still Here*.

> On an overcast August day in 1984, Edward J. Logue, head of New York City's South Bronx Development Organization (SBDO), surveys the ten cream-and-coffee-colored ranch houses improbably plunked down on Charlotte Street, a startling vision of suburbia in an old Bronx neighborhood. . . .
>
> He rounds the corner to face the first five houses that went up, all immaculately maintained and alive with the cozy signs of family life: knick-knacks in a lace-curtained window, a plastic wading pool in a driveway, a swing set in the back. "When we had the dedication for Charlotte Gardens," says Logue, "I remember a guy at the back of the crowd yelling, 'These houses will be torn down in a week,' and Koch screaming back, 'The people who have bought them will defend them with their lives.'" He laughs delightedly at the recollection as children swirl by on roller skates.
>
> Down across Boston Road, Logue wades into waist-high weeds to show more sites prepared for the eighty houses that will complete Charlotte Gardens. All the abandoned tenements have been razed clear through to Jennings Street. Only the occasional rumbling of the elevated train and the

The turn from Wilkins Avenue, now Luis Nine Boulevard, into Boston Road, just south of Charlotte Street, November 1984. "Logue . . . surveys the ten cream-and-coffee-colored ranch houses improbably plunked down on Charlotte Street, a startling vision of suburbia in an old Bronx neighborhood."
—Jill Jonnes. The Bronx County Historical Society Research Library.

muted back-and-forth roar of a bulldozer demolishing vacant buildings intrude on the stillness of lower Charlotte Street and its enormous meadows. . . He trudges back up the street to Crotona Park, lush from plentiful summer rains, and over to Indian Lake. After years of neglect, it has been dredged and the muck conveniently dumped as fill for Charlotte Gardens. Yellow paddle boats ripple gaily across the lake's cool, dark surface. . . .

. . . Of all the efforts confirming the renaissance of the South Bronx, none has been more heralded than Charlotte Gardens, where the mere completion of two American Dream houses on an infamous street spurred a front-page story in the *New York Times.*

Aided by state and federal subsidies and lowered mortgage rates, Logue kept the cost of houses low. Local community leaders helped cull the best potential homeowners from among the applicants. Help also came from the Ford Foundation–backed Local Initiative Support Corporation.

In Logue's pantheon of local heroes, the Catholic clergy of the South Bronx occupy a high place. He sings their praises constantly, with special hosannahs for Brother Patrick Lochrane of Belmont, and Sister Thomas and

The Simpson Street area between Southern Boulevard and Fox Street, February 1982. "This outpost of urban resurrection is an oasis of twenty-one hundred new and renovated apartments, two dozen single-family homes, and clean streets shaded by ginkgo trees."—Jill Jonnes. The Bronx County Historical Society Research Library.

Father Gigante of Hunt's Point, locally referred to these days as Giganteland. This outpost of urban resurrection is an oasis of twenty-one hundred new and renovated apartments, two dozen single-family homes, and clean streets shaded by ginkgo trees. At Tiffany Plaza, in front of Saint Athanasius Church, the honey locust trees sway full and green in the breeze, a lively counterpoint to the solemn lions' heads set against a pale pink wall.

In this restful setting, two well-behaved lines form at a truck that serves a free lunch, underscoring the poverty that still permeates the South Bronx. . . .

Logue turns into Tiffany Street and gestures excitedly at a row of simple, red-brick houses, which were developed several years ago by SBDO for Father Gigante, under a now-defunct low-interest program, and then sold to families. The pride of ownership is manifest in the elaborate wrought-iron fencing and gates supporting statuary, in the charming flower gardens of hollyhocks, roses, and zinnias, and in the old-fashioned bright awnings shielding the windows. "When I first started going around the South Bronx," says Logue, "in the midst of the worst abandonment, you'd see these houses and the owners still in them, hanging on. So we started doing more like these in the '235' program. Well, look at them. It's wonderful." Across the street, more large weedy meadows await houses. Beyond that grassy landscape, the familiar vista of bombed out buildings shimmers in the August haze. . . .

The blue official car swerves onto Bathgate Avenue, once the home of a bustling Jewish market but now the site of the twenty-one-acre Bathgate Industrial Park. Immediately south of the Cross-Bronx Expressway, the eight blighted blocks were laboriously cleared and readied to lure businesses into the Bronx. . . .

. . . Down in Port Morris, a decaying industrial area on the Bronx's Long Island Sound waterfront, big warehouses and factory buildings are being reoccupied and refurbished, as skyrocketing rents in Manhattan ineluctably push industry north into the Bronx. . . .

Sweeping onto the Grand Concourse, the greatest of all the borough's boulevards, one notices the love and money lavished on its rebirth. "The first thing I said when I got up here," says Logue, "is the Concourse is not going to die." Fordham Road bustles with shoppers, and the many stores lining the upper Concourse appear prosperous. (In October 1984 ground would finally be broken for the long-delayed Fordham Plaza, a major office building.)

Along the boulevard, virtually all the enormous apartment houses and edifices that made the Concourse so grandiose have been, or are now being, restored to their former splendor, thanks to City and federal rent-subsidy programs and low-interest improvement loans. . . . Roosevelt Gardens, that most public of disastrous abandonments, reopened in 1981. It has been completely renovated, down to the formal shrubbery out front.

. . . Only concerted reinvestment has revived the neighborhood. Black and Hispanic professionals . . . have discovered the glories of the boulevard's extraordinary apartments, with their spacious foyers, sunken living rooms, formal dining rooms, and eat-in kitchens. . . .

. . . And so the Concourse is slowly regaining its identity as the Grand Concourse, center of the borough and home to the upwardly mobile, though they are black and Hispanic, not Jewish. . . .

The Grand Concourse at 171st Street, the location of the Roosevelt Garden Apartments, October 1984. "Roosevelt Gardens . . . has been completely renovated, down to the formal shrubbery out front." —Jill Jonnes. *The Bronx County Historical Society Research Library.*

"The principal thing we have done," [Logue] says, "has been changing the perception within the community and outside about the prospects here."

—Jill Jonnes, *We're Still Here: The Rise, Fall, and Resurrection of the South Bronx* (Boston: The Atlantic Monthly Press, 1986).

The initial vision of city planners sometimes conflicted with what area dwellers wanted for their neighborhoods. Often, residents organized into local neighborhood groups to make their voices heard and to influence the process. The leaders of the area's churches tended to supply the galvanizing force. In April 1989, educator Jim Rooney witnessed some of the techniques used to influence the city over the restoration of three blocks in the Melrose neighborhood and noted it in his book, *Organizing the South Bronx.* The organization known as the South Bronx Churches wanted 90 two-story owner-occupied houses on three blocks; the city demanded 350 condominiums in three- and four-story townhouses on the same site.

Former City Housing Commissioner Abraham Biderman argued that this is really a dispute about density and the most productive use of this vacant land: "Does it make sense to build 70 affordable homes when you can build 350?"

To resolve that question, on a sunny April 2nd in 1989 the relentlessly efficient organizing efforts of South Bronx Churches filled these bulldozed stretches with thousands of people who gathered in knots under banners of forty Catholic and Protestant churches. The scale of the rally was unprecedented. As Father Jim Connally, the long-term pastor of Sts. Peter and Paul, said in awe a few days later, "The last time I've seen so many people come out in the South Bronx was back in the seventies when the Pope came to Yankee Stadium." The congregations of these forty churches, which only a few decades ago would have been almost entirely Irish, German and Italian, are now exclusively Hispanic and Black. The tens of thousands of Jews who once lived in the now destroyed buildings are also only a memory on these streets.

At the rally the angry crowd fanned out from the south facade of the Gothic church where a temporary stage and podium were set up and where fiery speeches merged florid religious imagery with blood-pumping class antagonism.

Perhaps the most electrifying speaker that afternoon was Rev. John L. Heinemeier, pastor of St. John's Lutheran Church, which is ten blocks north in the Morrisania section of the South Bronx.

. . . Earlier that day, he warmed up for the rally with a stem-winding sermon that shook the rafters. . . .

. . . He began slowly, almost softly: "South Bronx Churches wants to build homes on Site 404, not apartments. *Single-family homes*," he emphasized with exaggerated deliberation, savoring every word. "Homes that have a front yard where you can park your car and a backyard where you can barbecue. Homes that have a full basement that you can fix up and party in." His pace accelerating, he continued to sketch out the dream: "Homes with two [*pause*] even three bedrooms. And these homes will sell to our people for a little over $43,000. You have to put about $5,000 down, and the monthly payments would be about $380."

His voice rose and, in an abrupt shift in tone, dripped with contempt as he continued,

Tony Aguilar, associate director of South Bronx Churches, addressing the rally for Nehemiah Houses, April 2, 1989. "'South Bronx Churches wants to build homes on Site 404, not apartments. Single family homes.'"—John L. Heinemeier. The Bronx County Historical Society Research Library.

> The leaders of this city, just like the Pharisees and Sadducees are extremely jealous of that. Because it shames them. *Their* developers, the ones who build *their* apartments, are the ones who contribute more as a single group to their reelection campaigns than any other group in the city. Their developers receive $20,000 to $25,000 on each apartment they build. Our developers will receive $1,000 per single family home. And they are grabbing the best piece of land on which to build, Site 404.

He pounded home a class-driven analysis to his parishioners, most of whom live in the mammoth and dangerous Claremont Village public-housing project which sprawls through a large section of this neighborhood. And to this audience, keenly receptive to any hope of improved housing, he continued, "And *they* asked The Partnership, that's Chase Manhattan Bank, American Express, and the Rockefeller Family and folks like them to build *condos* on Site 404 to sell for over $100,000 each!" Gesturing dramatically, with his robust voice echoing off the vaulted ceilings, he roared, "Condos, not homes. Apartments! People on top of you; people below you; people over here; people over there; in front and in back. They are *telling* us; giving us strict orders not to give them any more grief about that site. They are saying it's settled. You folks in the South Bronx: Be still!". . .

In his church service, Rev. Heinemeier underscored his central message: a rally was planned for that afternoon, and all parishioners were most emphatically urged to attend. . . .

After that rousing warmup, Heinemeier was ready to spark the eight thousand demonstrators at the afternoon rally with stirring oratory. He was one of four principal speakers, and his job was to contrast dramatically the housing goals of South Bronx Churches with that of the city's Department of Housing Preservation.

—Jim Rooney, *Organizing the South Bronx*
(Albany: State University of New York Press, 1995).

Through different strategies, South Bronx Churches and other neighborhood groups had an effect on the rehabilitation and rebuilding of the area. Often an amicable compromise was reached. Their efforts came to the notice of journalist Alan Finder, who reported his observations to the *New York Times* in 1990.

With a sweep of her hand, Charlene Moats traces the cycle of devastation and renewal that has changed the face of her Bronx neighborhood.

Not long ago, all five blocks along Southern Boulevard from East Tremont Avenue north to the Bronx Zoo were lined with shells that once housed hundreds of people. "I've been here thirty years," Ms. Moats said, "and I remember when this whole block was abandoned."

Today, every apartment building is either rebuilt or under reconstruction. "It makes me feel good," said Ms. Moats, who will soon become the manager of a handsome five-story walk-up nearing completion at East 181st Street and Southern Boulevard. "People used to be running. Now they're not going anywhere. We have a new laundromat, new stores opening up. It means a lot to the community."

The building, along with one across the street and two others nearby, has been restored by a nonprofit community group called Build, one of two dozen local agencies that represent the most successful nonprofit component of New York City's effort to create tens of thousands of apartments in the city's poorest neighborhoods. . . .

The local groups vary considerably in size and experience.

Mayor Edward I. Koch to the left and Bronx Borough President Stanley Simon, center, at the dedication of the Beck Street Housing Rehabilitation Project, April 1984. "Today Banana Kelly is a major developer in Longwood and Hunts Point and manages buildings containing more than 700 apartments." —Alan Finder. The Bronx County Historical Society Research Library.

Some, like the Banana Kelly Community Improvement Association and Build—an acronym for Bronx United in Leveraging Dollars—have been in the forefront of local housing development for a decade or more. . . .

Today Banana Kelly is a major developer in Longwood and Hunts Point and manages buildings containing more than 700 apartments. It has supervised the reconstruction of eight large abandoned apartment buildings through sweat equity, said Getz Obstfeld, Banana Kelly's president, and has organized a similar effort at five small abandoned buildings on Fox Street.

The group has also overseen the moderate renovation of 20 occupied but rundown buildings taken over by the city after landlords defaulted on their property taxes. And it runs a program in which 30 young people are learning construction by renovating, under supervision, a five-story abandoned structure. . . .

"The not-for-profits bring something that dollars and cents can't measure," said Felice Michetti, the acting Commissioner of Housing Preservation and Development. "They know neighborhoods as no private developer could know them. They look at tenants as neighborhood residents; there's a difference between a tenant and a neighborhood resident."

—Alan Finder, "Nonprofit Community Groups Rebuild Housing in the Bronx," *New York Times* (March 11, 1990).

It was not just the building of new housing or the restoration of abandoned shells of buildings that had a postive effect. The creation of the Longwood Historic District, filled with early twentieth-century semidetatched townhouses, also affected its surrounding area. Journalist Daniel S. Levy detailed his observations in his 1989 essay, "Surviving Urban Blight."

Life abounds on streets made stable by the presence of longtime residents, private homeowners, and the work of the Longwood Historic District Association (LHDCA), which was formed 12 years ago. Salsa music swings from small grocery stores and children play on jungle gyms and slides in the middle of the block. On Sunday afternoons large extended families dressed in their Sunday best stroll from church. Men tinker with their highly polished, jacked-up cars, young couples lug laundry bags, girls skip rope. An old woman sets a plate of food on her stoop for stray cats. . . .

Outside the district, there has been a resurgence of business and social life over the last few years. Many of the lots bordering Longwood Avenue and the other neighboring streets have been cleaned and turned into gardens, with regimented rows of wooden vegetable troughs. Others are used by children playing catch or shooting hoops. Large architectural murals and lifelike reliefs decorate bare party walls. To the east of the Longwood Historic District run Southern and Bruckner boulevards with their auto repair shops, signed stores, and grocery marts. To the north rumbles the overhead Number 2 train. P.S. 39 on Longwood Avenue has been turned into a studio space for artists, and also serves as the headquarters for the LHDCA. Spanish restaurants, unisex hair salons, plumbing and heating stores, bakeries, and social clubs now do business on the thoroughfare.

. . . On Fox Street, east of Longwood Avenue, old tenement buildings have been gutted and renovated with new walls, plumbing, and electricity, new sewer pipes are being buried. A block away stand rows of new aluminum-sided houses—complete with ersatz mansard roofs, cast concrete lion statues, and driveways enclosed with wrought-iron gates—constructed a few years ago by the South East Bronx Community Organization.

—Daniel S. Levy, "Surviving Urban Blight," *Metropolis* (July 1989).

Local residents not only tackled the rebuilding of much of the South Bronx, but also turned to combat the social problems that had plagued the area. In 1999, journalist Vic Ziegel chronicled the story of one of them, Felix Velasquez, who became the executive director of PROMESA, located in on Clay Avenue.

His first meeting, his new neighbors told him what they needed. A mailbox, because the only one available to them was almost in another zip code. A park, because all the kids had was an empty lot covered by garbage.

Velasquez started writing letters, posting flyers, making calls, reaching out to local merchants. "It wasn't easy," he said. "It took time."

He got a mailbox for Clay Ave. And two years ago, they cut a ribbon and opened Villa Promesa Park. Its services include affordable health care, psychiatric counseling, nursing services and HIV/AIDS counseling. It has a substance abuse program and a career guidance center. The organization also owns and manages 200 low-income apartments reclaimed in abandoned buildings. . . .

"Two weeks ago," he said, "we graduated 70 people from our drug program. It's the culmination of what we do, and it gives me happiness."

Corporate America has noticed.

"I've been offered positions," he says, "nice-paying positions. I've been wined and dined by people who want me to run for public office."

He shakes his head, and makes another promise. "This is where I belong."

—Vic Ziegel, "Promises Keep Him in Bronx," *Daily News* (March 20, 1999).

The organized battle to combat drug use in the South Bronx could not be won without local youngsters realizing that the quick riches earned in illegal activities were ultimately unrewarding. In the novel by Abraham Rodriguez, Jr., *Spidertown*, the fictional Miguel, a drug runner for the notorious Bronx crack kingpin called Spider, has often watched his peers die at the hands of the police. Now, he aspires to a better life, which means breaking away from Spider, starting anew, and trying to achieve success honestly. Cristalena is his sweetheart.

He had been weary of fetters, had encouraged looseness in all his relationships until he'd met Cristalena. She ratified a belief dormant in him that there was more to life, that maybe he had to think about doing something besides staying in a rat hole, part of the pack. He didn't know why he was different, but early on he had seen the decay in Jimmy's face, the death dancing in Jokey's eyes, the emptiness of the street joy, the crazed gun thrills, the pop of the NINES, the splintering glass raining down singing like pretty wind chimes, the ineffectual cop cars cruising by all of it, a nowhere land, a nothing experience. Miguel could rattle off names of a few kids he had known by face by name but not much else, kids that were walking tall, rocking hard, like you couldn't even look at them a certain way without them popping a scene on you. Each one ended up sliced and splintered and bitten by shells and who knew why? Miguel remembered cop lights swirling like disco strobes and he and his buddies craned and pushed and shoved to see who it was and who'd got it.

"Oh, thass Michael."

"Holy fuck, they got Rolando."

"Uch. Lookit how they shot up Shorty."

"Oh shit! I tole Joey nah t'go in there tonight! Fuck, lookit how they iced his ass!"

Even Spider had to be careful and on the run. Spider was no show-off. Some guys made their drops from the back seats of limos; Spider stayed small. He spun his web and ran there and here in scummy clothes with bloodshot eyeballs. When he rode the subway business types and blond women in pretty office wear would move away from him. There was a distinct Spider aroma: sweat piss armpit dirty sneakers.

"This is the American dream," Spider was always telling him. "We livin' it, bro'. We climbin' the ladder, man." But Spider was wrong. Miguel was the one with the American dream, of making it to the top honestly and cleanly.

—Abraham Rodriguez, Jr., *Spidertown* (New York: Hyperion, 1993).

With the swift pace of housing construction and rehabilitation, the assault on the drug problem, and changing personal values, the perception of The Bronx began to change. The revival of the South Bronx led to the creation of a whole new district dedicated to selling antiques. This was noted in 1995 by journalist Cathy Asato in "Old Furniture Is Big News on Port Morris Antique Row."

The Loop Exchange is one of a half-dozen antique dealers that have helped revitalize a once-blighted strip of abandoned storefronts on Bruckner Boulevard between Willis and Alexander Avenues in Port Morris. Low rents drew the dealers to the area.

Bruckner Boulevard at the corner of St. Ann's Avenue, spring 1988. "'Everything was vacant in 1980, but store by store it began filling up and it has turned the neighborhood around,' said Lou Newkirk, the owner of Bruckner Antiques. . . . After Newkirk, several others followed, establishing what has become known as Antique Row." —Cathy Asato. The Bronx County Historical Society Research Library.

Recognizing the potential that the growing antiques market offered, the city began making improvements to the area in 1989, moving wires and poles behind the buildings and lining the street with trees. . . .

"Everything was vacant in 1980, but store by store it began filling up and it has turned the neighborhood around," said Lou Newkirk, the owner of Bruckner Antiques. "It used to be so dirty, sanitation wouldn't come around."

World-of-mouth brings antique devotees from as far away as Massachusetts and Pennsylvania. In Port Morris they can find a square grand piano from 1864 and a 1955 *"Handbook of Pediatrics."* The stores are crammed with thousands of items dating back to the 19th century—wooden tables, chairs, desks, bureaus, sofas, chandeliers, tea sets, china, vases, cuckoo clocks and toys.

Newkirk was the first to move to the neighborhood, in 1979. The sign outside his store reads, "We buy anything old." After Newkirk, several others followed, establishing what has become known as Antique Row. . . .

Shopkeepers like the location because the area is easily accessible by train, bus or car. The strip can be seen from the Major Deegan and Bruckner expressways, both heavily traveled routes into Manhattan from the north. And Bruckner Boulevard leads right to the Third Avenue Bridge.

> —Cathy Asato, "Old Furniture Is Big News on Port Morris Antique Row," *The Bronx Beat* (March 13, 1995).

At the same time, The Bronx experienced a booming visual arts renaissance. The borough's primary exhibit space is the Bronx Museum of the Arts on the Grand Concourse and 165th Street. Others include galleries at the Hostos Community College, the Bronx River Arts Center, Io Gallery in Tremont, En Foco, and many others. These have attracted young and emerging artists to the borough.

World-class art is nothing new to The Bronx. Over the decades, prominent artists have called the borough home. The noted sculptor Elie Nadelman, whose work is in the collections of the Museum of Modern Art and the Whitney Museum, among others, had a studio in the Riverdale section. Similarly, the noted Realist painter and etcher Isobel Bishop was a long-time Riverdale resident and kept a studio there. Bishop used Bronx working-class women as models for her famous paintings of Union Square shopgirls. Other lesser-known WPA and Depression-era artists and sculptors lived and worked in the cooperative apartment houses of The Bronx.

Today, as in the past, artists have flocked to the area, although recently the center of interest focuses on the South Bronx. Spurred by their interest in graffiti art, many world-famous artists such as Jenny Holzer came to the borough in the 1970s to exhibit at the legendary Fashion Moda, a South Bronx storefront gallery. Some of them have remained. Generally, the work of today's Bronx artist is highly experimental, ranging from spray-paint murals to plaster casts to video installations. In addition to placement in exhibit space, these works can be viewed all over The Bronx—in schools, subways, courtrooms, hospitals, and on the facades of buildings.

Journalist Holland Cotter surveyed the scene in the borough in his article, "Way Up in the Bronx a Hardy Spirit Blooms."

> Art in the Bronx . . . is a resilient, clamorous, multifaceted thing, cosmopolitan in outlook but imbued with a spirit of place. . . . And it turns up in unexpected places.
>
> —Holland Cotter, "Way Up in the Bronx a Hardy Spirit Blooms," *New York Times* (May 7, 1999).

Like the visual arts, music and musical organizations have blossomed in The Bronx. The Bronx Arts Ensemble and the Bronx Opera Company receive favorable notices for their classical offerings. In the Highbridge neighborhood, Bruno Casoleri reached out to the community to form a choir.

A renovated garage in one of the poorest neighborhoods in The Bronx is home to the Highbridge Voices, a choir of 140 youngsters between the ages of nine and thirteen. The group was selected several years ago from among the more than three thousand neighborhood children who auditioned. The former garage has recently been expanded to provide more rehearsal and classroom space, a counseling area, and additional practice rooms. The expansion will hopefully enable the organization to add a training choir for younger children and a chamber choir of fifty hand-picked students who have the potential to pursue a professional musical career.

The youngsters in the Bronx choir are primarily African-American and Hispanic. Most live in low-income housing, with a small percentage living in shelters. Most come from lower middle-class, working fam-

Longwood Avenue, one block from Westchester Avenue, February 1982. Note the mural on the apartment house wall. "Art in the Bronx . . . turns up in unexpected places." —Holland Cotter. The Bronx County Historical Society Research Library.

The debut concert of Highbridge Voices. "The choir director, Bruno Casoleri, has selected an ambitious professional repertoire that ranges from Broadway musicals to Schubert, traditional Hispanic folk music to Bach, Hebrew songs to gospel music. On an average concert program, the choir might sing in four different languages." —Barbara Unger. Highbridge Voices photograph.

ilies and attend neighborhood public schools with weak or nonexistent music programs.

Choir members work hard. Each youngster participates in two weekly two-and-one-half-hour chorus rehearsals, a weekly private one-on-one lesson, and a weekly music theory class. After-school tutoring and the services of a social worker are also provided in order to assist the youngsters with academics as well as other issues they face while growing up in The Bronx. This intense and demanding program helps to impart life skills, such as self-discipline, hard work, and responsibility, that will help the youngsters achieve success in life.

The choir has a positive influence on the future goals of its members. Prior to their experience in the Highbridge Voices, few of them had future educational plans. Today, many aspire to a career in music, while others are motivated to improve their grades and possibly earn college scholarships.

The choir director, Bruno Casoleri, has selected an ambitious professional repertoire that ranges from Broadway musicals to Schubert, traditional Hispanic folk music to Bach, Hebrew songs to gospel music. On an average concert program, the choir might sing in four different languages. The vocal faculty has been drawn from among graduates of the Julliard School of Music, Manhattan School of Music, and the Mannes School of

Music. The choir's annual budget comes from a nonprofit social services corporation, the Highbridge Unity Center. Highbridge Voices performs at fifteen to twenty events a year, ranging from local concerts to street fairs and, although it is only a few years old, has already sung with the pop diva Celine Dion and at Manhattan's St. Patrick's Cathedral.

Meanwhile, Highbridge Voices continues to strive for excellence. During rehearsals, the youngsters are told, "As a chorus we are only as good as our weakest member, so if the person next to you isn't singing, then he or she takes us all down; so do something about it! Tell them to get with the program."

—Barbara Unger, "Highbridge Voices," unpublished article.

Even popular music performers drew inspiration from The Bronx. Latina actress Jennifer Lopez, who grew up in the Castle Hill area of the borough, recalled her Bronx roots on her 1999 debut record album, *On the Six*. The title refers to the Number 6 subway train she took to her dancing lessons in Manhattan, and the music and lyrics related to her ethnic roots, her family background, and her old neighborhood.

New theaters presenting professional live productions have also opened in the borough. The Belmont Italian-American Playhouse and the Pregones Theater at Hostos Community College present plays in both English and the neighborhood ethnic language. The Live from the Edge Theater mounts productions at the arts center in Hunts Point called The Point.

Yet again, new immigrant groups have begun to sink roots in the borough and add their own vitality. By the end of the century, 47 percent of the population was Hispanic, but the proportion of Puerto Ricans declined as many climbed the socioeconomic ladder and followed their predecessors out of the borough. Their place was taken by Dominicans, Cubans, Mexicans, and other people from the Central American Republics and South America. In addition, significant numbers of Jamaicans and other English speakers from the Caribbean arrived. There was also a noticeable influx of Asians from Korea, Vietnam, Cambodia, India, Pakistan, and Bangladesh. Both Arabs and Israelis from the Middle East came as well. Likewise, there were arrivals from West Africa, notably Ghana, Guinea, Senegal, and Nigeria. In addition, European immigrants from the former Soviet Union, Greece, Albania, and Ireland came to settle in The Bronx. By the end of the twentieth century, The Bronx was more ethnically diverse than ever before. Often, people from different continents peacefully inhabited the same neighborhoods, and even found themselves residing in the same apartment houses with their children attending the same schools. For the first time, Buddhist temples and mosques thrived in the borough.

The economic difficulties in Ireland in the 1980s caused many Irish to seek jobs in the United States. Attracted to the still Irish neighborhoods of the northern Bronx, several decided to remain illegally after their student or temporary work visas expired. Janet Noble in her play *Away Alone* traces the varied destinies of a group of young Irish illegal immigrants who share adjoining apartments in the Norwood neighborhood. Their meeting place is the fictional Old Sod bar on Bainbridge Avenue. Liam, who has just arrived from Ireland, chats with Mario, the bartender.

> MARIO. . . . So, what do you think of New York?
> LIAM. I saw nothing. Come straight from Kennedy. *(Pause.)* If you told me a week ago I'd be in America today, I would have called you crazy. I never planned to come. I was happy staying where I was. Helped me da in the shop a bit. Made posters for the youth council.
> MARIO. What changed your mind?
> LIAM. Peter Kelly came back from Brooklyn to fix his mother's roof. They live at the end of the road. He fancied me sister. One night, he asked her out for a Chinese dinner. She didn't care to go out with him alone, so she

*An Irish pub on Bainbridge Avenue near 207th Street, 1972. "*LIAM. *. . . And here I am . . . wherever I am.* MARIO. *This is the Bronx." —Janet Noble. The Bronx County Historical Society Research Library, gift of Ralph Marx.*

asked me would I go along. I told her no. I was only hanging about the house, but jaysus . . . I hate Chinese food! But then, at the last minute, I changed me mind. *(Pause.)* And possibly me life.

MARIO. He gave you a job?

LIAM. Sure, I thought he meant on his mother's roof 'til he handed me the money for the ticket. You could have knocked me over. And here I am . . . wherever I am.

MARIO. This is the Bronx. . . .

Later, Liam is initiated into the life of an illegal Irish immigrant in The Bronx. In an apartment with other immigrants, he is warned about how to handle himself both inside and outside the neighborhood. Craic, pronounced "crack," is Irish slang for fun.

MARY. You'll get to know your way around soon enough. We'll show you where to get the papers from home. And Mario's grand at The Old Sod. He'll cash your checks for you.

LIAM. That there bar seemed sound enough. How's the crack?

PADDY. Oh, jaysus, lad . . . that's a word you're never to use!

OWEN. Crack over here is a different thing entirely.

MARY. It's a form of cocaine they sell in the streets. You've never heard of crack? Where've you been, Liam?

BREDA. There's none of that in Ballylicky . . .

PADDY. Don't be throwing that word around. First thing, they'll have your money off you, the crack'll be up your nose and your life a living hell from here out.

OWEN. Six blocks in any direction here and the scene gets pretty rough.

PADDY. Best not to leave the neighborhood.

LIAM. How'll I get to Brooklyn?

BREDA. What do you want to go to Brooklyn for?

LIAM. Me job!

DESMOND. You have a job?

MARY. Take the subway. It's at the end of the block.

OWEN. No problem on the subway.

MARY. Just don't be traveling alone late at night.

OWEN. The important thing to remember is . . . keep your mouth shut around strangers.

PADDY. The immigration is everywhere.

—Janet Noble, *Away Alone* (New York: Samuel French, Inc., 1990).

Starting in 1992, some 250 Jewish families from the former Soviet Union moved into the massive Co-op City high-rise complex in the northeastern corner of The Bronx. They chose that place precisely because the 15,372-apartment development was ethnically diverse, and they would be forced to learn English and to assimilate. Journalist Maria Newman tells their story, including that of the Yakobson family, in "Émigrés Who Want to Assimilate Pick Co-op City."

Leonid Yakobson and his wife, Alla, arrived in the United States more than two years ago, after having tried to emigrate for about 10 years. Their daughter, Regina, 14 months old, was born in New York, and one month ago the family moved into a one-bedroom apartment in Co-op City. The Yakobsons had lived in Brighton Beach, which is home to about 100,000 Soviet immigrants, and also in the Pelham Parkway area, a much smaller Russian community. But they say they prefer Co-op City.

Mr. Yakobson, a doctor and speech therapist in Kiev, Ukraine, is learning English, which he speaks haltingly but determinedly. His wife is also studying English, but she is shyer about speaking it. Both say the best way to adapt is to immerse themselves in the vast community of Co-op City.

A friend, Mikhael Scotland, who dropped by their apartment to tell the couple that a mutual friend in Kiev had received permission to travel to the United States, agreed with them about the need to adjust quickly. "If you want to live in America, you have to speak the language and be a regular citizen," he said.

—Maria Newman, "Émigrés Who Want to Assimilate Pick Co-op City," *New York Times* (February 9, 1992).

Often, the immigrants brought new energy, ideas and vibrancy to their new homes and had a positive impact on their neighborhoods. In 1991, journalist David Gonzalez told the story of Astin Jacobo from the Dominican Republic.

Entranced by the vision of an innocent era, a man transforms a field into a shrinelike ball park that attracts hundreds of eager visitors.

Kevin Costner acted the role in "Field of Dreams."

Astin Jacobo lived it in the Bronx.

The 59-year-old school custodian built the Mapes Athletic Field six years ago in Crotona, taking a brick- and garbage-strewn lot that symbolized the borough's struggle with ruin and transformed it into a broad patch of green that embodied his dreams for the area's rebirth. . . .

But when Mr. Jacobo arrived in Crotona from the Dominican Republic in 1970, street lights was an idea well on its way to becoming an oxymoron.

Despite the new houses and ballfield he cadged from Mayor Edward I. Koch during a testy confrontation at a public meeting in 1983, the streets remained dark, desolate and sometimes dangerous.

His solution was to bring night games to Crotona.

"There was something we did in the Dominican Republic that we want to see here," he said in his raspy island-tinged English. "When we played baseball, our parents used to come to the park and play dominoes, cards, have a barbecue and everybody stayed in one place minding each other. That is the future we are thinking of seeing."

Relying on his political savvy, Mr. Jacobo and his coalition received money from the office of the Bronx Borough President, Fernando Ferrer, and assistance from the city Division of Youth Services. Lights and bleachers were installed at the field, which is used for baseball and football. . . .

The Marine Corps anthem ushered in the new era of night games last week, when a fatigue-clad drill team marched into the hard-packed yellow dirt, filling the night air with thumping bass drums and chiming glockenspiels.

—David Gonzalez, "An Immigrant's Field of Dreams Transforms a Dingy Patch of the Bronx," *New York Times* (November 12, 1991).

Other immigrants made their contribution by starting businesses. Several opened restaurants. Such was the case of Jerry Stephanitsis from Greece, as told by journalist J. D. Heiman in "A Day in the Life of a Greek Diner."

When Stephanitsis bought the diner in 1982, people snickered. Much of the Bronx was being torched or abandoned, and thousands of middle-income residents were fleeing the borough. The lonely spot where the restaurant was located—just off the New England Thruway in a multi-ethnic, working-class neighborhood—was surrounded by acres of junkyards.

"There was nothing here," says Stephanitsis. "Everybody thought I was crazy to want to run a diner in the Bronx."

But now the area is booming. A giant Home Depot has opened across the street from the diner, and the huge Bay Plaza shopping mall sits just across the highway. "I was here first," says Stephanitsis. "The Bronx is now a great place to do business, and I like to think we helped turn this area around."

—J. D. Heiman, "A Day in the Life of a Greek Diner," *Daily News* (March 21, 1999).

Another immigrant restaurateur, Mohammed Abdullah of Ghana, wanted to acquaint local residents with his native cuisine. His story was told by journalist Jonathan Stempel in "From Gaseteria to Gastronome."

> Mohammed Abdullah cast his eyes along the walls of his restaurant, a kaleidoscope of acrylic paint and fabrics depicting Ghanaians hunting, carrying well water and dancing in celebration.
>
> The murals are the focal point of the 38-seat African American Restaurant in Morris Heights, where Abdullah, 45, and his second wife, Geordina, offer West African tastes that his family purveyed in the open-air markets of his native Accra, Ghana's capital.
>
> When he first opened in 1986, he said, the South Bronx had no good West African restaurants. "I wanted Americans to know African food," he said. "Many people don't know what African food tastes like. I decided not to modernize it, to make it authentic.". . .
>
> One of 14 children, Abdullah came to the United States in 1980 and started working at a Gaseteria on Jerome Avenue and 181st Street. After beating back immigration officials' efforts to deport him, and while trying to provide for his first wife and three children on $140 weekly salary, he started to prepare West African entrees at home and sell them at the station.
>
> People wouldn't believe that Abdullah, now a father of 10 children, was the chef. "They said, 'You're lying,' and I said, 'No, no, I'm not lying,' and so I started selling it, and there was first one person, then two, then three people, then 10 and 15," he said. "People started to know me. So I decided to get a place."
>
> —Jonathan Stempel, "From Gaseteria to Gastronome," *The Bronx Beat* (April 12, 1999).

As The Bronx became more ethnically diverse, so did the population of its schools. The leading secondary school in the borough is the Bronx High School of Science. Founded in 1938 as an educational institution for the intellectually gifted, it has produced more Ph.D.'s among its graduates than any other secondary school in the country. Although it started with a predominantly Jewish student body, the demographic changes in the borough and the city ensured that those admitted to Science High by passing a special examination came from an increasingly ethnically diverse background. This change, the continuing excellence of the institution, and the hope it aroused, are reflected in Shirley Pollan-Cohen's poem "Turns."

> and still they come
> small quiet

with their solemn slant eyed babies
with their darkly adolescent girls
their boys with fine rimmed round spectacles
they are telling us something
they are saying to us
here are your scientists your physicists your mathematicians
they are saying to us we will make neighborhoods again

and still they come
the changing leaves the shorter days
the city voices light upon the cooling evening air
as they have come for
all the days for
all the years
I have seen them
each in their wave of time
brittle leaves
shortened days
the Whites
the Blacks
the Puerto Ricans
the flourishing
the revolution
the devastation

and still they will come
broken hearted
toward some limitless expectations
when my last leaf has fallen
when my shorter days will end
when the city voices are too far for me to hear.

—Shirley Pollan-Cohen, "Turns," unpublished poem.

In 1970, New York's City University system inaugurated Open Admissions and remedial education programs, which enabled Bronxites who were not fully prepared to attend college. Many of them took the opportunity to enroll at Lehman, Bronx Community, and Hostos Community colleges, units of the City University in the borough. Some, along with students from all over the world, attended the many private colleges in "the Borough of Universities," a title first bestowed upon The Bronx by Borough President James J. Lyons in 1937.

Certainly, by the last year of the century, it could justly be said that The Bronx had risen from the ashes like the mythical phoenix. This is noted by journalist Trish Hall in "A South Bronx Very Different from the Cliché."

> Few urban areas have ever had a worse image than the South Bronx in the 1970's, with hundreds of buildings abandoned, stripped, burned and rotting. The neighborhood became a synonym for disaster—a warning, perhaps, of where cities might be heading.
>
> That wasn't very long ago, but in parts of the South Bronx it seems like another century. Where surreal decals of flower boxes and window shades once adorned burned-out buildings, those derelict structures have been renovated and real people with real furnishings have moved in. The population is growing, not falling. Artists, antique stores and other businesses, symbols of growth rather than decay, are arriving. . . .
>
> Crime rates are significantly lower, and like many other urban areas, parts of the Bronx are beginning to be transformed. In the last 11 years, 57,000 units of housing have been built or rehabilitated in the borough as a whole. . . .
>
> . . . But the area's image has still not recovered, and people who work and live there say that visitors are still shocked at the extent of the revival.
>
> On a two-block stretch of Bruckner Boulevard, a street infamously immortalized by Tom Wolfe in "The Bonfire of the Vanities" as a threatening place, charming antique stores have been popping up, and above them, renovated apartments rent for $1,000 a month. . . .
>
> Over in Hunts Point, new houses and apartment buildings have replaced the weeds that thrived in abandoned shells. On Manida Street, where two-story, century-old town houses with rounded facades survived the difficult years, a group of artists are living and working to create a vital cultural life, through the Point Community Development Corporation, at Manida and Garrison Streets. . . .
>
> Within walking distance, a huge outpost of ABC Carpet and Home, one of the most stylish stores in Manhattan, doubled its space three months ago at 1055 Bronx River Avenue and began offering the same kind of merchandise sold at its other stores. . . .
>
> Throughout the South Bronx, residential and commercial projects are being built; loan rates are more affordable in the economy as a whole, but even more important, banks are making loans at rates comparable to those in other regions. . . .

But the vitality of the South Bronx is so unmistakable, and the improvements so profound, that even though there is much to be done, people who never expected to return have been lured back.

People like Majora Carter, who is in the process of acquiring the house on Manida Street where she now lives. Ms. Carter returned to the neighborhood where she grew up in 1995, when she was getting a master's degree in creative writing at New York University and found there wasn't enough money for rent in Manhattan and tuition. Because of the compatible people she found in the neighborhood, artists, writers and others with a lot of energy and optimism, she has decided to stay. . . .

Also back is F. Maximo Soba, who works as a salesman in the furniture section of ABC while he studies historic preservation at Mechanics Institute in Manhattan. He never intended to return to a place with such unhappy memories, he said, a place where his mother suffered from drug addiction, contracted AIDS and died.

He fled as soon as he could, he said, moving to Manhattan, to Brooklyn, and eventually to Puerto Rico, where he ran a gallery and store selling antique Spanish furniture. When the roof literally caved in on the operation, he went back to his grandmother's home in the South Bronx three years ago, to regroup.

Like Ms. Carter, he found the area so changed he decided to stay, and last year moved into a town house floor-through on Manida Street with three bedrooms that rents for $750 a month—a price, he said, that wouldn't even get him a studio in Manhattan. . . .

The vacancy rate in the South Bronx is very low. Apartments of any kind are hard to find and tend to be passed around by word of mouth, not advertising. . . .

It is a comment often made about people who didn't flee the South Bronx in the 1970's: They have hung on, and they don't plan to go even if they have the means to do so. The Bronx is being restored primarily by the people who lived through the grim time when landlords were torching their own buildings for the insurance money.

—Trish Hall, "A South Bronx Very Different from the Cliché," *New York Times* (February 14, 1999).

It is true that the people of The Bronx still face severe problems. Many schools are among the poorest performing in New York City, and the borough's unemployment rate is too high. However, considering the renaissance of The Bronx, its residents can look to the future with optimism. The story of The Bronx is still a work in progress.

INDEX

About the Authors

Lloyd Ultan is a professor of history at Fairleigh Dickinson University, based at its Tea-neck–Hackensack campus in New Jersey. A life–long Bronxite, he also holds the appointed governmental position of Bronx Borough Historian. He served as president of The Bronx County Historical Society from 1971 to 1976 and founded *The Bronx County Historical Society Journal.* Ultan has appeared as a guest on numerous talk shows to speak about Bronx history, has also appeared in documentaries, and has been quoted in the local and national press on Bronx issues. He has written over three hundred articles on Bronx history, and has authored or co–authored five books on the subject: *The Beautiful Bronx (1920-1950)*; *The Bronx in the Innocent Years: 1895–1925*; *Legacy of the Revolution: The Valentine-Varian House*; *The Bronx: It Was Only Yesterday: 1935–1965*; and *The Bronx in the Frontier Era: From the Beginning to 1696.*

Barbara Unger is a professor of English at Rockland Community College of the State University of New York. She is the author of a book of short fiction, *Dying for Uncle Ray and Other Stories*, and five collections of poetry: *Basement: Poems 1959-1961*, *The Man Who Burned Money*, *Inside the Wind*, *Learning to Foxtrot*, and *Blue Depression Glass*. Her work has appeared in such publications as *The Nation*, *The Beloit Poetry Journal*, *The Massachusetts Review*, *Denver Quarterly*, and *Carolina Quarterly*, and has been widely anthologized. Her many honors include awards for her poetry from the National Endowment for the Arts, the New York State Council on the Arts, and the State University of New York. She has been a Squaw Valley Writers' Colony fellow and has received residencies from VCAA, Ragdale, the Djerassi Foundation, and the Edna St. Vincent Millay Colony for the Arts, among others. A Bronx resident from 1936 to 1960, she currently lives in Suffern, New York.